THE LAST SOLDIERS OF THE COLD WAR

FERNANDO MORAIS is one of Brazil's most important contemporary writers and journalists. He has received the Esso Award three times and the April Award for journalism on four occasions. Morais's works have sold more than two million copies in more than nineteen countries.

THE LAST SOLDIERS OF THE COLD WAR

The Story of the Cuban Five

◆

FERNANDO MORAIS

Translated by
Robert Ballantyne
with Alex Olegnowicz

VERSO
London • New York

First published in English by Verso 2015
Translation © Robert Ballantyne with Alex Olegnowicz 2015
First published as *Ultimose Soldados da Guerra Fria*
© Companhia das Letras 2011

1 3 5 7 9 10 8 6 4 2

Verso
UK: 6 Meard Street, London W1F 0EG
US: 20 Jay Street, Suite 1010, Brooklyn, NY 11201
www.versobooks.com

Verso is the imprint of New Left Books

ISBN-13: 978-1-78168-876-2
eISBN-13: 978-1-78168-877-9 (US)
eISBN-13: 978-1-78168-878-6 (UK)

British Library Cataloguing in Publication Data
A catalogue record for this book is available from the British Library

Library of Congress Cataloging-in-Publication Data
A catalog record for this book is available from the Library of Congress

Typeset in Garamond by MJ Gavan, Truro, Cornwall
Printed in the US by Maple Press

To Helena and Clarisse, the light of my eyes

CONTENTS

1 Veteran of the Angolan War, René Steals a Plane in Cuba, Lands in Miami and Receives a Hero's Welcome   1

2 A MiG Commander Swims Seven Hours Across the Shark-Infested Guantánamo Bay. Arriving at a US Naval Airbase, He Emerges From the Sea Shouting: "I'm a Cuban Officer, I'm Defecting!"   15

3 Overnight, 130,000 People Flee Cuba for the United States and Defeat Jimmy Carter and Bill Clinton   31

4 The Cuban Gerardo Hernández Abandons His Diplomatic Career, Changes Identity and Lands in Miami as the Puerto Rican Manuel Viramóntez   51

5 By the Middle of 1995 the Cuban "Wasp Network" Has Thirteen Secret Agents in Anti-Castroist Organizations. But the FBI Is Already Watching Them   69

6 Love Attacks the Secret Agents: Tony Marries Maggie and René Manages to Bring Olga and His Daughter to Miami   83

7 José Basulto Defies the White House and the Cuban MiGs and Decides to Fly Once More Over Havana   99

8 The Cuban Control Tower Authorizes the MiG Fighters to Shoot: Seconds Later, Two Cessnas Are Reduced to Dust Over the Florida Straits   115

9 The Mercenary Cruz León Didn't Want to Kill Anyone.
His Dream Was to Be Just Like Sylvester Stallone   131

10 For $7,500, the Salvadoran Returns to Cuba to Plant
Another Five Bombs in Hotels and Restaurants   147

11 The Cuban Intelligence Services Set Two Traps, but Fail
to Catch Big Paunch, the Recruiter of Mercenaries Hired
by Miami   169

12 Fidel Castro Sends Bill Clinton a Letter With Accusations
Against the Extreme Right-Wing Florida Organizations.
The Carrier Pigeon Is Nobel Prize Winner Gabriel García
Márquez   185

13 Six FBI Agents Arrive Secretly in Havana and Return to
the United States With a Crate Full of Reports on the Florida
Organizations Produced by Order of Fidel Castro   199

14 A Portrait of Cuban Miami: The Militant Anti-Castroist
Rodolfo Frómeta, the Pro-Cuban Journalist Max Lesnik and
the Marxist Writer Norberto Fuentes   221

15 Leonard Weinglass, Attorney to Jane Fonda, Angela Davis
and the Black Panthers, Joins the Defense of the Cuban Five,
but for Them the Die Had Already Been Cast   237

Afterword by René González   253

Epilogue   263

Acknowledgments   267

List of Interviewees   269

Bibliography   271

VETERAN OF THE ANGOLAN WAR, RENÉ STEALS A PLANE IN CUBA, LANDS IN MIAMI AND RECEIVES A HERO'S WELCOME

It was really hot in Havana in that late autumn of 1990. Nature's only blessing, at that time of the year, is that nightfall comes early, before six o'clock in the evening, sweeping the city with a fresh Caribbean breeze. It was a Saturday—December 8, 1990, she would never forget the date—and Olga had decided to spend her day off catching up on work at the Tenerías Habana, the state company where she worked as an engineer. Around seven o'clock on that overcast night, she got off the bus on tree-lined Fifth Avenue and walked a block to the modest apartment where she lived with her husband, René, and daughter, Irmita, in the once elegant neighborhood of Miramar, half an hour from the capital's center. As they left home late that morning, Olga had suggested to René that the six-year-old girl spend the day with her grandmother, freeing the parents to see the Brazilian film *Estelinha*, directed by Miguel de Faria Jr., which was opening the Latin American Film Festival at the Yara cinema downtown that evening.

Back home, Olga noticed that the apartment lights were out. René was late and the film festival would have to wait for another day. Inside, with the lights on, she saw that Dandi, her daughter's dog, had chewed up a pile of old newspapers, spreading bits of paper all over the place. When she went to the kitchen to get a broom, she heard the neighbor's voice:

"Look, the lights have come on. She's back."

Seconds later there was a knock at the door. Opening it, she came face to face with two solemn-looking men.

"Are you Olga Salanueva, René González's wife? May we come in?"

Her reaction was immediate: her husband, a pilot and parachute instructor, had had an accident. What else could it be?

The man tried to calm her down:

"We're from the Ministry of the Interior. Please, sit down, we'll explain everything."

"Explain what? My husband! What's happened to my husband? Is he injured? Is he alive?"

"You knew your husband was going to fly today?"

"Yes, I knew. What happened to him?"

The answer, she would remember later, was like a blow to the head:

"Your husband has defected."

"René? Unbelievable! René is a veteran of Angola, a Party militant! Where did you get this idea?"

"René stole an airplane from San Nicolás Airport and fled to Miami."

"I don't believe it! I don't believe it! This is an insult!"

Despite her distress, the man went on dryly, unflappable:

"Do you have a radio? If you do, switch on Radio Martí."

Olga's tiny, battery-operated radio could tune in on shortwave to Radio Martí, a station created in May 1985 by American President Ronald Reagan to broadcast anti-Castro propaganda to the Cuban public. With her heart racing, Olga heard her husband's crystal-clear voice spreading through the house in an interview that had been broadcast over and over all afternoon:

"I had to flee. In Cuba there's a shortage of electricity, a shortage of food, even potatoes and rice are rationed. The fuel for our planes is counted drop by drop."

Olga's anguish was understandable. René, thirty-four and six feet tall, lean with a rough face, prominent nose and faint shadows around his bright eyes, was a war hero decorated by the Cuban government. They made a handsome couple. Olga, a few inches shorter and three years younger than her husband, was an attractive woman, with distinctive eyebrows, abundant hair and a determined air. Apart from being workers' children, they had both been admitted a few months earlier into the Communist Party where they were militants. And they shared a love of children and dogs. The main difference between them was that Olga was a true *habanera* on both sides, whereas René, an American citizen, had been born in Chicago. His father Cándido, a metal worker and a card-carrying communist, had emigrated to Texas in 1952 in the hope of becoming a professional baseball player. At that time, baseball was the national sport of both Cuba and the United States.

His cherished career as pitcher, however, would never go beyond the odd training session on the fields of the major league teams. Faced with a choice of going back to Cuba, where the repressive dictatorship of Fulgencio Batista (1933–59) awaited him, and trying his hand as a manual laborer, he chose the latter. He moved to Chicago, where he married Irma Sehwerert, the granddaugher of Germans and the daughter of Cuban emigrants, with whom he had two sons—René was born in 1956 and Roberto in 1958. It was while living in Chicago that the family heard the news that Fidel Castro had put an end to the Batista dictatorship. In April 1961, after the attempt by the United States to invade Cuba at the Bay of Pigs, Cándido decided that it was time to return to his native land with his wife and children.

From that day until this, René had never again set foot in the country of his birth. When Olga met him in 1983, he was working as a flight instructor at various flying clubs around the country. Aged only twenty-seven, René was a veteran of the Angolan War— not unusual in Cuba, where more than half a million people, or 5 percent of the adult male population, had taken part in military missions abroad. But René stood out among the roughly 300,000 Cubans who fought on the side of the People's Movement for the Liberation of Angola (MPLA). The MPLA was backed by the USSR, which opposed the National Front for the Liberation of Angola (FNLA) and the National Union for the Total Independence of Angola (UNITA). The FNLA was sponsored by the United States, China and Zaire, and UNITA by South Africa. After two years in the jungles of Africa, where he performed fifty-four combat missions driving Soviet tanks armed with 120-millimeter guns, René quit military service, but wore a medal officially designating him as an Internationalist Combatant by the government in Havana.

December 8, 1990, started like any other day. René woke at five and ran eight kilometers through Miramar's tree-lined avenues. Back home—an apartment so small that the only place to stretch and do some exercises was the tiny space by the side of the couple's bed—he took a cold shower, woke Olga and together they shared a quick breakfast. They had little time for conversation. At seven sharp, René had to catch the bus that took him and the other workers fifty kilometers to the San Nicolás de Bari civil airport, where he had been working for two years as an instructor. As they said goodbye Olga reminded him of their evening engagement:

"Don't be late, because we are going to the cinema at eight."

"I'll be back at six, don't worry."

Still tormented by what she had heard on the radio, Olga didn't notice the men leaving. It didn't sound like a fake recording, nor did it seem that René had been forced to speak such nonsense. She switched off the radio and called her brother-in-law Roberto, a lawyer who had also done his stint in Angola. Lacking the courage to give the news over the phone, she said only that something had happened with her husband and asked him to come over right away. Roberto was not alarmed. He knew his brother was an expert pilot, and that the planes at San Nicolás were regularly overhauled—sometimes by René himself. The flying club's planes were so safe that if he wanted or needed to, the pilot could even cut off the engine in mid-flight, glide and then land safely somewhere. At worst, he would have been forced to make an emergency landing. There was no need to worry. The calmness lasted only until he opened the door and found Olga, eyes swollen from crying. She hugged her brother-in-law:

"René has defected, fled to Miami."

He opened his eyes wide:

"You're crazy, who told you that?"

"Listen to Radio Martí."

She switched on the radio and the air was filled with the sound of the interview, repeated for the umpteenth time. In his unmistakable voice, René was denouncing the problems that had turned him into what is considered in Cuba a traitor to the Revolution: food was short, money to buy food was short, transport lacking, shortage of this, shortage of that. Roberto shouted:

"Turn off that radio! I don't want to hear this guy talking shit! That bozo is not my brother!"

"That's not the René I married either; he's not the father of my daughter. Roberto, this must be some set-up by the gringos!"

It wasn't. At noon, after launching Michel Marín, the last parachute student of the morning, René saw that the little airport was half empty. He took advantage of the two control tower employees' lunch hour to cut the cables of the radio communicator with pliers, and stuffed the microphone into the pocket of his overalls. He went bounding down the stairs and got into the cabin of the only plane parked outside the hangars. It was a yellow, double-winged, Antonov An-2, made in the Soviet Union forty years earlier, and used in Cuba as a crop duster and for towing gliders. When the ground crew realized that something strange was going on, the plane was already in the air.

René knew that although the tower had no communications, it was a matter of moments before the Cuban radars would be warned of the escape. He also knew that as soon as his plane was detected, Soviet-made MiG fighters would take off from the military base at San Antonio de los Baños, minutes away from Havana, and force him to return. To outwit the control he flew almost hugging the ground, below the reach of the radar network. And, contrary to what any pilot headed for Florida would do, he did not take off in a straight line for Key West, a route that would take only forty minutes. He crossed over Cuba, and when he reached the sea, he made a turn to the northeast, pointing the plane in the direction of the Bahamas. Only when he was sure he was beyond the twelve miles of Cuban airspace did he swerve the plane round to the west, making a perfect zigzag through the air. The maneuver worked, but it almost cost the pilot's life: when René sighted the first islets of Florida, an hour and a half had passed since he had taken off from Cuba. There was only enough fuel for another ten minutes of flying. His hands sweating, he tuned his radio to the control tower of the naval air station at Boca Chica, thirty kilometers north of Key West, announced that he was a Cuban defector and that his airplane was running out of fuel. He received authorization from the US Navy to land on one of the military base's three runways and when the Antonov's heavy wheels touched down on American soil, its fuel tank was practically empty. "Bold Defection" and "Dramatic Return" were the headlines the next day, celebrating the feat. "After starring in a story of heroism, valor and compassion," said the *Miami Herald*, "the bold René González" would have no problems being accepted by the Cuban community in Miami.

The new hero of the north shore of the Florida Straits, the stretch of sea between Cuba and Miami, René had left a trail of desolation among family and friends on the south side of Havana. Olga and Roberto's first painful duty was to break the news to both of their parents. It was especially tough telling the truth to Olga's laborer father Esmerejildo, and Roberto's mother, Irma, both old communist militants, Party members since before the triumph of the Revolution. From the anguished look on the faces of her son and daughter-in-law, Irma knew something bad had happened. Olga looked terrible and it was obvious she had been crying. They had barely walked in when Roberto punched the wall:

"René betrayed us, Mother. He's betrayed us!"

The old lady was incredulous:

"It's not possible! I can't get my head round that. It's not possible!"

Unsure what to do, Roberto took her to the back of the house and told her in no uncertain terms:

"Mother, he has betrayed us and there's nothing we can do but accept it. In time we'll get used to it."

With tears in her eyes, the white-haired Irma refused to believe what she had heard. She couldn't understand how a person like her son, so immune to consumerist temptations, could do such a thing. Deep down, not even Roberto was able to decipher his brother's gesture. It might be understandable had there been political differences, but to see someone with his ideological background defect "because of food" was, as Cubans say, like pouring vinegar on the wound. Although they were both American citizens, neither René nor Roberto had ever considered going to live in the United States. Unlike many people who dreamed of emigrating, the brothers had stayed in Cuba because they wanted to, as a matter of personal choice. Both had gone to Angola as volunteers. "We weren't brought up to bother about material goods," Roberto would often say. "Potatoes and beans were never the center of our lives."

In spite of the widespread incredulity, the reality was that René had stolen a plane and gone into exile in Miami—full stop. This was the hard reality his family would have to live with. Roberto encountered an extreme variety of reactions. People who had known his brother seemed genuinely surprised, unable to understand what had driven him to leave. Others reacted as if it were the most natural thing in the world. "Don't give yourself a hard time over this," he heard several times, "because René was just one more. It's over, forget it." Some didn't hide their admiration. "Good for him. What's a competent pilot going to do here if there isn't even fuel to fly with?" said others. "This place is a piece of shit, he did the right thing leaving."

Only 160 kilometers from Havana, the deserter was being feted by the Cuban community in Florida. Upon landing, all he had to do was present his birth certificate, proving his American citizenship, for the military authorities in Boca Chica to release him. Once in Miami, he spoke to waiting journalists—among whom was the Radio Martí reporter, whose retransmission hours later would put Olga and Roberto's doubts to rest in Havana. Showing no sign of regret, he seemed sure of what he had done. He said he had felt like "a true Christopher Columbus" when he spotted the first *cayos*, the string of islets of southern Florida, and revealed that it was a long-hatched plan: "Planning the escape took three months, but I had already said goodbye to Cuba many years ago."

As time went by, Roberto's "we'll get used to it" took on a prophetic note. Deep down, however, Roberto, Olga and Irma continued to find it difficult to understand. And it was many months before René sent news. The sparse, scattered information that reached Olga about her husband's doings came over the waves of what Cubans call *radio bemba*—the grapevine of whispers and rumors. Some said he was working as a laborer, while others swore he was an employee at Miami Airport. But all of them agreed on one point: René had gotten mixed up with organizations of the extreme right in Florida.

The *radio bemba* was spot on. In the first year he worked as a flight instructor at the airport in Opa-Locka, a township close to Miami, and as a roofer, among other odd jobs. In addition, he had become involved with armed anti-Castroist organizations throughout southern Florida. The Cuban diaspora was intensely excited about the self-dissolution of the Soviet Union. The foreseeable damage that the disappearance of the communist power would cause to the structures of the Cuban Revolution rekindled the hope of accomplishing a thirty-year-old dream, even among the most conformist: overthrowing Fidel Castro, reinstating capitalism on the Island and recovering the assets confiscated by the Revolution. Faced with such a promising outlook, the former owners of banks, factories and sugar refineries—many of whom had had their businesses expropriated in the early 1960s, only to rebuild their fortunes in exile—opened their coffers to the many factions and tendencies within their community. More precisely, the United States was home to forty-one anti-Castroist groups, led for the most part by Bay of Pigs veterans who were openly in favor of armed confrontation with Cuba.

In early 1992, after a year of roaming from place to place, René joined one such organization, the recently-founded Hermanos al Rescate, or Brothers to the Rescue, led by an old acquaintance from Cuba: José Basulto. He wasn't just another defector, like René, but a sworn enemy of the Cuban Revolution. When they met each other,

Basulto was a prosperous building contractor. At the age of fifty-one, turning white at the temples, Basulto still had the looks of a soap-opera star, often accented by a sharp pair of Ray-Bans. And he hadn't given up his obsession: to overthrow the Cuban government by force. Trained by the CIA, he decided to form his own organization after personally carrying out a number of spying missions and terrorist attacks on Cuban soil and frequenting several anti-Castroist groups in Florida. Registered, like all the others, as a "nonprofit institution with no political aims," Brothers called itself "a humanitarian organization," although Basulto himself was the first to stress that one of its missions was "to promote and support the efforts of the Cuban people to free themselves from dictatorship."

Brothers came into being prompted by the reappearance of a character from the Cuban landscape: the rafter—the migrant who took to the sea on small boats, improvised rafts or even inner tubes, seeking asylum in the United States. For its initial activities the organization relied on a squadron of three O-2 planes—the military version of the Cessna 337—retired after years of service in the United States Air Force during the Vietnam War (1955–75) and in the Salvadoran Civil War (1980–92). Basulto had been given the aircraft on the orders of President George Bush, at the request of the Cuban-American congresswoman Ileana Ros-Lehtinen. In the following months the fleet would incorporate a Seneca 859C, two Cessna 320s and two Piper Aztecs acquired through donations from Cuban businessmen exiled in Florida. Among the donors were prominent names such as Jorge Mas Canosa, the multimillionaire figurehead of anti-Castroism in exile and president of the Cuban American National Foundation (CANF), created in 1981 at Ronald Reagan's suggestion and the most powerful of the anti-Castroist organizations. Before it was two years old, Brothers already owned a reasonable fleet of small and medium-sized airplanes, some donated by personalities sympathetic to anti-Castroism, including the Cuban-American musicians Willy Chirino and Gloria Estefan, and the octogenarian Argentinean actress-singer Libertad Lamarque, who would end her days in Miami.

Officially, the organization's objective was to fly over the Florida Straits in search of refugees, throw them food and first aid kits, and transmit their location by radio so that the American Coast Guard could lead them safely to the United States. Still in force at the time was the Cuban Adjustment Act, enacted in 1966 by President Lyndon Johnson and conceived with the explicit aim of encouraging the exodus of Cubans dissatisfied with the Revolution. Popularly known as the "wet-foot, dry-foot policy," it guaranteed that any Cuban who set foot in the United States would be admitted as a permanent resident, and a year later would receive a coveted green card, ensuring them the same rights as a citizen born in the United States.

Although benefitting from a privilege not offered to any other foreigners, recently arrived Cubans in Miami had to work as hard as other immigrants. It was no different for René, who went to live in a one-bedroom apartment on the top floor of a four-story building in the district of Kendall, in southeast Miami. Even though Miami wasn't among the most expensive cities in the United States, it wasn't easy to live on his monthly budget of $1,000. Four hundred went on rent, 300 on food and 200 on day-to-day expenses such as electricity, gas, telephone, cable TV and transport. He survived by doing odd jobs, such as fixing fences in the neighborhood, mowing lawns, washing dishes in restaurants—and flying planes for Brothers, at twenty-five dollars per mission.

The experience he had acquired in Cuba soon made René one of the organization's most sought-after pilots, on a par with veterans twice his age who had thousands more hours of flying, such as Basulto himself and the Brothers' co-founder, William "Billy" Schuss. Born in Havana in 1935, the cross-eyed, sixty-year-old Schuss was the son of an American who had been co-pilot to the legendary Charles Lindbergh, the first man to make a solo, nonstop flight across the Atlantic in May 1927 when he flew his single-engine *Spirit of Saint Louis* from New York to Paris. Like Basulto, Schuss was CIA-trained and had fought at the Bay of Pigs. After the invasion's defeat, he sought exile at the Brazilian embassy in Havana. When he left, he headed for the United States armed with a letter of safe conduct obtained by the Brazilian ambassador, Vasco Leitão da Cunha.

Thanks to his expertise and the trust Basulto and Schuss had in him, René carried out hundreds of flights over the Florida Straits in his first two years. He improved his resumé as a pilot, a profession where experience is measured mainly by the number of flying hours completed, and this increased his monthly income. Little by little he was able to dedicate himself solely to aviation and could stop being a *biznero*, a neologism among the Hispanic community in Miami for those who scrape by on odd jobs. In fact, many of the young volunteers who operated in Brothers—in addition to Cubans, there were Salvadorans, Guatemalans and Argentinians—turned up not only for ideological reasons, but also for the opportunity to fatten up their flight logbooks.

As the months went by, René realized that saving rafters was only a part of the organization's activities. With ever-increasing frequency, Brothers planes circumvented flight plans presented prior to takeoff at Florida's airports, entered Cuban airspace and conducted risky flights over Havana. When they were above the busy Malecón, the eight-kilometer seaside boulevard that snakes along the shoreline of the Cuban capital, the pilots would drop from the sky hundreds of thousands of *octavillas*—leaflets inciting people to rebel against the government—or plastic bags full of tiny aluminum medals engraved with the image of Our Lady of Charity of Cobre, Cuba's patron saint.

The first time he flew as Basulto's co-pilot on one of these sorties, René was taken aback by how bold the chief of the organization was. As he was preparing to cross Parallel 24, which divides the airspace between the two countries, Basulto took the plane perilously close to Cuban territory and announced his intentions to the Havana control tower:

"Good afternoon, Havana Center. This is November-two-five-zero-six calling [referring to the prefix of the Cessna N2506]. We are crossing Parallel 24 and will remain in your area for two or three hours. We will fly at an altitude of five hundred feet. Today our operations area will be the northern part of Havana. Cordial greetings from Brothers to the Rescue and its president, José Basulto, who is speaking."

From the Cuban capital, the flight controller answered politely, but warned him of the gravity of the intrusion:

"OK, OK. Received, sir. But I inform you that the area north of Havana is activated. If you go below Parallel 24, you will be at risk."

Basulto was a seasoned pilot who knew the meaning of the expression "activated area." It meant the space was being used for military air exercises and was thus out of bounds for civilian flights. According to international law, the Cessna, having been warned, could then be shot down. The threat didn't appear to deter him:

"We are aware that we are running a risk every time we enter the area south of Parallel 24 but, as free Cubans, we are prepared to do so."

The plane was flying so low that René could see, without the need for binoculars, cars gliding down the sunny Malecón, the Ameijeiras Hospital, the Hotel Nacional building and the colorful, run-down, colonial houses of Old Havana. Moments after the conversation between Basulto and the control tower, two almost imperceptible black triangles crossed the sky in front of the Cessna, leaving twin trails of white smoke. Both pilot and co-pilot knew what it meant: Cuban radars had detected their presence and sent up two MiG-23 fighter-bombers from the San Antonio de los Baños base to chase them off. One single missile of the six carried under their wings was capable of pulverizing the Cessna in midair, but Basulto, indifferent to the threat, continued to carry out maneuvers for over an hour before returning to Miami. This was no display of courage. The president of Brothers was certain of one thing: the Cuban authorities would think a thousand times before shooting down a plane flown by two American citizens, a move that could invite a ruthless response from the United States. Basulto knew that a mere six minutes was enough for the 200 F-15 tactical fighters stationed at the bases of McDill, Homestead and Boca Chica (where René had landed) to reach Havana, each one of them armed with eight tons of missiles and bombs.

Since the first airborne incursion from Florida into Cuban air-space, the country's foreign ministry had been sending written protests to the US State Department. Havana warned Washington of the risk of the aircraft being shot down—and pointed out that Basulto hadn't even gone to the trouble of disguising the origin of one of the airplanes used by Brothers, the single-engine Cessna N58BB, which still bore United States Air Force insignias on its fuselage. It wasn't the first time that the name of the US government had appeared clearly associated with aggression against the Island. Months earlier Cuba had reported the United States to the Biological Weapons Convention for spraying its territory with the eggs of *Thrips palmi*, unknown in the country until then, causing the loss of half the country's potato harvest. The cropduster that had spread the pest, a single-engine aircraft, prefix N3093M, was officially registered as belonging to the US State Department.

In addition to dumping poison, pamphlets, medals and plastic stickers with slogans like "Down with the Tyrant Castro," it was common for pilots to deliberately interfere with transmissions from the control tower at Havana's José Martí Airport, endangering the lives of thousands of passengers on commercial airlines with daily flights that crossed Cuban air corridors to and from the United States and Latin America. Frequently, when flying over Cuba, airline crews were surprised by a strange broadcast from Brothers planes in which someone, simulating the end of mass, would recite the Prayer to Our Lady of Charity of Cobre:

> Most Holy Mother of Charity, who came
> to us as a Messenger of peace,
> You are the Mother of all Cubans and to you
> we pray for help, Holy Mother,
> To honor you with love as your children …
> For our torn country, that we may be able to build
> a nation based on peace and unity …
> For our families, that they may live in fidelity and love,
> For our children, that they may grow strong …
> For those far from home,

For the Catholic Church in Cuba and its evangelist mission,
For its priests, deacons, religious and laity …
Mother of Charity! Blessed are you among women
and blessed be the fruit of your womb, Jesus!

After a brief silence, the voice would return, finishing the broadcast:

Let us recite the Lord's Prayer, three Hail Marys and a Glory Be to the Father.

In spite of Cuba's complaints and protests, the leniency shown towards the counterrevolutionary groups by the US government—indulging not only the airspace invasions, but also the placing of bombs and the armed attacks on Cuba—had made Florida a sanctuary where all this could be done in broad daylight. Press conferences were convened in the hangars of the Miami, Kendall, Key Marathon and Opa-Locka airports, from where the flights took off. To raise more money for the organizations, photographs of the Cuban capital taken from the planes were sold for $10 in kiosks in Little Havana, the neighborhood where Cuban exiles are concentrated. On countless occasions René would take TV crews from the two main local channels, Univisión and Telemundo, to film flights over the Cuban coast that would then be aired at prime time, often showing MiGs zigzagging menacingly around the invading planes.

In Cuba, Martí's TV and radio broadcasting of the Brothers' and other organizations' provocations was cause for increasing indignation among the country's leaders, whereas in Miami it became an incentive for new adventurers not only to cross the Florida Straits in search of a new life, but to join the aggressive anti-Castroist groups. That was how, thirteen months after René's escape, a high-ranking officer of the Cuban Air Force disembarked in the United States following a feat even more reminiscent of a Hollywood blockbuster than the one that inspired it.

2

A MIG COMMANDER SWIMS SEVEN HOURS ACROSS THE SHARK-INFESTED GUANTÁNAMO BAY. ARRIVING AT A US NAVAL AIRBASE, HE EMERGES FROM THE SEA SHOUTING: "I'M A CUBAN OFFICER, I'M DEFECTING!"

The new and larger-than-life character who was to become one of the leading anti-Castroists of the Cuban diaspora in Miami was named Juan Pablo Roque. Thirty-six and a major in the Revolutionary Armed Forces, Roque would soon be known as 'the exiles' Richard Gere." On Saturday, February 22, 1992, taking advantage of a weekend off, he embarked on a commercial flight in Havana bound for the city of Guantánamo, 800 kilometers from the Cuban capital. There he bought a train ticket for a little fishing village called Caimanera. An experienced MiG-23 fighter pilot, with many years of service in the former Soviet Union, Roque was traveling alone, in civilian clothing, and his baggage consisted of only a nylon backpack slung over his shoulder. From Caimanera's railway station he walked a few kilometers until he reached the edge of a cove at Joa, a place where Guantánamo Bay resembles an enormous pond. At that spot was the perimeter of the 120-kilometer-square airbase that the United States had occupied on Cuban soil since 1903—and which at the start of the twenty-first century would be transformed into a prison for Afghans and others accused of terrorism by the United States. Roque sat on the sandy beach and waited for nightfall. When it was completely dark, the only lights visible were the searchlights of the Cuban Coast Guard boats that patrolled the waters twenty-four hours a day. At eight o'clock, the soldier decided the time had come. Hidden behind a wall of rocks, he took off his clothes and shoes, and, wearing only his underpants, removed from his backpack the equipment he used for diving, his favorite hobby. He put on the worn neoprene suit, the flippers and a facemask and snorkel. Around his neck he hung a small water-proof bag containing his documents and the photo of a friend, the Cuban general Arnaldo Ochoa. Condemned to death and shot by firing squad three years earlier in Havana, Ochoa had been accused of leading a smuggling and cocaine-trafficking network. He tied to his waist the serrated knife he used in his underwater hunts and slipped silently into the water, careful not to attract the attention of the coast guards.

The roughly nine-kilometer swim took almost seven hours. Every time he came up and saw the lights of the Coast Guard boats sweeping the surface of the water, he dived down, careful not to go too deep as the area was infested by sharks. At one point Roque noticed that the zipper on his suit had burst, leaving it to gape open in the middle. The two halves of the suit had created resistance, doubling the efforts needed to breathe and paddle with his arms. He took the knife from his waist, cut the neoprene material from top to bottom, freed himself from the hindrance and carried on wearing only his underpants. It was already past three in the morning when Roque surfaced and filled his lungs with air, relieved. Through the blurry lens of his mask, he could make out the American flag fluttering on an illuminated pole, and he read the inscription on a huge gate guarded by armed marines: "US Naval Base Guantánamo Bay." He'd made it. He came out of the water and walked shakily along the sand until he came across a group of uniformed recruits with rifles pointed in his direction. He raised his hands and shouted in Spanish and English:

"*¡Soy oficial del ejército cubano y estoy desertando!* I am a Cuban army officer and I am defecting! I'm Cuban! I'm defecting!"

Taken to the officers' mess, Roque handed over his documents and briefly listed the reasons that had led him to abandon his country and request asylum in the United States. He received some olive-green overalls and made a joke when a soldier appeared with a hamburger and a Coca-Cola bought at the base's McDonald's: "For someone who's been eating McCastro's for years, a real McDonald's is a delicacy!"

Surrounded by servicemen, he told how his differences with the island's government had begun after the shooting of General Ochoa, and got worse as soon as he came out in defense of perestroika, the political movement led by President Mikhail Gorbachev that had culminated in the self-dissolution of the USSR. The last straw had been the imprisonment of his brothers Alejandro and Raúl, also MiG pilots, after their unsuccessful attempt to flee Cuba. Under suspicion from his superiors, banned from flying and transferred to an office job at the airport in Havana, Roque decided to leave his wife Amelia and their two small children and abandon the country. The American immigration services responded quickly, and three weeks later the travel authorization arrived. Around the middle of March he hitched a ride on a plane from the military base and disembarked in Miami, a city he'd never been to before.

The rank of superior officer and the prominence given by the international press to his defection did not lessen the difficulties that he, like all Cubans, faced in the early months of exile. Without a cent in his pocket, Roque initially moved in with his aunt Aurora, his mother's sister who had emigrated with her family during the first years of the Revolution. He later went on to share a room with his cousin, Denayf Elias Roque, an agent of the FBI. During the day he wandered around Little Havana looking for a job. Any job. Since the classified ads had few openings for supersonic fighter-jet pilots, he worked as a laborer paving streets, as a pizza delivery boy and as a personal trainer for people who lived in the elegant neighborhoods of Coral Gables and Coconut Grove. When Hurricane Andrew devastated southern Florida in August of that year, killing fifty people and causing $30 billion-worth of damage, Roque called upon his skills as an amateur joiner, repairing doors and windows and rebuilding wooden houses. At that time, the only steady job he managed to get was as a truck driver for the United Parcel Service.

The pilot's fate began to change only when he got close to two compatriots, Alberto Cossío, a young and active businessman in Miami, and Nico Gutiérrez, leader of an association of former Cuban farmers whose lands and sugar mills had been expropriated during the Revolution. It was through them that he reached José Basulto, who soon invited him to join the Brothers. His days as a *biznero* were over. His pilot's logbook, packed with thousands of flying hours as a MiG commander, immediately qualified Roque to become part of the organization's top team, composed of Basulto, Billy Schuss, Arnaldo Iglesias—all Cubans—and the young and personable Argentinian, Guillermo Lares, an anti-Castroist adventurer and friend of the then president of Argentina, Carlos Menem. The group called themselves the Kamikazes, a reference to the Japanese suicide pilots who flew their planes into allied targets during World War II. Remembering this, eighteen years later, Roque would insist that the nickname was no act of bravado:

"We were violating all the laws of the air and were ignoring basic safety parameters, whereby the amount of a pilot's time off should not be less than eight twenty-four-hour periods per month. Think about it! We went as far as flying nine hours a day, seven days a week, all month long."

To achieve that level of performance, airplanes with a flying range of less than four hours, as in the case of the Cessna 337s, were fitted with internal fiberglass fuel tanks, doubling the distance they could cover but subjecting crews to potentially fatal risks. "Basulto himself lost a single-engine plane and narrowly avoided death," Roque would recall, "attempting an emergency landing at Cayo Sal, in the Venezuelan Antilles."

On the southern shores of the Florida Straits, the Cuban government insisted on reacting diplomatically to the encroachments on their national airspace by planes from the United States. On each incursion, the ministry of foreign relations would send an official note to the US Interests Section in Havana, installed in a modern seven-story concrete building on the Malecón. The letters were practically identical, the only difference being the dates and the prefixes of the invading planes:

The Ministry of Foreign Relations respectfully offers its compliments to the United States of America's Interests Section and takes the opportunity to transmit to it its concern regarding the serious situation created in the Flight Information Region of the Republic of Cuba. The Cuban authorities have detected that airplanes coming from North American territory, originating in the airports of Opa-Locka, Miami and Marathon, have violated the airspace of the Republic of Cuba; they made undue use of the radio frequencies responsible for air traffic control; they interfered in such controls, thereby risking the safety of international civilian flights that use Cuban air corridors. These irresponsible and provocative violations took place at distances of between 1.5 and 5.5 nautical miles off the Cuban coast. Such violations were perpetrated by aircraft of the make Cessna, model 337, with North American prefix numbers N58BB, N108LS and N2506. The Ministry of Foreign Relations demands that the North American authorities adopt effective measures to prevent any recurrence of these events.

With the handy excuse of rescuing rafters lost at sea, and encouraged by the indifference of the US authorities, the Brothers became more and more daring. In the summer of 1992, Cuba presented evidence to the United Nations Security Council that on two occasions Basulto's organization had passed information from the air to the flotilla of a Miami group called the Democracy Movement, indicating to the anti-Castroist boats the location of Cuban Coast Guard launches. By avoiding these the anti-Castroist groups could gain the beaches of Varadero and Villa Clara, where they intended to place bombs. Paying no heed to the Cuban complaints or the diplomatic conflicts that their actions provoked, the Brothers continued their flying missions to the Island.

As time went on, Roque became the star of the organization. His daring escape, fighter-pilot past and Hollywood looks made him a regular fixture on television programs as well as in newspaper and magazine interviews. A frivolous weekly magazine went as far as offering him $5,000 to take part in a "fabrication"—a false news story. To get the money he would have to pretend to be Richard Gere and be photographed from a distance, surrounded by women on a Miami beach, by a fake paparazzo. The fee was tempting but propriety won the day. What's more, the major, who like René had left his wife and children in Cuba, was already romantically involved with a Cuban-American woman.

The flirtation had begun a week after his arrival in Miami. Accompanying his aunt Aurora to Sunday worship at a Baptist church in Coral Gables, Roque had been introduced by his cousin Denayf to Ana Margarita Martínez, an attractive girl five years younger. At the age of six, Ana and her family had been passengers on one of the Freedom Flights organized by President John F. Kennedy to allow opponents of the Cuban Revolution to seek exile in the United States. She had never been an anti-Castroist militant, but she had turned into a character typical of the Cold War landscape in the Gulf of Florida: she considered herself an American, and it had never crossed her mind to go back to her country of origin.

On returning to the Brothers' hangar at Opa-Locka after a flight, months after meeting her, Roque confided to his friend René González his plans to marry Ana Margarita. René replied that, unlike him, he had never stopped loving the woman he'd abandoned in Cuba. "I'm still in love with Olga, and can't take it any more, I'm missing her and our daughter Irmita so much," he confessed. "And I'm willing to do whatever it takes to convince them to come out to Miami."

As he must have realized from the infrequent and curt letters he was getting from home—almost always confined to news of their daughter—René's faithful passion was not returned by his wife. For Olga, all that remained of her love for René fitted into half of a small wardrobe. As time went by the memory of her husband would come up only for a few moments each day, when she was choosing what to wear after her shower and her eyes fell on his pants and shirts, hanging in a corner of the cupboard, briefly reminding her of the best years of her life.

But irritation soon overcame the fond memories until the only thing she managed to do was repeat to herself in silence the promise she postponed every day: "I must give those clothes away to someone." On a wooden shelf above the coat hangers, safely out of reach of the inquisitive Irmita, lay the little bundle of red-and-blue-edged envelopes, the colors of the US mail, containing the letters René had sent her months after his escape. Written in an affectionate tone, they spoke of life in exile, and invariably ended with a plea that little by little turned into a supplication: that Olga forgive him for his desertion and that she and their daughter go to Florida, where they could all live together once more. The only time she replied, it was to state bluntly that her feelings had not changed since he had gone: she was not interested in moving to the United States, much less in allowing her daughter to be brought up by a traitor. Nearly two decades later it was still possible to make out Olga's handwriting on the onion-skin paper, blurred by the tears René had shed when reading the letter.

Olga's main worry was the repercussions their situation might have on Irmita's upbringing. Every time the girl enquired about her father, Olga would repeat the same lie. She pretended that he was abroad, as many other Cubans were, on commercial missions in an attempt to minimize the effects of the US economic embargo. It wasn't such an implausible excuse. In the so-called special period that followed the end of the Soviet Union, Cuba dispatched dozens of employees all over the world to set up "private" companies dedicated to contravening the American embargo, seeking out markets for products previously sold to the USSR—mainly sugar, tobacco and nickel—and buying basic essentials, like petroleum, food, agricultural supplies and medicines.

When she turned nine, Irmita received an affectionate letter from her father, apparently posted in Mexico. René had enclosed a simple birthday present, a little puzzle made up of colored tiles, a memory game for two or more people to play. After a little practice the girl became an expert with the toy, beating not only her classmates, but even grown-ups like her mother and her uncle Roberto. When her elder cousin Sergio came to visit, she soon challenged him to a game. She won repeatedly. By the tenth victory, she couldn't resist and gloated over her opponent:

"I'm three years younger than you, but I won them all. I'm the champion!"

The cousin, stung, answered straight back:

"Sure, you're the champion. But your father is a *gusano* and mine isn't!"

In revolutionary Cuba there was no insult more offensive than *gusano*—synonymous with "worm"—a derogatory term for someone with no scruples. It was also indiscriminately used to designate critics of the regime and the hundreds of thousands who decided to go into exile after the triumph of the Revolution. In tears, Irmita flew at her cousin with such violence that the adults had to separate them. That night, before going to sleep, she asked Olga if the accusation was true. Her mother said no, that her cousin was a bad loser, and repeated the story that René was traveling overseas to help the Cuban economy. And that he would soon be coming home.

Perhaps because it was less painful, the young girl went along with the lie invented by her mother. But now and again she would have her doubts. One occasion was when Olga gave to a friend, who had just had a baby, the wooden crib René had made so carefully for his daughter at a neighbor's carpentry workshop. Later, Irmita noticed that her uncle Roberto and her grandfather began showing up at weekend visits in clothes she knew belonged to her father. The affection she felt for her uncle and her grandfather was such that she never said anything to them at the time, but the growing child took note. "To me it wasn't as if we were getting rid of the crib or the pants or the shirts," she would recall as an adult, "but of my father himself." She had news of him only sporadically, mostly when she asked her mother about him point-blank. René kept on writing to Olga, never losing hope that she and their daughter would move to the United States. Olga rarely replied, and when she did it was to say no. She had no desire to take her daughter to be brought up "alongside a mafioso terrorist like José Basulto."

Unknown to Olga, however, René had left his work with Basulto in order to operate in another extreme-right organization—the National Democratic Union Party (PUND)—a small anti-Castroist group with little or no political presence that was also dedicated, at least officially, to rescuing rafters lost at sea. His only work tool was a solitary twin-engine Beechcraft Baron 55, donated by a Cuban businessman exiled in El Salvador. Installed on the second floor of a bar on the corner of 17ᵗʰ Avenue and 5ᵗʰ Street, in southwest Miami, the PUND had been created at the end of 1989 by Sergio González Rosquete, encouraged by the idea that the perestroika implemented by Gorbachev in the USSR might end up leaving Cuba high and dry. Rosquete had served some years in prison in Havana, and on being freed in 1969, he fled to the United States. His two lieutenants were the Cuban Héctor "El Tigre" Viamonte, ex-bodyguard to Jorge Mas Canosa, and the seventy-year-old American Frank Angelo Fiorini. Public opinion only knew of Fiorini under his alias, Frank Sturgis, the name with which he had graced the front pages of the international press on two occasions. First at the start of the 1960s, when he was suspected of involvement in the plot that led to President Kennedy's assassination, and later in 1972, as one of the CIA agents caught removing electronic devices from the Democratic National Committee office in Washington, the episode known as "the Watergate scandal" that would culminate in President Richard Nixon's resignation.

The appeal that the PUND held for René was the fixed salary of $175 a week, paid religiously every Saturday morning in cash at the counter of the bar, no matter how many flights he did. Learning of his new activities, friends warned him of the rumor that the PUND was nothing but a front for the smuggling of drugs from Central America to Miami, which explained the abundance of funds in the hands of such an insignificant organization. Although he had no wish to fall foul of the Drug Enforcement Agency (DEA)—the powerful antidrug watchdog of the American government—René believed that the accusation was just one of the many intrigues that contaminated the anti-Castroist world. If the PUND was indeed a front for drug running, it was a convincing one, as René himself had more than once witnessed groups of exiles receiving heavy weapons in the small bar on the first floor and going off in several vehicles for military training. And months earlier the Cuban police had arrested one of the PUND's leaders, Humberto Real Suárez, when he and six other militants tried to unload a shipment of arms and explosives on a beach in Villa Clara province. A man who witnessed the unsuccessful infiltration was shot dead, a crime for which Real Suárez would receive the death sentence (later commuted for lack of evidence).

However, after a few months' work, René began to suspect there was some truth to the stories about drug trafficking. The flight plans presented to the Miami airports always declared trips over the Florida Straits in search of rafters, but half an hour after takeoff the planes banked steeply, headed south and landed at clandestine airstrips on the Caribbean fringe of Honduras. The planes never stayed on the ground for long; sometimes the pilot never even got as far as switching off the engine. Just long enough to load some mysterious packages that nobody on board was allowed to touch. Once back in Florida, the packages were transferred to vans waiting on the runway and, hey presto, the operation was over. Now suspicious, René decided to share his fears with his friend Juan Pablo Roque. Ana Margarita, who was still engaged to the Cuban major, would recall years later that whenever they wanted to talk safely away from indiscreet ears, "the two of them communicated in Russian, a language they both appeared to speak fluently." Roque suggested a meeting between René and agent Slingman, his cousin Denayf's boss in the FBI.

Slingman was the code name of Oscar Montoto, a naturalized Cuban-American. Pale, tall and thin, with an almost bald head and an unhappy look, Montoto was an experienced FBI agent who was deployed on important operations. Years later he would travel to Brazil, as a legally registered State Department observer, to follow the Brazilian police investigations into the assassination of the American-born missionary Dorothy Stang by land-grabbers in the Amazon. Drug trafficking was not his area of operations, but Oscar "Slingman" Montoto listened with attention to what René had to say and then proposed another meeting a few days later. He came to this one accompanied by Alejandro Barbeito, special agent of the FBI Anti-Drug Squad, a policeman, as René would remember later, whose politeness bore little resemblance to the Feds he was accustomed to seeing in films and TV shows. He had a long talk with the

Cuban but reached no firm conclusions. It seemed obvious that this was a case of drug trafficking, but Barbeito preferred to err on the side of caution. He knew how much political power and influence the Cuban community wielded in Florida.

The exiles' votes determined city councilmen, governors and state and federal congressmen. What is more, no American president, Democrat or Republican, had ever reached the White House without first subjecting themselves to the "hand-kissing" of the leaders in Miami's Cuban diaspora. Every four years, a Committee of Political Action—a kind of NGO authorized to collect funds for political causes—made up of the elite of the Cuban community flooded the electoral campaigns with around 400 candidates for federal congressional representatives and senators, and giving donations as high as $10 million. Those favored did not necessarily need to be of Cuban origin and it was of little importance whether they were Republicans or Democrats. All that mattered was that they defended the interests of the Cuban diaspora: that they were committed to the continuation of the embargo against Cuba, and to all forms of struggle to end the communist regime on the Island. Political observers unanimously agreed that the power of the Cuban lobby in Congress came second only to the exceptionally well-funded American Israel Public Affairs Committee (AIPAC)—America's pro-Israel lobby. So it was clear that opening an unfounded investigation into the leader of any anti-Castroist organization—even a small one like PUND—could lead to a few months in the refrigerator, if not an unexpected transfer to some remote FBI office thousands of kilometers away from cozy Miami. Barbeito requested a few weeks for "consultations," after which they would get together again.

At the policemen's suggestion, they always met in cheap diners or in a McDonald's or Burger King. This time the venue was the Palacio de los Jugos, a fruit juice franchise on 57th Street in Little Havana. "Alex Barbeito seemed to me to be an enthusiastic young man genuinely committed to the fight against narcotraffic," René would say many years later. "He arrived with two Americans of ruddy complexion"—one of whom was federal agent Al Alonso, as the pilot would later discover—"who wrote down everything that was said at the meeting." Having obtained carte blanche from Lloyd King, Florida's assistant federal attorney, the lawmen went straight to the point: if he agreed, René would begin to regularly provide the FBI with information on the PUND's suspect activities, a task for which he would receive a monthly fee of $1,500. Thanks to an apparently deliberate indiscretion from Barbeito, René then learned that Roque had been providing similar services to the FBI for over a year already, for the same monthly payment. Only after weeks of tests with micro-recorders taped to his body beneath his clothing, always monitored by FBI technicians, did Irmita's father feel confident to start recording his conversations with PUND leaders.

Some months of work elapsed before the law decided it was time to pounce. One Friday, René was instructed by Barbeito to make up an excuse not to go along with Héctor Viamonte on his flight the following morning. On Saturday the PUND's twin-engined plane took off from Cayo Marathon, picked up some packages at a small Honduran airport, made a brief stop in Nassau, in the Bahamas, and returned to Florida. Upon landing in Miami and entering one of the airport hangars, the plane was surrounded and searched by dozens of armed police. Once the packages that had been loaded in Honduras were opened, the suspicions were confirmed: it was a cargo of cocaine. Viamonte and his co-pilot were arrested on the spot. Under Cayo Marathon's palm trees, René's brief career as a police informer came to an end, as he preferred to have no further involvement with the FBI.

The loss of the job was not so serious. While still at the PUND René had received an offer to work for the Democracy Movement. This organization was founded and directed by Ramón Saúl Sánchez, a pale and skinny Cuban businessman, with glasses and a thick mustache, who had moved to the United States in 1960 at the age of six. Unlike the Brothers, Sánchez's organization was active not only in air operations but also at sea. In the beginning, the air sector consisted of only three planes, but the naval operation could count on a flotilla of dozens of boats of various sizes that undertook dangerous incursions into Cuban territorial waters. Before founding the Democracy Movement, Sánchez was a militant in various aggressive anti-Castroist groups based in Florida, like the Cuban National Liberation Front, Alpha 66, Young People of the Star, Organization for Cuban Liberation, Omega-7, and Cuba Independent and Democratic. On various occasions his name appeared linked to pirate attacks, bomb plots, kidnappings and armed operations against the Island. Summoned in 1984 to testify in New York at the Grand Jury convened to investigate responsibility for an attack on the Cuban Interests Section in Washington, Ramoncito, as he was known, refused to appear in court. As a result he was sentenced to four years in jail, of which he served only two, since he was pardoned in 1986 by President Reagan.

As René went about his activities in the Democracy Movement, his friend Juan Pablo Roque, who had stayed with the Brothers, informed the publishing world that he had written a book about his experience as a defector. Roque sent a brief letter outlining the project to various publishing houses in Florida, New Jersey and New York, and sat back to wait for the best offer. The synopsis promised a bomb that could shake the foundations of the Cuban Revolution:

> I am an ex-major of the Armed Forces of Cuba and a MiG-21 and MiG-23 fighter pilot. I attended the Lenin Political-Military Academy in Moscow for four years and returned to Cuba as deputy commander of an airborne regiment of the Anti-Aircraft Defense Troops. I was also head of the political section of the Communist Party, responsible for twenty-five PCC nuclei and for eighteen founding committees of the Union of Young Communists.
>
> I arrived in this country from the Naval Base at Guantánamo, which I managed to reach by swimming all night. Since my arrival I have been writing about a variety of internal topics relating to the Armed Forces and the Cuban Air Force. I managed to bring photographs with me from Cuba of high-ranking army and air force personnel, also of the Ministry of the RAF—Revolutionary Armed Forces—under the command of Raúl Castro. None of these documents has ever been seen before and they are in my possession. I have

written a book with the following details, which will be made public for the first time:

... Disagreements between the different generations within the Revolutionary Armed Forces (RAF), their motives and disillusions.

... Perestroika: internal view of the topic within official circles and how the central political directorate of the RAF deals with this question.

... The case of General Arnaldo Ochoa and the true opinion of the RAF and the Ministry of the Interior on the subject. Ochoa's imprisonment and my meeting with him two weeks before his detention.

All of these issues, as well as a large quantity of photographs and documents, form part of the book, making for a new vision of the RAF today. It is the point of view of a pilot who grew up and developed within the machine that condemned him and his two brothers, also pilots, who remain imprisoned by the regime.

My thanks in advance for the time and attention you may give to this matter, in hopes of an early and satisfactory reply.

Yours sincerely,
Juan Pablo Roque

Although there are dozens of publishing houses in Florida specializing in Cuban subjects, the highest bidder was CANF Editors, the editorial arm of the Cuban American National Foundation, based in Washington. What the author actually had ready was barely a rough draft. The signing of the contract in 1994 coincided with a new wave of migration from Cuba, brought on by the worsening economic crisis. The resurgence of the rafters increased the demand for experienced pilots, and Roque did not have much time for writing. The book as such would still take months to be delivered.

The more the economic crisis worsened on the Island, the greater the number of Cubans who risked leaving the country by the most dangerous route: by sea. Added to the economic problems was the toughening of the State Department's policy of visa concessions to Cubans for legal entry to the country, which produced endless queues at the door of the US Interests Section in Havana.

The Washington authorities were stingy when it came to giving out visas, while maintaining the "wet-foot, dry-foot policy" that acted as a spur to risky crossings and boat thefts. Seeing it was also a problem for the American government, since it was becoming more and more difficult to absorb and house the illegal immigrants arriving in Florida, the Cuban government decided not to try to prevent the growing number of escapes.

Any Cuban adult knew that leaving the country by sea was extremely foolhardy. Whoever managed to sail, whether on buoys, rubber dinghies or rafts, up to the twelve-mile territorial limit and get into American waters, had to pray to be located and rescued by the US Coast Guard, who would take charge of castaways and occupants of vessels in danger. Whoever could afford it paid dearly to be picked up on the Cuban coast and taken as far as Florida's first keys—the small islands to the south of Key West that, seen from above, call to mind a string of pearls. The new exodus created a short-lived but lucrative activity for sailors and owners of motorboats and other vessels in Miami who charged between $8,000 and $10,000 per head to carry exiles to Florida. At the limits of despair, some Cubans went as far as selling everything they had to get enough money for the crossing.

The dire situation that René had alleged as his reason for going into exile in 1990 seemed to have deteriorated even more. Cuba's main source of income was still sugar. However, as 85 percent of the harvest was mechanized, and there was now no gasoline to feed the cutting machines, the combine harvesters and the trucks, the annual crop of over 8 million tons—in the last year of the USSR's existence—had dropped to a little over 3 million tons. Rationed for the sugar industry, fuel was practically nonexistent for private cars, meaning that cars disappeared from the streets, leaving Havana and the other provincial capitals looking like ghost towns. In order to replace them, some sugar and nickel production was exchanged with China for one million bicycles, enough for 10 percent of the population.

The crisis also changed the country's cultural face. Gone were the days when printings of 100,000 copies of classics like *Don Quixote* or *One Hundred Years of Solitude* disappeared from bookshops in a matter of days. The average number of books published annually, which was 45 million copies in 1990, had fallen to less than 1 million. The impossibility of importing newsprint suspended the circulation of the majority of publications. Traditional magazines like the University of Cuba's *Alma Mater*, in operation since 1922, the weekly *Bohemia*, founded in 1908, the monthly cultural magazine *Casa* of the Casa de las Américas, and even *Verde Olivo*, the official vehicle of the Revolutionary Armed Forces, had to close their doors. The daily *Granma*, official organ of the Communist Party and the country's main newspaper, which had in times of plenty circulated with over sixty pages, was now reduced to a tabloid of six pages.

The strict rationing of energy subjected the population to additional hardship. A severe system of rotation imposed on the country obliged everyone to spend sixteen hours a day without electricity. The blackouts generated peaks of telephone use between eight-thirty and nine o'clock at night, causing congestion on the precarious local network. On investigating the phenomenon, the authorities discovered that what was on television at that hour had become a passion among Cubans: Brazilian soap operas. Whoever had electricity would call a friend who was in the blackout zone and place the phone by the television speaker, so that the friend could at least hear that day's episode.

For René and Roque, the extent of the crisis could be seen from the skies, in the mass of crafts that again crowded the strip of sea separating the two countries. The average number of flights made by René in the United States had tripled in the first months of 1994. By the end of March 1994, when the number of rafters taken into Florida in that wave of migration surpassed 30,000, the phantom of the so-called Mariel Exodus of 1980 came back to haunt the White House. In April of that year, at the end of a TV debate between presidents Jimmy Carter and Fidel Castro, no less than 130,000 Cubans had left the country from the port of Mariel bound for Miami.

3

OVERNIGHT, 130,000 PEOPLE FLEE CUBA FOR THE UNITED STATES AND DEFEAT JIMMY CARTER AND BILL CLINTON

Migration crises were far from a novelty in the harsh and tumultuous relationship between the United States and Cuba after Fidel Castro came to power in 1959. The first of these arose shortly after the triumph of the Revolution and lasted until 1962—a period in which 200,000 people, almost 3 percent of the Cuban population, departed for the United States. The exodus produced a sharp demographic leap in Miami, whose population rose from 300,000 to almost half a million. Up until the Cubans' arrival, the census registered that out of every ten local residents, eight were white and only two "nonwhite," a category that included blacks and Hispanics. Although the first wave of migration included torturers from the Batista government, drug traffickers, bookies and pimps, statistics showed that the great majority was made up of liberal professionals—above all doctors, given that health was one of the first sectors nationalized by the revolutionary government—as well as businessmen, bankers, landowners and industrialists who had had their property expropriated. The components of this first wave fostered the illusion that what had happened in Cuba was just one more Latin American military coup. The coup d'état backed by the CIA in Guatemala six years earlier, when President Jacobo

Arbenz had been overthrown after decreeing an agricultural reform program that affected the interests of the American multinational United Fruit Company, was still fresh in everybody's mind. The United States would never tolerate a communist government in Cuba, 160 kilometers from its coastline. "Entire families, with their servants and dogs," wrote the Cuban specialist and academic Jesús Arboleya, "embarked for Miami in the hope they would soon return home."

Cubans still lived with the trauma of the mass escape organized when the Catholic Church joined forces with the opposition. At the height of the first confrontations between Havana and Washington, the CIA and the archbishop of Miami, Coleman Carroll, orchestrated a dreadful plan for the mass transfer of children from Cuba to the United States with the indispensable support of the Cuban Church. Christened Operation Peter Pan and later inspiring books and films, the action began on an October night in 1960 with a distressing proclamation from an announcer on Radio Swan, a station set up by the CIA in Miami to broadcast programs to Cuba: "Cuban mothers! The revolutionary government is planning to steal your children!" cried the announcer. "When they are five, your children will be removed from your families and only come back again at eighteen, transformed into materialist monsters! Watch out, Cuban mothers! Do not let the government steal your children!" The second step came the following morning when hundreds of thousands of pamphlets were scattered throughout the country with the text of a fictional law, written by members of the CIA, that would allegedly be put into effect "at any moment" by the Cuban government. Packed with legal considerations, the apocryphal document was signed "Dr. Fidel Castro Ruiz, Prime Minister" and by the then president of the Republic, Osvaldo Dorticós. The threat that would terrify mothers and fathers appeared in three articles and two paragraphs:

Article 3 — ... From the date of implementation of the present law, minors below the age of twenty will become wards of the State.
Article 4 — ... Minors will remain in the care of their parents up

to the age of five, from which time their physical, mental and civic education will be entrusted to the Children's Circles Organization, which will be responsible for the guardianship of the aforementioned minors.

Article 5 — … With a view to their cultural education and civic training, from the age of ten years onwards, any minor may be removed to a place more appropriate for the attainment of such objectives, always taking into account the best interests of the nation.

Paragraph 1 — From the date of publication of this law, it is prohibited for all minors to leave the country.

Paragraph 2 — Noncompliance with the precepts contained in the present law will be considered a crime against the revolution, punishable by imprisonment from two to fifteen years depending on the gravity of the offense.

The man chosen by the archdiocese to carry out the plan was Bryan Walsh, a six-foot-tall, fifty-year-old Irish priest with the body of a boxer, who had lived in the United States since his youth. Arriving in Havana a few weeks after that October night, carrying in his baggage no less than 500 blank entry visas to the United States, Walsh found a society in a state of shock. The denials of the revolutionary government had done little to soothe the fears of Cuban families. In addition, parish priests all over the country, especially in the countryside where the less-educated population lived, took it upon themselves to spread the gruesome rumor that the children separated from their parents were to be removed to Moscow and transformed into canned food for consumption by the Russian population. It was not the first time that such a ghastly and implausible story had been used for political ends. The anecdote about communists eating people had been born at the end of World War II, when the fascist propaganda machine flooded Italy with leaflets affirming that Italian soldiers who surrendered to the Red Army would be killed, ground up and fed to the starving millions in Stalinist Russia.

Towards the end of 1960, the Cuban Revolution had already implemented radical changes such as agrarian reforms, the nationalization of the banking system and the "forced expropriation" of almost a thousand industries, among which were a hundred sugar mills and some giants like the Bacardi rum factory and the American DuPont chemical company. In spite of the revolutionary nature of these measures, when Operation Peter Pan was conceived Cuba and the United States still maintained normal relations. Hundreds of travelers crossed the Florida Straits daily in both directions, on flights that connected the Cuban capital with Florida; the air bridge between Havana and Miami was the route chosen by Bryan Walsh to put the operation into practice. The CIA demanded children should not be accompanied by their parents. The 500 blank forms the priest had taken on his first trip would not be enough, as it turned out, to cover even 5 percent of the little candidates for salvation from the communist hell. Many years later, Fidel Castro would comment on the episode in a television interview. "We thought that the Revolution should be a voluntary act on the part of a free people, and we placed no restrictions on departures from the country," recalled the Cuban leader. "The response of imperialism, among other hostilities, was the implementation of Operation Peter Pan."

According to the American NGO Pedro Pan Group, altogether 14,048 girls and boys were smuggled out. Some would become distinguished figures in American public life, like Republican Senator Mel Martínez, Tomás Regalado, the former mayor of Miami, and the diplomats Eduardo Aguirre, nominated as ambassador to Spain by President George W. Bush, and Hugo Llorens, ambassador to Honduras in 2009 at the time of President Manuel Zelaya's deposition. Initially put into Catholic orphanages and charitable institutions, thousands of these evacuated children would never see their fathers and mothers again. The beginning of 1962 saw the end of Operation Peter Pan, one of the most dramatic and painful episodes of the Cuban Revolution.

The third wave of migration occurred at the end of 1966, after President Johnson signed into law the Cuban Adjustment Act— which was simply the legal recognition of a situation that had existed since 1959 and survived under the complacent eye of the American authorities. Without parallel in any other country, the law offered

Cubans arriving in the United States, even if illegally, privileges not conceded to foreigners of any other nationality. The benefits offered by the government were a tempting invitation: political asylum and documents granting permanent residence. In other words, authorization to work and claim social security—rights that were extended to spouses and to children below the age of twenty-one. It was the opposite of the treatment dispensed to the hordes of Latin Americans who tried to enter the United States via the Mexican border. In the four years to follow, an air bridge linking the seaside resort of Varadero to Miami carried more than 270,000 Cubans.

The fourth and noisiest crisis began on the afternoon of April 1, 1980, when six Cubans invaded the mansion that housed the Peruvian embassy in Havana, hurling a bus against the garden fence. The only impediment to entry, a lone soldier guarding the doorway, was gunned down. Minutes later, once inside the house, the six were declared political refugees. Cuba demanded that all of them be returned, since by killing a soldier they had become common criminals. The Peruvian ambassador, however, would not budge: his country had decided to grant them political asylum. The gravity of the situation put Fidel Castro in direct confrontation with General Francisco Morales Bermúdez, head of the Peruvian government, who had toppled the similarly ultranationalist General Juan Velasco Alvarado in 1975. On receiving the six invaders as asylum seekers, Bermúdez imagined he had Fidel in a corner with no way out: were he to concede safe conduct for the group to leave Cuba, the government would be setting a serious precedent, that in order to get out of the country, all it would take was to set foot inside an embassy, even if it involved violence. But to deny permission would turn those six Cubans into martyrs, and once again brand Cuba a country that violated human rights. All of these outcomes had the potential to cause a diplomatic impasse with unpredictable consequences. What General Bermúdez could never have imagined, however, was that Fidel would react with an extraordinary decision. The response came in a short article published on the front page of the April 4 edition of *Granma*, which ended in an unusual way:

In view of the Peruvian government's refusal to hand over the delinquents who caused the death of the soldier Pedro Ortiz Cabrera, the Cuban government reserves the right to withdraw the embassy's protective guard. The diplomatic mission mentioned, therefore, is open to all who wish to leave the country.

What seemed to be an isolated incident turned first into a commotion, then a stampede, and two days later there were 10,000 people camped out in a six-bedroom residential property. Frightened by the presence of the rabble that had taken over every inch of the house, Ambassador Edgardo de Habich abandoned the premises, taking with him his entire diplomatic staff except for his business attaché, who became responsible for the legation. Two weeks after the occupation, and with the swarm of people still inside the embassy, Peru capitulated and admitted it was unable to receive 10,000 people at a moment's notice.

It was at this point that Jimmy Carter entered the fray. Of all the occupants of the White House since the triumph of the Cuban Revolution, Carter was the one who maintained the best relations with Cuba. He had been responsible for lifting all the restrictions on the exiles for travel to the Island and for the creation of the Interests Sections in Havana and Washington so that, in his own words, "a minimum of diplomatic exchange could be carried out." In July 1977, in an interview with the Brazilian magazine *Veja*, Fidel recognized that something was changing in the United States. "Eisenhower, Kennedy, Johnson, Nixon and Ford were committed to a policy of hostility towards Cuba," affirmed the Cuban president to the weekly, "and this is the first US government in eighteen years that is not committed to that policy. Nixon was a buffoon, an individual without ethics of any kind. I don't think the same of Carter."

Three years after these declarations, however, the domestic scene in the United States had changed a lot. The conservative American majority had fumed at Carter's treaties with the Panamanian president Omar Torrijos, pledging to hand over control of the Panama Canal in 2000. Public opinion also considered Carter to have been soft on the USSR for ignoring the 1979 invasion of Afghanistan by Soviet troops. But what would put an end to his popularity happened on the night of April 25, 1980, when the White House–approved Operation Eagle Claw ended in catastrophe. Aboard eight helicopters and six Hercules C-130 planes, ninety men from a USAF antiterrorist commando took off from the Kingdom of Bahrain and from the aircraft carrier *Nimitz*, anchored in the Indian Ocean. The operation's objective was to set free fifty-two Americans taken hostage six months earlier by a group of young Iranians who had occupied the United States embassy in Tehran. Thrown off course by sandstorms in the Dasht-e Kavir desert, already in Iranian territory but still 500 kilometers from the capital, the mission was aborted when one of the helicopters crashed into a transport aircraft. Eight American soldiers died, and the hostages remained in the hands of the Iranians.

The crestfallen survivors of Operation Eagle Claw returned to Washington nineteen days after the Peruvian embassy in Havana had been taken. In the face of the timidity shown by the international community—Peru agreed to receive only 1,000 of the 10,000 people who had taken refuge in the embassy, Canada 600 and Costa Rica 300—the American president, who would run for reelection in October of that year, thought that here was an opportunity to recover his popularity. Contrary to the moderate diplomacy he had adopted in relation to Cuba since he came into the White House, Carter called a press conference and announced a bombshell. With the new name of "Open Hearts and Open Arms," the old Adjustment Act was resurrected: all Cubans who managed to reach the United States would receive political asylum, permanent resident status, permission to work and to register with social security, and the rest.

Fidel Castro replied on the same day and in the same tone: in view of Carter's offer, from that moment onwards the port of Mariel, fifty kilometers to the west of Havana, was open to whoever wished to take refuge in the United States. The decision stressed it was valid not only for the 10,000 tenants of the Peruvian embassy, but for any one of the 11 million Cubans who might wish to leave. Hours later, the 160 kilometers of sea that separate the port of Mariel from Key West were speckled with boats of all shapes and sizes coming from various points in Florida, ready to transport passengers in what would be the largest wave of migration in the history of the Cuban diaspora. If Bermúdez got a fright when Cuba freed not six, but 10,000 people, the White House's plan had also gone awry. Carter could not have foreseen that in the following weeks 130,000 candidates for American citizenship, more than 1 percent of the population of Cuba, would cross the Caribbean Sea headed for Miami.

The president of the United States only became aware of the size of the problem when the CIA informed him that around 40,000 *marielitos*—as the exiles who left at that time became known—were mentally ill or common delinquents, many of them serving long sentences for drug trafficking, robbery or rape. The reports were alarming: Cuba was exporting its criminals and madmen to the United States. The Cuban government denied that it had forced anyone to leave the country. However, according to information spread by the *radio bemba*, soon after the opening of the port of Mariel, Cuba's madhouses and prisons had indeed been visited by government officials who repeated the same offer to the sick and to prison inmates: whoever wished to emigrate to the United States, with all the advantages offered by Carter, only had to bundle up his things and get to the port at Mariel. Many years later, Max Lesnik, a Cuban exile in Miami who never stopped being a friend of Cuba, would be outspoken as to the selection process of those who became known as the *undesirables*:

"These lunatics were in Cuban psychiatric hospitals, in the care of the Revolution. Someone would show up and ask the inmate: where are your parents? In the United States? All right, take him to Mariel. His family can look after him in Miami."

Be that as it may, 40,000 people left mental health institutions and prisons and embarked for Florida. Once again the problem switched sides and was no longer Cuba's: what future could be given to all those people? How to resettle 130,000 people and offer them, overnight, the minimum required for survival? The CIA expressed an additional worry that made matters worse: Fidel would never pass up this opportunity to plant a few dozen intelligence agents among the multitude of refugees.

The first step Carter took was to share the problem with his allies and distribute the unexpected guests among the states governed by Democrats. The news that tiny Arkansas would be assigned 20,000 Cubans, of which statistically 6,000 were criminals or mentally ill, made the young state governor's hair stand on end—he was thirty-four-year-old Bill Clinton, elected two years earlier. The municipality selected to receive the Cubans was Fort Smith, situated 200 kilometers from the state capital of Little Rock. It was a quiet, conservative town of 60,000 inhabitants, of whom 50,000 were white Protestants. Fort Smith was chosen because of its military camp, Fort Chaffee, largely inactive after 1961, but used as a processing center for refugees from South Vietnam following the end of the Vietnam War in 1975.

Stunned by the news, Clinton contacted the White House in hopes of dissuading Carter. Just like the president, he was up for reelection that year—in Arkansas at that time the term of office was two years—and the worst thing that could happen to his ratings was to foist 20,000 Cubans on the state's population. Eugene Eidenberg, the presidential aide entrusted with the job of dealing with the "Cuban question," tried to reassure Clinton by reminding him of the favorable results of the experience with the South Vietnamese. The governor retorted that in that case a screening performed in the Philippines and Thailand had filtered out the undesirables. He suggested that the 20,000 Cubans destined for his state be put on board an aircraft carrier anchored in the Florida Straits, where a screening could be performed. Eidenberg dismissed the idea, insisting that there was no room for so many people. In Clinton's autobiography, *My Life*, he tells how he lost patience with Carter's advisor:

"Sure there is! We still have a base at Guantánamo, don't we? And there must be a gate in the fence that divides it from Cuba. Take them to Guantánamo, open the door, and march them back into Cuba."

In the governor's opinion, Fidel was "making America look foolish and the President look powerless. Jimmy Carter already had his hands full with inflation and the Iranian hostage crisis." Defeated, Clinton would see not 20,000 but 25,390 Cubans arrive in Arkansas at the end of May 1980. And it soon became clear that his fears were well-founded. There were disturbances inside the fort. After a week, 200 exiles escaped from the camp. Worried about the risk of a bloody confrontation, Clinton spoke with Carter by phone and requested federal troops to maintain order and secure the Cubans inside the base. "I was afraid people in the area were going to start shooting them," he wrote. "There had been a run on handguns and rifles in every gun store within fifty miles of Chaffee." On June 1, armed with sticks, stones and bottles, another thousand refugees broke out and set off on a protest march on the highway between Fort Smith and Barling, a small town ten kilometers to the south. Faced with the inaction of federal troops and fearing a "bloodbath," Clinton ordered the state troopers to stop the advance of the fugitives. The Cubans confronted the troops with stones, but ended up turning around and going back to the fort. When the smoke cleared, the disturbances had left a total of sixty-two injured, from both sides, and two buildings burned down. The only fatality would be the governor's ratings. When they were opened, the ballot boxes of the December election revealed what Clinton feared most: the *marielitos* had defeated him. In his place, the electorate had chosen the Republican Frank Durward White. On a national level, the Democratic disaster was identical. Jimmy Carter lost badly, and handed over the White House to the ultraconservative Ronald Reagan.

The wave of migration that interrupted Clinton's career and helped to bury Carter's lasted only five months, but it would be considered officially over only four years later, in December 1984, when Cuba and the United States signed a provisional agreement to resume normal immigration practices. In accordance with this document, Washington would concede 20,000 visas annually to Cubans who intended to emigrate, with priority given to political prisoners and their families and to those who had relatives with

American citizenship living in the United States. In exchange, every year Cuba would take back around 6,000 "undesirables," rebaptized by the American authorities as "excludables."

The Cuban influx profoundly changed the face of the Miami that René González and Juan Pablo Roque knew. Whites, who in 1960 represented 80 percent of the population, were reduced to a mere 12 percent by 1990—the great majority was composed of Hispanics (62 percent) and blacks (24 percent). Miami was on its speedy way into the *Guinness Book of Records* as "the city with the largest foreign population"—of every ten inhabitants, six had been born in another country. Among the rights that the Cubans acquired upon setting foot on American soil was that of voting and of being voted for, which gradually came to confer a respectable political and electoral importance to the community. And in the complicated American electoral system, Florida's Electoral College constituted a keystone for reaching the presidency, whether the candidate were a Democrat or a Republican. The tens of thousands of rafters that René and Roque saw landing on American territory at the start of 1994 were not simply numbers to boost the Hispanic demographic in Florida. The White House knew that it was once again facing a "Cuban question," and that there was only one way to staunch that hemorrhage: negotiate a new migration deal with the communist government of Cuba. A choice that would end up interfering with the life of René González, Juan Pablo Roque and the majority of anti-Castroist organizations in Florida.

Roque divided himself between his activities as a pilot, writing the promised book of memoirs and preparing for his wedding to Ana Margarita, while René persisted with his obsession to bring his family to Miami. And, for the first time, he felt that wasn't the illusion of a husband in love. The years that had passed since his desertion had softened Olguita's heart somewhat. Although she never shared such thoughts with her parents or her closest friends, in the scarce letters sent to René she began to show signs that perhaps she would consider going to live with her husband again. Like him, Olga had never really stopped thinking about the possibility, but every time she weighed the pros and cons she came to the conclusion that it made more sense for her to forget René, bring up her daughter Irmita in Cuba, and who knows, maybe one day find a new relationship. Moving to Miami and living alongside the *gusanos* René hung out with meant throwing away everything she had learned and defended all her life. What's more, if she ever did agree to emigrate, she would only do it legally, with a visa given to her by the US Interests Section in Havana. Although the Miami radio stations that could be heard in Cuba hammered nonstop at the heads of its listeners, urging them to leave the country any way they could, she would never dream of crossing the sea with her daughter, a risk that had already cost the lives of hundreds, perhaps thousands of Cubans. And in the middle of a migration crisis like that at the beginning of 1994, the chances of getting an American visa were one in a million. The single argument in favor of going into exile was, though, too strong for Olga to simply to discount: her love for René, which had never really disappeared.

While these doubts robbed her of a good deal of sleep, on the other side of the Straits Olga's husband was working feverishly to get permission from the American Immigration Services (USCIS) for safe conduct passes to be issued so that she and Irmita could leave the Island. René knew that the chances of success were slim and that he would face difficulties from both governments. As part of the lobbying campaign against the Cuban Revolution, the State Department gave priority in granting visas to political prisoners or to those persecuted for crimes of conscience. And Olga, a disciplined Communist Party militant, was far from being a dissident. On top of this, even if authorization for admission were given by the United States, René would still have major obstacles to overcome in order for Cuba to allow their departure. His hopes rested on a single point: that the governments of both countries, forced by the rafter crisis, might sign a new migration agreement, reactivating the policy of mass distributions of visa quotas for entry into the United States.

Even before knowing if Olguita would accept being an exile, René took the initiative to request the visas for his wife and daughter at the USCIS. If his status as an American citizen assured him of some small privileges, like not having to pay fees and being able to access counters with little or no queues, he knew that even so his request would gather dust with the other tens of thousands of identical requests made by Cuban-Americans who wanted to bring their families over. But he entertained hopes that in Miami, as in any government department anywhere on the planet, a political friend at court might help him through the tortuous bureaucratic maze. And the man who could show him the quickest route was José Basulto, with whom René was still friendly. During one of their chats in a hangar used by the Brothers, René disclosed his situation to his former boss:

"As you know, I intend to bring my family to Miami, but since the queue of applicants is so long, I need your help. I know you have contacts with influential politicians in Washington and it would really be helpful if one of them could push my application forward in the Immigration Services."

Polite as always, Basulto explained that it was of no use getting the help of some congressman if Cuba weren't going to give Olga and Irmita the safe conduct pass known as the "white card," granted to those authorized to leave the country legally. In any event, he recommended that everything should be done with the utmost discretion:

"If this becomes a political case and it gets into the press that you are having trouble getting your wife and child out of Cuba, the situation will get worse. Right there the Cubans won't give them the exit visa. I can try to help you in Washington, but what you really need is someone with access to the Cuban government to obtain the authorization for them to leave the country."

To intercede on their behalf with Havana, the name of the young reverend Jesse Jackson came up. Jackson was a black pastor who had twice been a candidate for president of the United States, and who had become Fidel Castro's friend. Before setting things in motion in Cuba, however, it was necessary to get someone to back René's case in Washington. It could either be a congressman or senator, as well as someone from the State Department who was supportive of Florida's anti-Castroist organizations. Finally they decided to focus their efforts on House Representatives Ileana Ros-Lehtinen and Lincoln Díaz-Balart, and on Senator Bob Menéndez.

Born in Cuba, the two Republicans represented electoral districts in Florida. Ros-Lehtinen had arrived in the United States at the age of six and had been the first Hispanic woman to be elected to the House of Representatives. Díaz-Balart was the nephew of Mirta, Castro's first wife and mother of "Fidelito"—Fidel Castro Díaz-Balart, the Cuban leader's eldest son. Menéndez, the then Democratic senator for New Jersey, had left Cuba still inside his mother's womb in 1953. With free access to the Oval Office, the trio prided themselves on representing the most radical sectors of anti-Castroism in Congress. Once introductions had been made by Basulto, René left for Washington. Even though he had no personal contact with any of the politicians, he was well received by their advisors. In the three politicians' chambers René heard optimistic forecasts on the result of his request, especially since it was a humanitarian one, rather than an attempt to get someone who opposed the regime out of the Island. But everything would depend on Havana and Washington restoring the visa quota system for Cubans who wished to emigrate.

It wasn't only René, however, who was worried by the new wave of rafters. As the Cuban roamed the Capitol's corridors in search of any friendly hand that could help him bring Olguita and Irmita to the United States, President Bill Clinton followed the unfolding of the latest migration crisis between the two countries with apprehension. At dinner at the writer William Styron's house, on Martha's Vineyard off the coast of Massachusetts, Clinton took advantage of the presence of his literary idol, the Colombian Gabriel García Márquez, to do something that the embargo against Cuba prevented him from doing personally: send a message to President Fidel Castro, whose friendship "Gabo" had enjoyed for a long time. Walking alone with the writer on the lawns of Styron's house, Clinton asked him to transmit a warning to the Cuban leader: if the new wave of migration went on, Cuba would receive a very different response from that given by Carter in 1980, after the Mariel exodus. "Castro has already cost me one election. He can't have two," he told Márquez.

The first result of Clinton's message to Fidel was the setting up of a top-secret operation, put into motion weeks after the dinner on Martha's Vineyard. Shrouded in secrecy, the initial contacts were made by a Cuban and an American official who met up in the corridors of supermarkets, in overcrowded subway carriages or in Starbucks—and always in New York, a city where three dozen Cuban diplomats accredited to the United Nations can circulate freely. At the end of the meetings, each of the negotiators personally delivered a report to his superiors on the progress of the talks—on the American side six high officials from the State Department, the CIA and the FBI, and on the Cuban side the same number of representatives from the Ministry of Foreign Relations and the Department of State Security (DSS), an organ of the Ministry of the Interior that brings together Cuba's secret services.

The main difficulties in reaching an agreement lay in the fact that each side insisted on including tit-for-tat demands in the document. When Cuba proposed a suspension of the radio broadcasts from Miami picked up on the Island, the American representative retorted that his country's Constitution guaranteed freedom of expression and the subject was not up for discussion. If the US negotiator sought to include imprisoned dissidents among the candidates for exit visas, he would be told that there were no political prisoners in Cuba, only people convicted of common crimes. At the end of ten weeks of negotiations, both sides concluded that it was time for the twelve officials, whose job it would be to draft the migration accord that was to be submitted to presidents Bill Clinton and Fidel Castro, to meet in person.

But there was still one problem: how and where to secretly assemble twelve officials of the highest rank, six Americans and six Cubans? Not even in the most critical moments of relations between the two countries—like the Cuban Missile Crisis in October of 1962, when the world was on the brink of nuclear war—had such a large number of such high-ranking officials from these two governments come face to face. Both sides knew that if word of the meeting were leaked, the hawks in the United States government and the anti-Castroist organizations of Florida—both of them interested in prolonging the rafter crisis as a means to weaken the Cuban government—would try to abort the operation. Cuba and the United States were therefore out of the question. And if the meetings were to take place in another country this would have to be done in secret, without the knowledge of the local government.

Suggested by no one knows which side, an unusual solution to the problem came up in the middle of August. The following month reservations were made for six suites in L'Un et L'Autre, a small and elegant Canadian hotel costing $270 a night. Situated near the old port of Montreal, less than fifty kilometers from the US border, this chic location was a popular tourist destination for gay men. On a Friday in September 1994, L'Un et L'Autre received six discreet male "couples"—six Cubans and six Americans—who stayed for the next few days, deciding the fate of the Cuban immigrants.

Weeks later, René read in the *Miami Herald* news of the signing of the new migration accord, which could be summarized in four basic points:

> The entrance of illegal immigrants into the country is prohibited by the government of the USA; those rescued at sea will be taken to shelters outside the United States.
>
> The government of Cuba, for its part, will take measures to stop unsafe departures, using mainly persuasive methods.
>
> Both governments are committed to prevent the illicit transport of people bound for the United States, as well as to prevent the use of violence on the part of all persons who intend to arrive, or arrive in the United States coming from Cuba by means of forced deviations of airplanes and ships.

The part that most interested René—the doorway through which Olga and Irmita would enter Miami—appeared only in the final words of the document:

> The United States establish that the total legal immigration from Cuba to the United States will now be a minimum of 20 thousand Cubans per year, not including in this number the immediate relatives of North American citizens, who will receive priority treatment.

The communiqué also stated that new rounds of negotiations between the two governments had been scheduled to try to solve the two delegations' differing points of view. Since there was no longer any need for secrecy, future meetings would take place alternately in Washington and Havana. The sticking points were that the United States did not want to prohibit the radio transmissions picked up in Cuba from Miami that continued to encourage illegal departures. And the Cubans dug their heels in on two issues: they did not accept that the Guantánamo base be used as "a haven outside the United States," where people rescued at sea could be taken—after all, it constituted an enclave inside its own territory, to which Cuba had never ceased to lay claim. Also out of the question was the US demand for the repatriation of one more batch of the so-called excludables, the criminals and the mentally ill who had set off for Miami during the Mariel migration crisis. By the end of the new rounds of talks, only one of these outstanding items had been resolved: the United States accepted Cuba's demand that any rafters rescued at sea after the signing of the accord would now be settled at Camp Carmichael, an unused British base in Nassau, capital of the Bahamas.

As René quietly celebrated the new agreement, it was received by the anti-Castroist organizations as a declaration of war by Clinton's government. Congressman Lincoln Díaz-Balart used the House of Representatives as a rostrum from which to condemn the agreement and assert that he was not surprised by the government's insensibility towards the Cuban exiles. "This lack of solidarity with the Cuban people has existed for many years," said the Republican, "but, in spite of the Clinton administration, the republic and democracy will be reestablished in Cuba." Ever under the sway of the Cuban community, the press in southern Florida accused the White House of being "soft on a Communist dictator" and foresaw that the Democratic Party would get its payback in the 1996 elections, when Clinton would try to get reelected as president. Political analysts also reckoned that the accords would pour cold water on the plans of Justice Secretary Janet Reno to stand for governor of Florida. One of the most vociferous activists in the anti-agreement campaign was Juan Pablo Roque, who often traveled to Washington with groups of exiles to carry banners in protest marches in front of the White House.

In charge of explaining the measures and diminishing their negative impact on the leaders of the Cuban community was Richard Nuccio, the special policy adviser on Cuba (or under secretary for Cuban affairs: Cuba was the only country to enjoy the dubious privilege of having an under secretariat to itself within the State Department). In discussions with groups of exiles in Miami, Nuccio affirmed that the Clinton administration's policy with respect to Cuba could be summed up in two words: "pressure" and "contact." To deflect accusations of excessive tolerance towards the Cuban Revolution and to remove the White House from the sights of the Cuban community, Nuccio accused Latin America of complicity with Fidel Castro. "Many Latin American governments have never said clearly that they wish to promote a democratic transition in Cuba," he declared in a debate at the Biltmore Hotel in Coral Gables. "That's what's truly disgraceful."

The aggressive reaction from the Cuban community had an objective explanation. Since the 1980 crisis, when the rafters became an integral part of the negotiations between the United States and Cuba, it had become a lucrative business in Florida to set up a "humanitarian and nonprofit" anti-Castroist organization—as all of them claimed to be. Under the authorities' conniving eye, fortunes were being moved around without any external or fiscal control. To place the accounts belonging to these anti-Castroist groups under scrutiny, or to question the origin or destination of their funds, was a heresy that automatically turned the accuser into "an agent of Fidel Castro."

Not even the *New York Times* would escape. When in 1998 it published a series of interviews with the archenemy of the Cuban Revolution, the CIA agent and Bay of Pigs organizer Luis Posada Carriles, in which he made scandalous revelations about the anti-Castroist organizations' links to terrorism, the journalist Larry Rohter, then head of the *Times* bureau in Miami, got a whiff of the anti-Castroist mafia up close. On the day the first article appeared,

Rohter's telephone didn't stop. Voices with Cuban accents repeated the same threat:

"Hey, commie, be careful. We're watching you!"

Other callers accused him of being "the new Herbert Matthews," a reference to the author of the first long interview given by Fidel Castro to the *New York Times* in 1957, while he was still in the Sierra Maestra. Matthews had been harassed by the Cuban community, accused of deifying the revolutionary leader for all the world to see. It was nonetheless ironic trying to stick the label of "Castrophile" on someone like Rohter, who in 1980, during the Mariel crisis, had been expelled from Cuba for having written an article in *Newsweek* that had upset the Cuban leaders.

Indifferent to the threats, the newspaper continued to publish the interviews with Posada Carriles that Rohter had written along with his colleague Ann Louise Bardach. On his way to work, the journalist often tuned his car radio to radical stations like Radio Mambí and La Voz de la Esperanza (The Voice of Hope), but he didn't take the threats seriously. "I admit I didn't think they'd do anything to me, I thought that reaction was sort of a folkloric thing, a bit of what they call the Cuban *farándula* [theater]," Rohter would recall many years later. "Just to reassure my wife and two young sons, I changed the house phone number." On the evening of the day the third article appeared, he was at home with his wife in their private garden, in Pinecrest, a suburb south of Miami, when he heard a bang coming from the street. He ran out in time to see a car speeding away; a rifle shot had opened up a gaping hole in his front door.

Worried above all about the safety of his wife and children, he let the newspaper know about the attack and filed a complaint with the police who stationed two armed guards at the entrance to his house. But Rohter insisted to his bosses that the articles should continue to be published. Two days after the attack, Rohter went into the newspaper parking lot on Biscayne Boulevard, and noticed that the driver's window of his car was partly open. He felt a little ridiculous imagining that, like in a cop thriller, the car would be blown sky-high the moment he switched on the ignition. He switched on and nothing happened. He put the car in reverse and when he stepped on the brake, his foot went all the way down and his Chevy banged into the vehicle parked a few yards behind him. A quick check there and then revealed that the brake cables to all four wheels had been cut with pliers. That's when he understood the meaning of the pen split down the middle that had been left on the passenger seat. Just as the Italian Camorra leave a fish wrapped up in newspaper at the front door of a future victim, the Cuban mafia was warning that it would break him in two if he continued to publicize the activities of the anti-Castroist organizations.

While the majority of these radical opposition groups in Florida went into decline following the changes in immigration policy, the fate of the Brothers was perhaps the most indicative of the harsh blow that the new agreements meant for Cuban exiles on the extreme right. With no rafters to rescue, the organization saw its donations from businessmen and institutions like the Cuban American National Foundation dwindle overnight. The annual number of sorties, around 2,000 at the height of the rafter crisis, fell to less than 200. The group's budget experienced a proportional drop, from $1.5 million in 1993 to little more than $300,000 after the new agreements. When Florida's courts delved into the organization's accounts, it emerged that all of its leaders, starting with José Basulto, were receiving high monthly salaries and expense allowances. One of the Brothers balance sheets showed that Basulto had actually received $40,000 in one single payment by way of a refund for food expenses. The documents also showed that the Cessna 2506 that Basulto boasted about having donated to the institution had in fact been sold by him to the Brothers for $64,000. Now the only pretext for the organization to obtain funds from the American government and to continue passing the hat among the community's millionaires was to keep the planes in the air, but only for political activities, airspace invasions, provocations and the financing of mercenaries who were willing to carry out bomb attacks against tourist targets on the Island.

4

THE CUBAN GERARDO HERNÁNDEZ ABANDONS HIS DIPLOMATIC CAREER, CHANGES IDENTITY AND LANDS IN MIAMI AS THE PUERTO RICAN MANUEL VIRAMÓNTEZ

The drastic reduction in the operations of the "humanitarian organizations" ended up affecting both Roque's and René's lives and changing their daily routine. René had been forced to go out again looking for odd jobs to bolster his income. He thought of training to fly large jets, like DC-10s, so he could apply for jobs in the big US airline companies, but abandoned the idea when he discovered that he would need to shell out an unattainable $6,000 to attend the course. Roque went back to being a personal trainer, which left him more time for writing his memoir. After various postponements, he and his girlfriend Ana Margarita Martínez had decided to get married the following year. Hailed as "the wedding of the decade" by the tabloid press, the ceremony finally took place on April 1, 1995—a sunny Saturday, and April Fools' Day. The couple had chosen a Hollywood setting: the University Baptist Church, a small, pink, colonial-style building, nestled among the luxurious mansions in the heart of Coral Gables. The characters present at the ceremony were also like actors in a film. Male guests were dressed either in traditional pleated *guayabera* shirts, white with starched sleeves buttoned at the cuff, or in crisp tropical English suits. All the men sported showy rings, often worn in pairs or threes. Women floated in what appeared to be genuine Dior and Chanel dresses. Coils of white smoke spiraled skywards from the profusion of cigars held in the fingers of politicians, bankers, businessmen and heirs to large distilleries. Mixing with them were mercenaries and confessed terrorists—but all of them in suits and ties, or at least in a *guayabera*. Among the leaders of the main anti-Castroist organizations could be seen another famous defector, General Rafael del Pino, who had fled with his family in May 1987 aboard a Cessna 402. Every half hour Channel 51 made live announcements of their complete coverage of the ceremony coming up at eleven o'clock.

At the appointed time the black Mercedes-Benz carrying the couple gradually made its way between the guests. Pale and slightly plump, wearing a thick pearl necklace, the bride looked the part in her long white dress. Her hair was pulled high into a chignon and tied with a string of pearls the size of marbles. Roque was the incarnation of the classic matinee idol: handsome, muscular, tanned and anticommunist. Not much given to smiling, Roque stood erect and martial, wearing a long tailcoat, a pearl-colored vest, white shirt and bow tie. His left lapel displayed a white carnation and from his breast pocket peeped a pale silk handkerchief. It made no difference that everything, down to the handkerchief, as he would disclose much later, had to be returned twenty-four hours later to the tuxedo rental store. Judging by their appearance, Roque and Ana Margarita really deserved the title "couple of the decade."

The ceremony was short. Facing each other as they knelt on lace-covered hassocks, Ana Margarita and Juan Pablo Roque listened to the brief sermon and the blessing of their union by the priest. Declared husband and wife, they left in a convoy headed by Roque's Toyota Corolla (a vehicle bought secondhand, as the groom would later say), covered in paint and with empty cans tied to the bumpers. The party was a treat given by Luis Alexander, a discreet, gray-haired, middle-aged millionaire, the owner of several banks and a network of hospitals, among other businesses. Alexander and his wife Matilde had what the social columnists, who were plentiful in the Cuban colony's newspapers, called "the most coveted address in Florida." The Alexanders' mansion, often the setting for receptions given by the Cuban aristocracy, was a mandatory stop for any big shots passing through town who were committed to the end of the Cuban Revolution. Hailed as "one of the great icons of the historic exile," a "paladin of democracy" and "a fighter for the liberation of Cuba," Alexander opened up the doors of his mansion in South Miami for the anti-Castroist crème de la crème to celebrate Roque and Ana Margarita's wedding that Sunday.

Wearing a jacket and tie and standing in a corner of the main hall, René watched the couple dance to the sound of *Contigo en la distancia* (With You From Afar), sung by the Mexican Luis Miguel. After the first steps Roque handed his bride to the couple's best man, the smiling José Basulto, to continue the dance. For the wedding night the presidential suite at the Hyatt Regency Hotel in Coral Gables was reserved. The couple danced until midnight in the Alcazaba, the hotel's nightclub, and slept until eleven o'clock the next day. After breakfast they both left for the airport at Tamiami where the anti-Castroist Guillermo Lares handed to Roque the keys to a twin-engine Piper Aztec for the groom to fly them to Andros Island, a little paradise in the Bahamas, where they would stay for four days. "How idyllic, how romantic," Ana Margarita would recall many years later, "that my husband, like a Pegasus, carried me off on our honeymoon flying through the clouds."

Life seemed indeed to smile on the couple. Less than six months after the wedding, they decided to give a big party to celebrate three events: their decision to start a family, Roque's fortieth birthday and the launch of *Desertor* (*Defector*), the book he had now finished. At 140 pages and set in very small print, Roque's book, written entirely in the first person, was a thorough account of the author's life from his birth in Havana in 1955 right up to his arrival in Miami after his adventurous swim across Guantánamo Bay. Of the four back-cover endorsements, at least two were written by people who would be arrested for terrorism should they step foot in Havana: José Basulto and the broadcaster Ninoska Pérez Castellón. The other blurbs were written by a university professor and General Rafael del Pino. It's possible that it was no accident that the Cuban American

National Foundation had published the book so sloppily. It looked almost handmade, with poor-quality paper and crude printing. Nor did the content of *Desertor* live up to the promised bombshell of a memoir from a high official of the Cuban Air Force. It wasn't a bad book, even though the author was clearly more familiar with the joystick of a MiG-23 than a computer keyboard. But it was a narrative full of opinions and short on information, with nothing about the machinations behind the scenes of power in Cuba, nor did it provide any important revelations.

In the book, Roque maintained that the accusations of involvement in drug trafficking against General Ochoa were false, and described the trial as "a spectacle." He denounced the existence of privileges among high-ranking military officials, and said that any different political views held by young Cuban officials were seen by their superiors as *"cosa de maricón y marijuanero"* ("fags and pot-heads stuff"). Every time he referred to the United States' economic war against his country, he put the word "blockade" in quotation marks. One chapter was devoted to disparaging a falling star of Cuban politics, Carlos Aldana, who for years ran the ideological department of the Cuban Communist Party's central committee, and got as far as being considered "number three" in the power hierarchy, after Fidel and Raúl Castro. Three years earlier Aldana had been dismissed from his post and sent to supervise a military hospital out in the country. Another character who came in for rough treatment in Roque's book was the then minister of foreign relations, "Robertico" Robaina, a young man from the rank and file of the Communist Youth who had been appointed to that lofty post at age twenty-seven. The account wound up with a declaration of faith in capitalism:

> Days after arriving in Miami, I was surprised by this immense country, criticized and so badly rated by the government of my country. For the first time I was able to see a person be able to choose between fighting to win and resigning himself to almost nothing. I could understand, truly, the meaning of democracy. I could understand what led us to the Marxist abyss of Fidelism, to the tropical socialism bathed and

inoculated with standards of living contradictory to the right to be free.

Although *Desertor* was plainly not about to topple Cuba's government, the book launch turned into a big party that once again gathered together the most eminent anti-Castroists. In the great lobby of the Omni Colonnade Hotel in Coral Gables, waiters served wine and champagne to hundreds of guests as they awaited the author's arrival. On the way to the hotel, Ana Margarita, who was by Roque's side in the car, wanted to know why her husband seemed so tense and quiet on a day that seemed to hold such promise. He invented an excuse:

"It's nothing. I'm just worried because they told me there might be some kind of demonstration against me at the hotel entrance. They're expecting something organized by the Antonio Maceo Brigade, that pro-dialogue with Cuba group."

On the contrary, the sidewalk under the green canopy that ran the entire length of the hotel façade was packed with reporters, photographers and cameramen. The really big surprise was standing at the entrance with open arms—none less than Jorge Mas Canosa. There in person was the president of the CANF, the boss of bosses, the exiles' unanimous choice to succeed Fidel Castro in a hypothetical "free and democratic Cuba." Treated by all with the obsequious bows and curtsies normally reserved for heads of state, Mas Canosa had begun to behave like exactly that. His presence at Roque's book launch, for example, was not only a tribute to the author, but also a way to disprove before the TV cameras—as those in power often do—the rumors that he had serious health problems. The big chief of Miami was flanked by José Basulto and General del Pino. In a navy-blue suit and plaid tie, always hand in hand with his wife, Roque made his way through the applause to a rostrum onstage and performed the book-signing ritual: he gave the usual thanks, read some extracts and faced the queue of readers that stretched from the front door of the hotel all the way around the corner of the Boulevard Ponce de León. It was only after signing the last copy that Roque made his way with Ana Margarita to Le Festival, a French restaurant where a large group of friends had already gathered. Now it was Ana Margarita who seemed to be sulking. At her husband's insistence, she confessed that she was upset with him:

"I don't want to spoil your birthday, but you thanked more than ten people and didn't mention me once."

Roque pushed her hand away and replied without turning his head, looking out at the traffic:

"I didn't forget. This is a very political book, Anita. I don't want your name linked to it."

It didn't seem like a convincing excuse, but the gaiety and the affectionate welcome in the restaurant made her forget the incident. Couples moved around the enormous buffet table and while others tucked in, Margarita ran her eyes over the copy of *Desertor* that she had in her hands. She flicked all the way through it to the end, went back to the first pages, and realized that she'd been left out of the book, too. More than this: in the two photos in which she did appear, one with Roque and Mas Canosa and the other with her husband at an anti-Clinton rally, her name was not included in the captions. She felt sad, but had already made up her mind not to sour her husband's big day.

It was after eleven o'clock when they both returned home. She had made it to the end of the night without bringing up the subject again with Roque, but her discomfort kept her awake. She decided to take advantage of the insomnia and satisfy her curiosity about the book's contents, since at no point had he ever given her the original manuscript to read. She adjusted the light on the headboard so as not to disturb her husband's sleep and plunged into the book. She read jumping from page to page, skipping some passages and concentrating on those that most interested her. The second to last page of the book had a puzzling paragraph. In the epilogue, entitled "Brothers With a Heart in the Middle of Their Chest," the author paid tribute to the Brothers and remembered a get-together of the organization's pilots in Key West after a day's flying over the Florida Straits:

Hours later my companions and I shared lunch. What a lovely bunch of people we had there! What a class of men were there that day at the Key West Airport: Captain Danilo Paneca, frogman and ex-parachute instructor at the Naval Academy; Major Pedro Delgado, the engineer who had run the Cuban department of civil aeronautics; Tony Márquez, a pilot who escaped with an Antonov 24 to the Bahamas; Captain René González, who two years before my arrival deserted aboard an An-2. And of course, there was also José Basulto, Billy Schuss, Carlitos Tabernilla, Oswaldo Plá and other brothers.

The title of captain that Roque had applied to René sowed new doubts in her head. "Captain" can mean the military rank, but also a commander of ships and planes. Could it be that René was a serviceman, like Roque? What mystery was there here? And why had Roque wanted to disassociate her name from the book? At this point Ana Margarita began to have doubts about her bogus Richard Gere, about the prince charming she had chosen to father her son.

Such uncertainty was not an unusual feeling among the Cuban population of south Florida. Not trusting anything or anybody, in Miami, was never a cardinal sin. The atmosphere of mutual distrust, prevalent since the birth of the diaspora at the start of the 1960s, had turned into a kind of collective paranoia after the landing of the 130,000 *marielitos* in 1980. It was enough for someone to introduce himself at some organization's meeting as an "upright anti-Castroist"—*anticastrista vertical,* an expression used by those who swore never to bow down before the threats of communism—for him to be viewed with extra caution by the older veterans of exile. Not even icons of the anti-Castro struggle, like José Basulto, managed to escape unscathed by the whispers coming from the domino tables and bars of Little Havana. In these places Basulto's many failed actions had only one explanation: the Brothers leader was also a Castro agent. Over the years the Cuban community in Miami had ceased to be surprised when it found out that this or that extreme militant, who had proclaimed himself willing to die to put an end to the Cuban Revolution, was nothing but an intelligence agent sent by Havana. What was new this time was that Ana

Margarita's fears were shared not by her compatriots, but by the United States government.

Months before her wedding to Roque, a smiling, middle-aged American, with gray hair and rosy cheeks, had rented a furnished room on the fourth floor of number 8021 on 149ᵗʰ Avenue, in the Kendall district of southeast Miami. The small property had been chosen because of one peculiarity: from its only window it was possible to see, with the naked eye, what was going on in the apartment across the street, where René González lived. The tenant had no plans to occupy the place as a home, but rather to convert it into a Surveillance Operations Center (SOC), which in police jargon is also called a "stakeout." The good-natured American, who had used a false name and documents to rent the property, was Mark D'Amico, an experienced official from the FBI's Anti-Terrorist Squad. On installing himself full-time in Kendall, D'Amico was taking the first steps of a secret operation launched by the US Department of Justice to investigate clandestine activities among Cuban residents in Florida.

Taking turns with him on the stakeout—carried out with the help of powerful binoculars equipped with night vision capability —were FBI agents Julio Ball and Myron Broadwell, who jotted down every detail of the Cuban's routine: what time he left the house, how long he stayed out, what time he came back and what he did when he was in the apartment. Luckily for them, René's day varied very little: he woke up early, made breakfast, did some pushups in the narrow corridor between the bedroom and the kitchen, left the house and ran for forty minutes around his apartment building, which occupied the whole block. He would come back home, take a shower—almost always cold, to save electricity—spend half an hour in front of his IBM 386 microcomputer, and leave for work at around eight o'clock in the morning. He would come home between eight and nine at night, and sit at his computer until going to bed some time after midnight. Only when they were sure about his entry and exit times did the FBI start to make incursions inside the apartment. On their first visit, the phone was bugged and listening devices installed in both rooms. They were careful not to force entry, picking the locks instead. While one agent was busy in the apartment, the other would watch the entrance of René's building and the street through his binoculars. In the event of René breaking his routine and coming home early, the agent monitoring the street would warn his colleague via walkie-talkie in order for him to escape without leaving a trace. In most cases it was D'Amico who did the watching from their kitchenette, while Ball and Broadwell took charge of rummaging through René's apartment. Each nook and cranny, every drawer, every cupboard was photographed every day. At the end of the search a hard disk was connected to the Cuban's computer, copying every operation, including all messages sent and received the previous day.

A few weeks of this surveillance was sufficient for the FBI to unravel the mystery that years later would explode onto the front pages of American newspapers: a captain of the Revolutionary Armed Forces of Cuba, René was an intelligence officer sent by the Cuban government to infiltrate the United States. Far from being a hard blow dealt against communism, as the Florida press had enthused in 1990, the theft of that training plane from San Nicolás de Bari Airport and the pilot's risky escape to Miami, with barely enough fuel, were all part of a meticulous operation planned by the Cuban Department of State Security (DSS).

René's real identity, however, had not been the only thing that the FBI had investigated. What astonished the authorities was the discovery that he was just one part of a network of false defectors spread throughout southern Florida—all of them in fact intelligence agents trained by Cuba to infiltrate anti-Castroist organizations in the United States. And all of them, from then on, came to be kept under rigorous surveillance by the FBI, with their phones bugged and microphones installed clandestinely in their homes. Just as D'Amico, Ball and Broadwell were in charge of René, another fifteen agents were already watching and gathering information on around ten addresses scattered around Miami, Key West and Tampa.

The discovery of this shady ring of informants poses an unanswered question: what leads could the American police have used to get to the secret agents? On the Cuban side, the officials at the DSS swear to have no details that might help uncover the mystery. In Miami the enigma still remains, since the FBI has refused to make public any information other than copies of the vast correspondence between Havana and the infiltrated agents in Florida, collected from their computers. This paperwork sheds no new light nor does it suggest the existence of a traitor among the group, nor whether the FBI reached the network thanks to slip-ups made by one of the Cubans. As the first document confiscated by the FBI was dated December 1995, all that can be said for sure was that of the eight years they were active, the secret organization operated for at least five years without being discovered by the American authorities.

It is certain that Havana's decision to create a network of informants in the United States was born soon after the demise of the Soviet Union and, according to a colonel in the Cuban intelligence agency, the decision was made "at the highest level"—in other words, with the knowledge of Fidel Castro and his brother, Raúl. The prospect of overthrowing the Cuban Revolution by economic suffocation encouraged organizations in exile to resume their provocations against Cuba and intensify the attacks against tourism, the country's main source of income, and the lifeline that guaranteed the regime's survival. The severing of relations between the two countries left the Cuban authorities with few options for preventing the attacks coming from Miami. The vigilance at ports and airports was reinforced, but Cuba had to make sure that such security measures didn't deter tourists, who arrived daily in their thousands from all over the world—except from the United States, a country from which travel to Cuba was prohibited by law. While Cuban leaders tried to figure out how to fight an unequal war, they watched the number of attacks rise. The objective asserted by the anti-Castroist leaders of Florida was clear: "International public opinion needs to know," they reiterated in pamphlets and interviews, "that it's safer to go sightseeing in Bosnia-Herzegovina than in Cuba."

Indeed, since the collapse of the USSR there had been more than thirty attacks against hotels, tourist transport vehicles and places frequented by foreigners. Thanks to information received by its intelligence services, Cuba had managed to thwart various terrorist plots, among them an attempt to place 900 grams of C-4 plastic explosives inside the famous Tropicana nightclub in Havana, which on show nights can attract around a thousand visitors. The American authorities' complacency inspired extremists like Tony Bryant, leader of the Commandos L group, to announce to the Miami press his willingness to continue carrying out violent actions in Cuba to undermine tourism. There was only one way to contain the wave of attacks: infiltrate organizations of the extreme right in Florida, so as to obtain information on attacks while they were being planned. And this was a high-risk operation. Havana's reluctance to put such a daring plan into action disappeared with the intensification of the attacks and the successive invasions of Cuban territorial waters by vessels coming out of Miami loaded with weapons and explosives.

The twelve men and two women chosen to do the job were very young, and almost all of them had a university education. One of the oldest among them, René, had just turned thirty-five when he reached the United States, and was one of the few without a university degree. The majority had taken part in the Angolan War and at least seven of them, including one of the women, had military ranks bestowed by the Interior Ministry. One of those decorated was the youngest in the group, the good-natured Lieutenant Gerardo Hernández, who at twenty-seven years old was in command of the operation and responsible for transmitting to Havana the material gathered by the other spies. The façade used by each of the fourteen had one thing in common: like René, they were all "defectors"—some had abandoned their posts in Cuban embassies or consulates overseas, others had absconded from scientific, sporting or economic missions while traveling and requested asylum in the United States. The false defections and real activities of these agents in Florida were considered so top-secret that they could not even be shared with their nearest and dearest, parents, wives and children. All fourteen were Cuban citizens, and three of them, like René, had been born in the United States. Only one was divorced. Seven were married, including the two women, whose husbands were likewise members of the *Red Avispa* (Wasp Network), the name with which the group had been baptized in Havana. The FBI knew all of these details, but there was still one piece missing from the jigsaw: the FBI did not know—and not even René knew at first—that Juan Pablo Roque was also an infiltrator, a false defector. Everything that the MiG pilot had done until then, from the escape via Guantánamo to the wedding with Ana Margarita, was part of a cover plotted in the old building of Villa Marista, in the center of the Cuban capital, the headquarters of the intelligence services of Cuba.

The group's presence in Florida only began to work as a live operation with the arrival of Lieutenant Gerardo Hernández, a year and a half after René's defection. If he'd had his way, Hernández would have served overseas not as a secret agent but as a diplomat. Brawny and almost bald, despite his youth, Hernández had completed the course in international relations at the University of Havana in the class of July 1989, but had never got as far as a desk job in the Ministry of Foreign Relations, the first step in a diplomatic career. He handed over his diploma to his beautiful young wife, Adriana O'Connor, who was still only eighteen, and volunteered as a fighter in Angola. On the night of July 14, 1989, the eve of their first wedding anniversary, along with another ninety men, Hernández boarded a ramshackle four-engined Bristol Britannia bound for Africa. Unlike the half-million Cubans who had fought alongside the Angolan troops to date, Hernández would spend only one year on the African continent, not three. Under the cease-fire signed that year by the Angolan president José Eduardo dos Santos and UNITA's leader, Jonas Savimbi, witnessed by eighteen African heads of state, the presence of Cuban troops were coming to have a merely symbolic character; in fact, under the US-brokered agreement of 1988, they had already begun to withdraw. Returning to Cuba in 1990, Hernández nurtured dreams of finally being able to begin his diplomatic career and start a family with Adriana. However, once more fate conspired against him. "It seems I caught the eye of the Cuban intelligence services when I was in Angola," he would remember years later, "because I had just arrived back in

Havana when they suggested the mission in the United States." The recruiting official had gone straight to the point:

"We know you studied hard to become a diplomat, and got a Gold at college, but we can no longer endure the attacks. We either put a stop to this or they put a stop to our tourist industry. We have to infiltrate the Miami criminal organizations, and we'd like to entrust you with this task."

Both his career and his plans to have children would have to be postponed. "I could have said no, that I'd rather be a diplomat, but we Cubans who grew up after the Revolution knew that the aggression from Miami forced the country onto a war footing," he recalled. "There wasn't a single Cuban who had not been a victim of terrorism, or didn't know someone who had. My life would have to be put on hold once more." To his wife Adriana, a small brunette with thick black eyebrows whom he nicknamed Bonsai, Hernández gave the explanation they had recommended at Villa Marista: he was going to spend a few months collecting data in Latin American countries for his master's thesis in international politics.

But the preparation for his disguise would still take some time. In the months that followed, he devoted himself to the complex process of changing his personality. He received from his new bosses—he was now officially incorporated into the intelligence service of the Ministry of the Interior—a twenty-page booklet that summarized the details of the character he would now have to play. In order to find him a name, Cuban agents had searched a cemetery of Cameron County, on the border of Texas and Mexico, to find a deceased person born more or less at the same time as Hernández. They chose Manuel Viramóntez, born a few months after the Cuban, who had died of respiratory failure at the age of three. In possession of the boy's birth certificate, provided by the town's notary public, it was possible to put together all the documentation that would sustain Hernández's cover in the United States.

Over the following six months Gerardo Hernández dedicated himself to reading and rereading his false biography created by the Cuban intelligence service. Only when he felt totally secure did he propose proceeding to the second phase: the interrogations. During interminable sessions that would last more than twenty hours, various intelligence officers took turns quizzing him, repeating the same question dozens of times, looking for some contradiction, some answer that might arouse suspicion. The work began at eight in the morning in a small room in the Villa Marista complex and, with short meal breaks, would often continue through the night. The officer's inquisition could start with Manuel Viramóntez's childhood or with any moment in his adult life.

"What's your name?"

"Manuel Viramóntez."

"Who are your parents?"

"Pedro Viramóntez and Rosalina Viramóntez."

"Where and when were you born?"

"I'm an American citizen. I was born in Cameron County, Texas, on January 26, 1967. In 1970 my parents went back to live in Puerto Rico, where they were born."

"What's your social security number?"

"584-82-5846."

"What's your present address in Puerto Rico?"

"Darlington Building, Muñoz Rivera Boriqueña Avenue, Apartment 6-C, Rio Piedras."

"What's the postal code?"

"00925."

"And the home telephone number?"

"765-8150."

"Describe the building where you live."

"It's a white building with eleven floors. On the first floor there's a salsa radio station called Radio Voz, and its antennas are on the roof."

"Where do you work?"

"At a company called B. Fernández & Hermanos, Inc."

"Where's it located?"

"On Dr. Mario Juliá Street, in the industrial district of Pueblo Viejo, in San Juan."

"What's the telephone number there?"

"797-7272."

"What do you do there?"

"I'm a salesman."

"What's your salary?"

"Nine dollars an hour, fixed, plus commission. All told, it comes to a little more than two thousand dollars a month."

"Where did you study?"

"Always in San Juan. From 1972 to 1979 I went to kindergarten and then I did first to sixth grade at the Eugenio María de Hostos School, on Constitution Street, between Cojimar and Camagüey, in Hato Rey. Primary school I did between 1979 and 1982 at the Rafael María de Labra School at Parada 18, Ponce de León, Santurce. From 1982 to 1985 I went to high school in University Gardens, between Columbia and Georgetown, Río Piedras. And in 1986 and 1987 I did the technical course in marketing at York College, which is on 3rd Street, in Puerta de Tierra."

"Do you remember the name of any teacher, classmate or employee at Eugenio María de Hostos?"

"Yes, some. Of the teachers I remember Miss Tillet and Miss Rosa, who were pretty old then and must be retired by now, and also Margarita Cornejo, Manuel Míguez, Aydée Vázquez. Classmates I remember Vivian Espinosa, Edgardo Ramos, Miriam González, Francisco Wong. The director was called María Elena Bartoli and her assistant, Lucy Delgado. Of the cleaning staff I remember two ladies called Cuca and Amapola."

Although his identity was false, all the names of people, places, streets, buildings and commercial establishments were real. If anyone took the trouble to check the details given by Gerardo Hernández on the Eugenio María de Hostos School, they would discover there the records of the old directors, teachers, pupils and employees listed in the interrogations. Every document, each bit of paper in Hernández's possession had a history. Should any authority want details on how he joined the video rental club Cine and Video, he had the answer on the tip of his tongue:

"To become a member of this video club, I arrived at the establishment on Magdalena Street that crosses Ashford Avenue. The rental place had two glass doors and to get in you have to knock.

If you want to be a member, they ask for some form of identification, which could be a driver's license, voter registration card, etc. I presented my driver's license. To rent films you need to show your membership card and pay three dollars for a new film or a new release."

With the same attention to detail, he could answer, should anyone ask, how and where he had obtained the driver's license he used to become a member of the video club.

"My present driver's license was obtained as a renewal, in September 1990. To get it, I went to the department of transport and public works, on the old naval base at Fernández Juncos Avenue, in Miramar, Santurce. When I got there, I went to the information desk where they gave me a form and explained how to proceed. I handed over the documents and they told me to wait, but I preferred to have it mailed to my house. It arrived a week later."

Nothing remained without an answer. When an intelligence officer wanted to know details of the company where he worked in San Juan, Hernández didn't hesitate:

"After graduating from York College, my family's financial situation allowed me to wait until I found a job I liked. That's why it was only in 1988 that I started to work in sales at B. Fernández & Hermanos Inc., a supplies and drinks distributor."

Seven months after receiving the booklet, Hernández was almost ready to assume the identity of Manuel Viramóntez. But it wasn't enough to be a native of the only associated free state of the United States; it was essential to also speak like one. In other words, he had to lose his Cuban accent and incorporate the idiomatic expressions, slang and swear words of Puerto Rico. Luckily he could count on an intial advantage: like *guajiros*, the Cuban hicks, Puerto Ricans swallow the consonants of words ending in *ado*, *edo*, and *ido*. Both, for example, pronounce *distinguido* as *distinguío*, or *disgustado* as *disgustáo*. They drop other consonants as well: when they want to say "*el pescado está salado*" (the fish is salty), both Cubans from the country as well as Puerto Ricans say "*el pecao tá salao*." Apart from these idiomatic similarities, Hernández learned that, unlike in Cuba, *arrebatado* does not mean "enthusiastic," but "drugged"; that *xota* is not the vulgar form for the female genitalia, but someone who is a big mouth, a chatterbox; that *pelado* doesn't describe someone who's bald, but someone with no money. All this had to be learned without even mentioning the hundreds of foreign loan words, such as those inherited from Yoruba slaves, like *chévere* from *ché egbéri* (very good), or borrowed from English, like *pana* (friend, stemming from *partner*), *raitru* (very true, originally *right true*) and *zafacón* (trash can, from *safety can*). By the end of 1991 the slow metamorphosis that had transformed Gerardo Hernández into Manuel Viramóntez was complete. The period of pretending was over, and the time had finally come to move to the United States and plunge into the belly of the beast.

5

BY THE MIDDLE OF 1995 THE CUBAN "WASP NETWORK" HAS THIRTEEN SECRET AGENTS IN ANTI-CASTROIST ORGANIZATIONS. BUT THE FBI IS ALREADY WATCHING THEM

With false documents in hand, Gerardo Hernández took a plane from Havana to Mexico, from where he headed to Memphis, Tennessee, and then on to Miami, without arousing any suspicion. He lived in a motel in Miami for three weeks, reading classified ads and visiting realtors, in search of an apartment that would fit the meager budget set by the Villa Marista headquarters. He chose a small apartment on the third floor of a four-story building, near the Sunny Isles beach, the start of a narrow strip of land that seems to want to break away from Miami and ends up on Ocean Drive, a spot enjoyed by wealthy tourists. A small balcony separated from the living room by a glass door compensated for the apartment's tiny size. The balcony opened onto a pleasant view of the palm trees decorating the building's entrance and, thirty meters away, the small apartment building where, some years later, the federal agents Ángel Berlinghieri, Vicente Rosado and José Orihuela would be tracking Hernández's every move. With a twenty-year career in the FBI, Rosado was part of the Computer Analysis and Response Team (CART), the department in charge of analyzing computer-generated evidence. After a lot of bargaining, Hernández-Viramóntez managed to persuade Henry Reizman, the landlord who also lived in the building, to lower the rent from $625 to $580, including taxes and condo fees. Apart from some basic furniture, Hernández's only other acquisition for his new home was an important work tool: a computer. He chose a piece of equipment that featured state-of-the-art technology—a sound and video graphics card, a super VGA monitor, a built-in fax modem and four gigabytes of memory. He paid $3,000 for it, the same amount he paid for a huge, ten-year-old Oldsmobile Delta, which was falling apart. Such a modest way of life was necessitated by more than his low income. The cover planned for him in Havana was that of a freelance newspaper cartoonist, a job he did have a talent for, but which allowed for no great extravagance.

It was only in early 1992 that the agents who would work under his supervision started to land in Florida. The first two he met did not come from Cuba, but from New York, and they were genuinely married. Nilo Hernández, codenamed Manolo, and his wife, Linda Hernández, Judith, were old employees of the Cuban mission at the UN and, according to the cover assigned to them by the intelligence agencies, had defected from the diplomatic service years before to set up a small medical instrument and computer peripherals export company in New York, which had been transferred to Miami when they entered the Wasp Network. They both had the rank of lieutenant in the Ministry of the Interior and, though they were the oldest in the group (he was thirty-eight and she was thirty-five), in the secret documents exchanged with the Main Center in Havana they were known as the Juniors. A few days after they settled into a rented house southwest of Miami, Nilo and Linda were told by Hernández-Viramóntez that their mission would be to infiltrate Alpha 66, one of the oldest and most aggressive anti-Castroist terrorist groups in Florida. Founded in 1966 by Eloy Gutiérrez Menoyo, Andrés Nazario Sargén and Antonio Veciana Blanch, the organization's first great sponsor was the American millionaire Henry Luce, founder and owner of *Time* magazine. Despite its long record of violence and attacks, Alpha 66 had a legal existence, being officially registered with Miami City Hall, and its headquarters were in Calle Ocho, the busiest street in Little Havana.

Along with the Juniors, other new Cuban agents were making a discreet arrival in Florida. The next one was twenty-nine-year-old Ramón Labañino Salazar—codenames Luis Medina, Allan and Urso. Labañino was an economist and a Cuban army captain. At six-foot-six and weighing 130 kilos, this thickly mustachioed, baby-faced giant was also passionate about martial arts, having won several Central American tournaments as a black belt karate fighter. Following the script penned by the intelligence services, he had moved to Madrid to work in a Cuban company for the purchase of hospital equipment, from which he had defected and moved to the United States. As with the other agents, the secret of his mission could not be shared with anyone, not even his wife, Elizabeth Palmiero, whom he had married the previous year.

Instead of going directly to Miami, Labañino was dispatched to Tampa, Florida. Although the city did not host any relevant anti-Castroist organizations, it was there that the leaders of some active and dangerous groups lived, such as José Enrique Cotera, Posada Carriles's deputy and a Bay of Pigs veteran, and Emilio Vázquez, who headed the local CANF branch. However, the Tampa resident who had most moved Cuban intelligence to assign Labañino to that city was Orlando Bosch, a man with a physique as amply filled out as his rap sheet. According to official documents divulged by the National Security Archive, an NGO based in Washington, the retired pediatrician, born in Havana in 1926, had started to cooperate with the CIA soon after Castro came to power. Bosch, easily recognizable thanks to a purple birthmark stretching from his lower lip to the tip of his chin, had been identified as "the mulatto sitting next to the man with an umbrella" during the investigations into John F. Kennedy's assassination, in a scene from the only footage of the crime, shot with a home movie camera by Abraham Zapruder. In the 1970s, never losing sight of Cuba as his main target, Bosch was at the service of the military junta that had overthrown the Chilean president, Salvador Allende, moving to Chile in December 1974. He had links to Operation Condor, a conspiracy organized by the intelligence services of the military dictatorships in Argentina, Bolivia, Brazil, Chile, Paraguay and Uruguay to persecute, repatriate and even physically eliminate any opponents of those governments. In the following three years—while also accused by the US government of masterminding mail-bombings of Cuban embassies in Latin America—the Cuban physician's name would be associated with a number of crimes committed under the auspices of Condor, most clearly the operation carried out in Washington in September 1976 that killed the former Chilean chancellor Orlando Letelier and his secretary, the American Ronni Moffitt. They were driving on Sheridan Circle, a small, wooded circle less than twenty blocks from the White House, when a bomb blew their car to pieces.

The list of Bosch's crimes did not end there. Two weeks after the Washington attack, on October 6, a Cubana de Aviación DC-8 took off from Georgetown, the capital of Guyana, headed to Havana, with scheduled stopovers in Port of Spain (capital of Trinidad and Tobago), Bridgetown (capital of Barbados) and Kingston (capital of Jamaica). The plane was carrying seventy-five people, including twenty-four fencers from the Cuban youth team who had just won gold medals in the Central American Championship, five North Koreans and eleven Guyanese, including students on their way to study medicine in Cuba. Among the other passengers was the CIA agent Hernán Ricardo Lozano, traveling with Freddy Lugo, both Venezuelans. They got off the plane in Barbados, at four o'clock in the afternoon, took a taxi from the former Seawell airport, made a quick stop at the United States embassy and checked in at the local Hilton Hotel, where they made a call to Central American Commercial and Industrial Investigations (ICICA) in Caracas, Venezuela, to give a short message: "The job has been done." At the other end of the line were Orlando Bosch and the owner of the private detective agency, Luis Posada Carriles. At a quarter past five that afternoon, the DC-8 left Bridgetown for Jamaica, the last stopover before landing in Havana. Eight minutes after takeoff, a bomb exploded in one of the toilets. Transformed into a giant fireball, the plane plunged into the Caribbean Sea, killing all sixty-eight passengers and five crew.

Arrested the following day, Lugo and Lozano confessed to the crime and revealed to the Barbados police the names of those who had given the orders: Orlando Bosch and Luis Posada Carriles. Tried in Caracas, Lozano and Lugo were sentenced to twenty years in prison. Posada Carriles spent nine years incarcerated in Venezuela until he escaped in 1985 from a maximum security prison, reappearing a few months later in El Salvador, where he joined the Contras, groups armed by the CIA to overthrow the Sandinista government in Nicaragua. Orlando Bosch, acquitted on procedural grounds, remained in jail while Venezuelan prosecutors sought to mount a new trial; he was eventually re-acquitted and freed in 1987. In 1988, he made it to Miami, but was arrested for violating the terms of his parole back in 1974. The Justice Department moved to have him deported, but the order was overturned by President George H. W. Bush in 1990. Bosch received a pardon, thanks in part to one particular champion, the governor of Florida, Jeb Bush.

When interviewed by a reporter about the attack in Barbados, Bosch gave a macabre answer. "All of Castro's planes are warplanes," he said. "There were no innocent people among the passengers on that flight."

In 2000, Posada along with Gaspar Jiménez and Pedro Remón, both Cuban, went to Panama where they intended to kill Fidel Castro, who would be there for an international meeting. Arrested and sentenced, the three of them would be pardoned in August 2004, on the last day of Panamanian President Mireya Moscoso's term in office, and released. The first authority to learn the news was the American ambassador in Panama, Simón Ferro. Unaware that her call was being secretly recorded—and that it would be disclosed worldwide on the Internet a few years later—Moscoso left a ten-second message on the diplomat's cell phone: "This is the president to inform you that the Cubans were pardoned last night. They have already left the country for Miami." According to what emerged later, the pardon had cost one million dollars, a helicopter and a yacht, paid as a fee to the Panamanian president by the Cuban American National Foundation.

After Ramón Labañino, it was the turn of another American agent to join the Wasp Network in 1992: Antonio Guerrero. At thirty-four years old and measuring six feet tall, Tony Guerrero was thin, with a narrow face and prominent upper teeth, as if keeping his mouth shut required some effort. He had been born in 1958 in Miami, but, unlike René, Guerrero's family had not gone into exile in the United States to escape Fulgencio Batista's dictatorship. His father, also called Antonio Guerrero, had been an amateur baseball player until a North American league spotter discovered him in Havana in the early 1950s. His first professional contract took him to the city of Odessa, Texas, where his first daughter, María Eugenia, was born in 1956. However, his professional baseball career would be short. Early in 1958, when he was playing for a Miami team, Guerrero sprained his left foot. Laid up in plaster for six months, unable to move without crutches, Guerrero was not the same when he returned to the field. He made some attempts to recover his old performance level, but his career had come to an end. At that moment, he and Mirta, who had just found out she was pregnant, decided to go ahead with a project they had often toyed with: going back to Cuba. But every time they consulted a Cuban relative or friend about the plan, the answer was always the same: "Don't come back! This place is going up in smoke!" The guerrilla war led by Fidel Castro was starting to impinge on the country's capital.

On October 16, 1958, Mirta was admitted to Jackson Memorial, the hospital complex of Miami University, a few blocks north of Little Havana, to give birth to her second child, Tony. Despite all the warnings, the family disembarked in Cuba on the day that Tony turned a month old. The plane that took them was forced to land in the inland city of Colombia, because the José Martí International Airport had been taken over by Castroist rebels for a few hours. Tony was not yet three months old when Havana fell to the Revolution, which, thirty years later, would send him back to the Florida city of his birth.

At the age of eleven, Tony saw his father die of a heart attack. A brilliant student, Tony was admitted in 1974 to the Young Communist League and five years later, on completing pre-university studies, he got a scholarship to study airport engineering at Kiev University, in Ukraine. Back in Cuba, he joined the Cubana de

Aviación works department, until hired to run the Antonio Maceo Airport expansion in the city of Santiago, in the far east of the Island. When the work was completed in 1987, the new wing was opened by Fidel Castro in person. At that time Tony was already the father of two-year-old Antonio, but his marriage to Delgys, a girl from Santiago de Cuba, would not last. In 1988 he returned to Havana, divorced and alone, and was recruited by the Ministry of the Interior to work as an intelligence agent. The months that followed were devoted to reaching "operational readiness," attending courses on intelligence and counterintelligence, disguises and false identities, visual espionage, surveillance and countersurveillance, cryptography, security measures, interviewing techniques aimed at recruitment, and methods for concealing information on computers, sending information by phone and decoding secret radio messages.

Early in 1990 he was assigned his first mission: to join a group of Cuban agents active in Panama, a strategically important country due to its geographic location and its canal connecting the Atlantic and Pacific Oceans. Tony's job, according to his rather uninformative personal file at the Ministry of the Interior, would consist of searching for political-military information by means of radio and visual intelligence, creating a sub-network of support agents, breaking into political and diplomatic facilities and gathering information on Panamanian groups deemed "special" by the Havana headquarters. Always using his real name and American citizenship documents, he followed the guidance he had received in Cuba to find and rent a home, look for a job that could justify his expenses and, if possible, establish a romantic relationship with a Panamanian girl as a way of making it easier to approach local groups and reinforce his American immigrant façade. A month after his arrival, Tony was already dating Nicia Pérez Barreto, the daughter of a local businessman, whom he would marry in October of 1991. The Panama that Tony discovered was at the height of political upheaval. In the first days of 1990, General Manuel Noriega, the commander of the National Guard and the de facto ruler of the country, had been deposed and imprisoned by American troops, accused of drug trafficking by President Bush—the same George Bush who had, years before, recruited him to collaborate with the CIA. Forcibly taken to Miami, Noriega was tried and sentenced to thirty years.

Tony's records at the Cuban interior ministry disclose little but they do suggest that his mission in Panama—whatever it might have been—was very successful, since at the beginning of 1992 he was promoted to the position of special agent, and awarded the rank of lieutenant. Along with the notice of his promotion, he received a new brief: to move from Panama to the United States with his wife, now four months pregnant, and join the Wasp Network that was being set up in Florida. Nicia was loath to be separated from her family and refused to go to the States, leaving Tony no alternative but to suggest a divorce, which his wife agreed to seemingly without any problem. When their son Gabriel Eduardo was born early in 1993, Tony had already gone north.

The script was the usual one: to find a place to live, to look for a job and to start a relationship with a woman. Like Ramón Labañino, Tony was not sent to Miami; his destination lay 300 kilometers south to Key West, a city with 20,000 inhabitants. It was a place famous for its homosexual communities, a feature noticeable by the profusion of rainbow flags flying outside bars, nightclubs and homes. The choice of Key West by Cuban intelligence bodies was not, of course, for its reputation as a gay paradise, but for its geographical location that made it the perfect kicking-off point for anti-Castroist organizations aspiring to invade Cuban territory. Lying at the southernmost point of the United States, Key West is only ninety miles from Havana. Besides being the perfect place for the surveillance of boating activity, the city offered a vantage point for anyone with binoculars to monitor the lights on the antennas of the huge blimps floating over the Straits of Florida—antennas transmitting the signals of Radio and TV Martí to Cuba. The use of the airships was the State Department's stratagem for bypassing the American law that prohibits the generation, inside US territory, of audio or video signals meant to interfere in any other country's politics. In the early years, the CIA would transmit programs from friendly Central American countries such as Honduras and El Salvador, but complaints from the Cuban government to international bodies compelled Washington to resort to the dirigibles that were then sent to fly over the no-man's-land of international airspace that separates the two nations.

Although Tony was carrying an engineering degree in his luggage, his first steps in the United States brought the same difficulties faced by his predecessors and by the Wasp Network members who would come afterwards. He did odd jobs such as mowing lawns, fixing fences, working as an electrician, as a plumber and as a stock boy in a local shopping center, until he got his first job with a fixed salary in a spa in a Days Inn, giving salsa lessons. His classes were mostly attended by men, many of whom were gay, but it would be two women enrolled in the course who would change his destiny. The first was Margareth Becker, a petite and alluring blond, with blue eyes and a Coco Chanel haircut, eight years his senior. Maggie, as she was known, was a vegetarian, Zen Buddhist and yoga practitioner, and had left her upper-middle-class family in Pennsylvania to live "in communion with nature" in the idyllic southernmost part of Florida. It was a typical case of love at first sight. As soon as Tony met her, he began visiting the little clapboard house, typical of Key West, where Maggie lived with a cat called Tai-Chi and worked as a masseuse.

The other female student, Dalila Borrego, also American, was an employee at the human resources department of the Boca Chica naval air base, the place where René González had landed his plane when he came to the United States. It was Dalila who told Tony that the Boca Chica command was accepting applications from civilians. It wouldn't be the best job in the world—the available openings were for janitors and handymen—but Tony was aware that in the United States an engineering degree from Ukraine had little or no value. Apart from the guarantee of a steady job, only a stroke of luck could put a Cuban spy to work inside a powerful American military facility. Tony easily passed all the interviews—his only difficulty was with English, a language he still didn't speak fluently. Soon after, he was summoned to join the 600 other civilians who worked at the naval air base, 10 percent of whom were Cuban-born. After having him clean windows and scrub floors for a few weeks, his superiors realized that the novice had more to offer, and promoted him to assistant lathe operator in the workshop that functioned inside the base. The new post did not provide access to areas restricted to military personnel, although the modest wage increase allowed him to abandon both the odd jobs and the salsa lessons, and also to improve his frugal lifestyle. To celebrate, he took out a small bank loan and bought a used Volkswagen Golf—second- or even thirdhand, but still in good shape.

Over the following months, the remaining members of the Wasp Network gradually arrived. Soon after Tony, a tall, thin, balding thirty-four-year-old sublieutenant named Joseph Santos moved to Miami. Born in 1960 in the tiny town of Weehawken, New Jersey, to Cuban parents, Santos moved to Cuba with his family when he was two. A revolutionary militant from a young age, he graduated in automation engineering at the University of Havana, where he met the cybernetics student Amarilys Silverio, a curly-haired brunette whom he would marry soon after graduation. Recruited to work as intelligence agents, after four months of training in a safe house in the city of Santa Clara, they were both sent to the United States during one of the many migration waves, and settled in New Jersey—his codename was Mario and hers was Julia. When the Wasp Network was created, the couple received orders from Havana to move to Miami, on which occasion Amarylis was also assigned the rank of sublieutenant. While her husband was out looking for employment, Amarilys soon found a job as a receptionist at the Peñalver clinic, in Little Havana. Four other Cuban agents would be incorporated during the following weeks, completing the group, but very little would ever be known about them other than their names and codenames: Ricardo Villarreal (Rocco, Horacio), Alejandro Alonso (Franklin), Remijio Luna (Remi, Marcelino) and Alberto Ruiz (Manny, Miguel or A-4).

The network functioned as a pyramid, with Hernández-Viramóntez at the top, where all the information and reports issued by the other members converged. Giro, as Hernández-Viramóntez was known in Cuba, was in charge of receiving, consolidating and summarizing information and reports, encrypting them with preset codes and sending them to the Main Center in Cuba. Of the entire group, he was the only one to communicate directly with Havana. However, as an additional security measure, none of the field agents had contact with him, or were even aware of his existence.

Just under Hernández-Viramóntez came the supervisors, who were in charge of collecting and conveying to him all the material gathered by the agents: Ramón Labañino, Ricardo Villarreal and Alberto Ruiz. Besides acting as a bridge between Hernández-Viramóntez and the other members of the group, these three agents also did fieldwork, searching for information within the anti-Castroist groups. At the base of the pyramid, responsible for the infiltrations and the production of the reports were René, always referred to by his nom de guerre Castor, Roque, Tony Guerrero, Alejandro Alonso, Alberto Ruiz and the couples Nilo and Linda Hernández and Joseph and Amarilys Santos. The compartmentalization of the team was almost absolute. Except in cases where both husband and wife were agents, none of the others knew their colleagues, nor were they aware of their existence; they didn't even know they were members of a group. Each of them could only contact their own superior, nobody else. The only exceptions were René and Roque, who had met by chance and become friends; neither of them however, knew that the other was also an intelligence agent.

The express recommendation to seek paid work was not only in order to provide credible false identities, but also because of the Cuban shortage of resources during that difficult period, especially when it came to US dollars. Far from the lavish lifestyle people are used to seeing in James Bond films and the like, the Cuban 007s spent their time counting pennies. The budget provided by Havana to keep the Wasp Network in operation didn't amount to more than $200,000 a year—and that included the upkeep of all the agents, their rents and their personal and operational expenditures. Half of the money was earmarked for the group's strictly personal and fixed expenses—rent, food and clothes—nearly $9,000 a year per capita, meaning each individual had less than $1,000 a month on which to survive. The operational costs amounted to nearly $70,000 a year, shared variably among the agents in accordance with their activities. While René, Roque and Tony, for instance, received slightly less than $5,000 a year, each one of the others was entitled to only half of that. The most significant share, amounting to $30,000 a year, was reserved for Hernández-Viramóntez who, with so little money, struggled to buy equipment—diskettes for computers, batteries, cassette tapes and so on—and still travel regularly to the Cuban mission at the UN (which was codenamed M-15) and the embassy in Mexico (codename M-2). Budget supplements would only be granted when an agent was called to Havana for a meeting, which usually occured once a year. Such trips were increasingly expensive, because with no air or sea communication between the two countries, the passenger was required to fly to neighboring countries like Mexico, Jamaica or the Bahamas, and from there on to Cuba.

It wasn't only in the distribution of resources that Hernández-Viramóntez received different treatment. Because he was the leader of the group and the only one to have all the information on the network and its operations, he had two other covers besides that of Manuel Viramóntez. According to guidance from Havana, "two sets of documents sufficiently reliable to ensure his departure from the United States" were required. As a first option, in the case of an emergency, he should assume the identity of Daniel Cabrera, a Puerto Rican born on June 28, 1961. The choice of Texas and Puerto Rico as places of origin for Hernández-Viramóntez's characters was made because both places have sizeable Spanish-speaking populations. These documents had been prepared two years before, when somebody provided the Wasp Network with the passport lost by the real Cabrera, a civil servant who lived in West Palm Beach, fifty kilometers north of Miami. The document was copied and the data used by the Cuban secret services to forge a birth certificate, a driver's license, a magnetic social security card and a membership card for a video rental store on Fisherman Island, West Palm Beach. With the second alternative cover, the Cuban would introduce himself as the photographer Damián Pérez Oquendo, born in 1965 in Hato Rey, Puerto Rico. As with the Viramóntez and Cabrera covers, Gerardo Hernández had been given a kit with the complete documentation on the third character, although the way it had been acquired would never be properly explained: a Puerto Rican identity card, a birth certificate, an American passport, a driver's license and a social security card.

Because he had the most relevant role in the Wasp Network, Gerardo Hernández not only got one escape plan from his superiors, but four. In case of any suspicion of being followed or monitored by the American authorities, he would avoid airports and leave Miami by land, heading for some neighboring city. When he was sure he was free of all surveillance, he would destroy all of Manuel Viramóntez's documents and assume the cover he deemed most appropriate for the circumstances—either as Daniel Cabrera or Damián Oquendo. Only then would he try, as quickly as possible, to choose one of the four options he had been given to leave the country. According to Havana's recommendations, he should avoid New York, Washington, Miami and Los Angeles airports, which at that time had the most stringent security systems in the United States. "None of these airports should be used," it was expressly stated in the instructions given to Gerardo, "either when starting the getaway trip or on flights that use them for connections before leaving the US."

The first escape route foresaw the agent taking a domestic flight from Miami to San Antonio, Texas and from there to El Paso, Texas, before walking across the border to Ciudad Juárez in Mexico. Choice number two suggested escaping on an international flight: having left Miami, Gerardo Hernández would decide on one of the three cities that provided nonstop flights to Mexico. He could either board in Atlanta and fly to Guadalajara, or fly from Columbia to Acapulco, or board a plane in Houston to take him to Mexico City. In all cases it would be important to make sure there were no stopovers in Cancún, Mérida or Veracruz, cities where security was stricter.

The third option had Managua in Nicaragua, Tegucigalpa in Honduras, or San José in Costa Rica, as alternative destinations, all capitals served by flights from Houston and New Orleans. In case of being unable to use any of the suggested routes, Hernández could choose the fourth option: to travel overland, either by bus or in a rental car up to Buffalo, New York, walk into Canada by way of the Rainbow Bridge in Niagara Falls, and from there head to Montreal or Toronto, where he would take a direct flight to Mexico City.

Of course, the document prepared by Havana for the Wasp Network's leader also envisaged the worst outcome of all: imprisonment. "If that happens, under no circumstances will you admit to being a member of the Cuban Intelligence Service. Confirm that you are Cuban and that you traveled to the United States via Mariel, in May 1980, on a boat where the captain was black, and strong, with a mustache—describe him as if he were officer Edgardo—and say that you paid $2,500 for the crossing." The final recommendation was not at all encouraging: "If they still keep you imprisoned, then ask for a lawyer."

6

LOVE ATTACKS THE SECRET AGENTS: TONY MARRIES MAGGIE AND RENÉ MANAGES TO BRING OLGA AND HIS DAUGHTER TO MIAMI

By the end of the first twelve months of operations, the secret agents of the Wasp Network had crammed the director general of intelligence's archives in Havana with more than 3,000 pages of reports. As time went by, the job of the agents entrusted with these clandestine infiltrations came to follow a routine that rarely changed. Communication between each individual and their immediate boss was by means of messages transmitted by pagers in alphanumeric codes devised and used for decades by the old Soviet Union. The first generation of cell phones was already available on the market, but their use had been discarded because of the price, beyond the group's modest budget, and because of the ease with which these devices could be tracked and bugged, a risk from which pagers were free. Every ten or fifteen days an agent would receive a coded message from his supervisor indicating a "spot"—the place where the material gathered during the period should be delivered. If the meeting involved just the passing on of a report, the method of choice, in the intelligence services' jargon, was the "brush pass"— handing over something covertly when bumping slightly into someone. In these cases agents would meet in one of the dozens of Walgreens pharmacies or Publix supermarkets spread over the

Miami metropolitan area, where material could change hands in the aisles without a word being said. In cases where, other than the handover of material, there was a need for discussion between the parties, the choice would always be some busy and noisy fast-food restaurant like McDonald's, Burger King, Dunkin' Donuts or Taco Bell. The frequent presence of anti-Castroist leaders and the high prices on their menus excluded from the list of "spots" some Little Havana restarants, like La Carreta and the Versalles. The material gathered in the period before each meeting was delivered to the supervisor on 5.25-inch diskettes with a capacity of only 800 kilobytes, real dinosaurs compared to the tiny pen drives that the world would come to know two decades later, capable of storing 30,000 times more data than their ancestors.

The mass of raw information gathered by the agents was organized by supervisors Ramón Labañino, Ricardo Villareal and Remijio Luna—who themselves had no connection to, or knowledge of, one another—and then passed on to Gerardo Hernández. It was he who gave the final form to the material, which, after being encrypted again, was sent to the Main Center. To communicate with Cuba, the chief of operations could choose between three options, depending on the circumstances. The simplest and safest was the small shortwave transmitter he kept in his apartment. At set times and on wavelengths previously agreed with Havana, he would put a recording on the air that sounded like the beeps made when pressing the buttons of a digital phone. Indecipherable to whoever might pick up the transmission, each beep stood for a letter or a set of letters that could only be decoded by DSS specialists. For security reasons the code would modify itself continually and automatically, so that the meaning of a certain tone would change from message to message. The second option was to use the *pitirre*, named after a little Cuban bird, a system of telephonic transmission of coded data to pagers in the Cuban mission at the UN in New York, and in some Cuban embassies in Central America. If for some reason it was impossible to use either radio or *pitirre*, Hernández encoded the data to be sent and printed it on sheets of bond paper, sealed everything in an envelope and put it in a street mailbox, addressed to a certain post office box in some Central American country. When the envelope reached its destination, someone from the Cuban embassy or consulate would collect it and send it on to Havana by diplomatic bag—very likely unaware of the item's origin and contents.

It didn't take long for results to appear. And it soon became clear that the risks run by the group of Cuban agents in the United States were justified. One morning in March 1995, when the Wasp Network had already completed a year and a half of full operations, two foreigners were discreetly pulled from a noisy line of Costa Rican tourists who had just landed at the José Martí Airport in Havana. After a few hours of interrogation at the airport, the pair confessed that they were traveling under false names and with false passports, that they were not Costa Rican and that they were not in Cuba to admire the sights. Their names were Santos Armando Martínez Rueda and José Ramírez Oro, Cuban Americans resident in the United States. It was the second time in a month they had trodden Cuban soil. The first time they had entered the country clandestinely by sea, to bury, in the town of Puerto Padre in Las Tunas province, a load of explosives, part of which would be used in an attack on the Hotel Meliá, a Spanish chain, in Varadero. On the present occasion they had intended to propose further targets for their local accomplices. Both confessed to taking orders from the Cuban American National Foundation. Martínez Rueda and Ramírez Oro, however, would not be the only terrorists caught by the Cuban police using information from agents based in the United States. In this first period of the network's activities, the reports sent from Florida to Havana enabled the Cuban police to thwart at least twenty attacks on its soil and to seize explosives, weapons and cash. The diligence of the intelligence services and the Cuban police led to the imprisonment of thirty terrorists, including Americans of Cuban origin, trained in camps in Miami, and foreign mercenaries paid by anti-Castroist organizations.

The most daring action planned by these groups was meant to have taken place in November 1994, and consisted of nothing less than the assassination of President Fidel Castro. From aboard a yacht, assisted by five mercenaries, Luis Posada Carriles himself managed to bring a small arsenal into the historic colonial town of Cartagena de Indias in Colombia, where the Fourth Ibero-American Summit was about to take place. Alerted by the Wasp Network, the Cuban authorities doubled their security measures around Fidel, and managed to thwart the crime. "I was standing behind the journalists and got as far as being really close to Castro's friend, Gabriel García Márquez," Posada Carriles confessed to the *New York Times*, "but I only managed to see Castro from a distance."

Also based on information produced by the Wasp Network, on at least three occasions the Foreign Ministry in Cuba succeeded in getting the United States Coast Guard to intercept boats from Florida, loaded with arms and explosives, that were headed for the Cuban coastline to carry out attacks on tourist spots. This resulted in the American police detaining nineteen mercenaries who were directly involved in the operations. Ten were freed on the spot by the FBI, and the nine remaining, though formally charged with acts of terrorism, had their cases shelved by Federal Judge Lawrence King, and were set free.

However, it was not always possible to prevent attacks. The pressures exerted by Cuba and its success in thwarting so many armed actions did not discourage the anti-Castroist groups. Under the conniving eye of the American authorities, the anti-Castroists persisted by dint of violence, bombs and bullets in trying to cut off the flow of tourists who were saving the Island from bankruptcy and impeding their dream of bringing the Revolution to its knees. Since the Network had installed itself in the United States, Cuba had been the victim of dozens of hotel attacks by invasion of its territory, and more than thirty violations of its airspace by planes coming from the United States—the large majority being Brothers or Democracy Movement planes, frequently flown by René or Juan Pablo Roque. The Guitart Hotel alone, a comfortable four-star hotel on Cayo Coco beach, was attacked three times during the year 1994 by motorboats from Key West—at one point, armed with machine guns spraying .50 caliber bullets at the beach, injuring some and terrifying the hundreds of foreign tourists who were there in high season.

In September 1993, the Mexican tourist Marcelo García Rubalcava, resident in the United States for more than thirty years, had been arrested as he disembarked in Havana. Inside the false tubes of toothpaste and bottles of shampoo that the traveler carried in his luggage, the police found enough C-4 plastic explosive to blow up a truck sky high. One link connected Rubalcava to the coming attacks on the Guitart Hotel: in both cases the financial backer was the octogenarian Andrés Nazario Sargén, a man just over five feet tall, and the founder and main leader of one of the oldest and most violent anti-Castroist groups in Florida—Alpha 66.

According to what Sargén himself would confess to the press, Alpha 66 had been responsible not only for the attacks on the Cayo Coco resort and for various attempts to smuggle in explosives, but also for the kidnapping of a passenger plane during a domestic flight in Cuba. After the plane had been diverted to the Fort Myers Airport, in southwestern Florida, the passengers were moved onto another plane back to Cuba. The original craft would never be returned by the United States government. Besides this one, another fifteen acts of air piracy took place during this period.

The radicalization of the exiles' relations with Cuba was whipped up by a dozen radio stations, legally installed in the Miami metropolitan area, whose programs were a permanent incitement to violence. A brief statistic gleaned by the Wasp Network between January 26 and February 25, 1993, from just seven of the stations—La Voz de la Fundación, La Voz de Alpha 66, La Voz de la Federación Mundial de Ex-Presos, Radio Rumbo a la Libertad, La Voz del Palenque, La Voz de la Resistencia and Radio Unión Liberal Cubana—conveys something of the atmosphere breathed in Florida. Those thirty days had seen the transmission of twenty messages urging the physical elimination of Fidel Castro, one hundred calls to carry out acts of sabotage against the Cuban tourism industry, and almost 500 exhortations to strike actively against the Revolution. Operating in shortwave, which allowed the signal to reach the ears of a good portion of the Cuban population, and protected by the Constitution of the United States with its guarantees for freedom of speech, some of these stations quite casually preached crime. It was common, when harvest time came along in Cuba, to hear the journalist Enrique Encinosa, announcer on Voz de la Resistencia, urge the population to boycott the sugar industry:

> The sugar cane harvest is about to begin. This year's crop must be destroyed. In the past, Castro promised ten million tons. Now, ten million acts of sabotage are necessary. People of Cuba: we call on each one of you to destroy the grinding machines in the sugar factories. Drop pieces of lead pipes or screws in the sugar cane that is being processed. Loosen or damage machine parts. Set fire to the plantations, pouring a little gasoline or other flammable fuel on a cloth bag; set fire to the bag and let it burn for a few minutes then put it out. At night throw the bag into the plantation. Next morning the heat of the sun will take care of lighting the fire again.

The resourcefulness of the organized anti-Castroist groups, their preaching of violence, their formidable and aggressive propaganda against the Revolution broadcast by radio and TV stations and by the Florida press, all gave the agents of the Wasp Network a clear idea of the inequality of the war they were engaged in. Such circumstances spurred them to redouble their efforts in the pursuit of information that would allow the Cuban government to stay a step ahead of the aggressors, frustrate the attacks, arrest the perpetrators and, if possible, identify the masterminds.

Nevertheless, the correspondence between the Cuban agents and Havana, which the FBI began intercepting in 1995, reveals that no matter how immersed in feverish and stressful activities, the Cubans were not immune to ordinary personal issues like passion, homesickness and loneliness. A case in point was Tony. At the height of the network's activities, he let Gerardo Hernández know that he wanted to marry Maggie, or at least move in with her on a permanent basis, now that he was staying at her house so often. Apart from the emotional reasons, she had found a steady job as a masseuse at the Hilton Hotel in Key West, which increased the couple's financial stability. The exchange of correspondence between Tony, Hernández and the Main Center is revealing on the nature of the intelligence services' relationship to their agents. In the first message on this topic to his superiors in Havana, sent as usual by way of Hernández, the agent made it clear that his involvement with the American woman would not take priority over his work, or imperil the activity he was part of in the United States:

> She brings up the subject once in a while and I try to get out of it, as best as possible. ... We must begin with what is required by the work; that is to say, if we are considering that intensifying this relationship with Maggie, moving into her house first, and even have a child with her at a later time, does not come between our projections, and is positive for the objectives planned for me, then we must move ahead and take some action in this regard. If on the other hand, we consider that living with Maggie and having a child with her is contrary to our work projections, then we must direct our actions at cutting off this relationship.

At the same time he was sending on the request to Cuba, Hernández gave Tony his personal opinion. It wasn't the first time he had made honest comments on his life and behavior. Giro had previously shown concern over Tony's excessive weight loss, the result of the vegetarian diet he had adopted under Maggie's influence. As for the couple living together, the first and obvious concern of the network chief was with security and secrecy, which would have to be amplified if indeed this were to happen. After all, Maggie "didn't know nor should she even imagine" anything about his intelligence work. Although he was seven years younger than Tony, Hernández spoke to him like an older brother:

"You've already been married, so you know that having a wife is not the same as having a girlfriend. Consciously or not, a sense of ownership develops and it's normal for one to ask the other for explanations about the things they have in common. And, as you must have noticed in your earlier relationships, a woman picks up signs about things that you didn't even mention or discuss with her."

Before deciding on their answer, the men from the DSS wanted to know under what legal conditions the two would get married and what would be the consequences for him should they divorce. As they were deliberating over the issue, they suggested to Tony that he delay the wedding "as long as possible." Only after some months did Gerardo Hernández receive and forward the green light to Tony from Havana, which came with a list of recommendations on the care that the agent should take with this move:

> To avoid by all means having a child with Maggie because of the sentimental and legal inconveniences that this might have at some future time … using the problem of Maggie's age (forty-five years) as a reason, which can put at risk the child's life or health and Maggie's life as well.
>
> Periodically review the hard drive of the machine and in case he detects reports sent to us, or any operational information, erase it with Wipe-Info; the latter is a program that the agent has and was sent to him by the comrades from M-XV [code that identified the Cuban embassy at the UN].
>
> Maintain the working disks with other disks that contain commercial programs and information. He must keep them in such a way that only he will be able to identify them.
>
> Separate his disks from Maggie's.
>
> Use the computer for the purposes that he had planned (making of videos) or for other purposes that justify the purchase of the equipment.
>
> Select a place in the house where he will have privacy for working with the equipment. Preferably choose a place that doesn't look out on the street.
>
> Maintain privacy from Maggie at the time when working on the computer apart from the fact that he may be using it for the purpose of cover. Avoid attracting her attention, that something improper is being done and show her concrete results of how he's using the equipment.

One week after receiving Havana's *nihil obstat*, Tony gathered up his scanty belongings from his motel room and moved them to

Maggie's small, cozy house on Poinciana Road. Like the majority of houses in Key West, Maggie's was made of white clapboard, with a living room, a kitchen, a bathroom and two bedrooms. One of the bedrooms had been turned into a massage room, where, from Wednesday to Saturday, Maggie received clients attracted by an advertisment she had placed in the Yellow Pages. On Sundays, Mondays and Tuesdays, her job at the Hilton Hotel kept her busy. In his new house, which was much closer to work, Tony got an extra hour of free time every day, which he filled with morning yoga exercises. His work hours were from seven in the morning until five in the afternoon, with an hour for lunch in the mess room at the aeronaval base. At the end of the day he would drive to the local headquarters of the Democracy Movement where he would stay late at meetings. He would come home, make a frugal meal— the contents of which never included meat, fish, fowl or any food derived from living creatures, like honey, eggs, milk or cheese— and only then would he sit down at the computer, to record onto diskettes the information he would transmit to Gerardo Hernández or to one of the three assistants who supervised him. Since his job on the base at Boca Chica did not allow him access to any restricted or secret sector, Tony received a new and tedious daily task from the DSS directors: to count and identify the planes that landed and took off on the three runways at the military unit. Such caution was warranted, since any attack that might be mounted by American forces against Cuba would obviously come from Key West, the closest point to the Island. It still seemed odd, however, that the Cuban intelligence services should assign to a secret agent a mission that could be done by any ordinary mortal: as the fence that protects the Boca Chica base is scarcely twenty meters from the busy highway that runs from Key West to Miami, the coming and going of planes and helicopters could be monitored and even photographed by any of the thousands of tourists who circulated daily around the place.

If Tony Guerrero's love life was taken care of, the indefatigable René González still had a long road ahead of him to achieve the dream he nurtured from the moment he landed in the United

States: to get the family he had abandoned in Havana five years earlier out of Cuba and into Miami. Still unaware that René's theft of the plane and his defection had been a front set up by the DSS and that the father of her daughter had not turned into a *gusano*, by the middle of 1995 Olguita seemed to have finally capitulated in the face of René's convincing appeals. Although he did not intend to move to another house or change his standard of living, the husband knew that the pay he received from Havana, even augmented by odd jobs and sporadic temporary work, was not enough to sustain a family of three. With the help of his influential friends he eventually managed to get a position as a co-pilot at Arrow Air, an air cargo company based at Miami International Airport. Also, thanks to the good relations he had established with elite anti-Castroist activists in Florida, a few weeks after receiving his wife's "yes," René found out that the American Immigration Service had approved Olguita and their daughter as residents of the United States.

Swallowed up by Cuban bureaucracy, however, the government's authorization for the two of them to leave the country would only be given in December 1995, six months after their initial decision. Before beginning to chase up the paperwork for departure, Olga would be called for an interview in a Ministry of the Interior safe house, where she was greeted by a young, smiling intelligence officer. It was Gerardo Hernández, the Manuel Viramóntez from Miami, who happened to be in Havana on one of his visits. Without beating about the bush, Giro went straight to the point and told her the truth about her husband, an account she listened to in complete astonishment: René was not a traitor to the Revolution. The theft of the plane in San Nicolás de Bari, the escape to Key West and the interviews given to the American press had all been acts in a pantomime set up by Cuban intelligence to hide his real mission: to infiltrate organizations of the extreme right in Florida and to try to prevent terrorist acts against his country.

Although in a state of shock at the news, Olga was overcome by a profound feeling of relief. The revelation put an end to five years of nightmares, sleepless nights and crying all alone. A whirlpool of memories took hold of her: her perplexity at the discovery of his desertion, the humiliation of being seen as the wife of a traitor to the homeland, the five years of loneliness, during which she lived in the unheard-of situation of being at the same time a widow, a married woman, and single—while in actual fact not being any of those three. Gerardo awakened her from these recollections to end the interview, not without having first reiterated a recommendation of the utmost importance for the safety of the operation and of all those involved: no one else should know of what she had just heard. Not even René's brother or his mother, and much less Irmita, who would go to live with her parents in Miami.

In the midst of the stupor that followed Hernández's story, Olga was excited at the thought of the trip, but the family's reunion would still depend on overcoming a calvary that both husband and wife knew well: the lethargic, sleepy local government departments. Even after the departure authorization was conceded, Olga had to suffer for weeks, filling in forms and facing endless lines at crowded counters. Part of this time would be taken up getting an apparently banal document: a declaration by the Ministry of Light Industry, to which Tenerías Habana, where she worked as an engineer, was attached, releasing her from her contract and confirming that the employee "owed nothing" to the State company. On the night of December 20, 1995—a Wednesday—Olga arrived home exhausted from her toings and froings for the paperwork on top of a long day's work. Tiredness gave way to eagerness when she spotted on the table an envelope from the Cuban Immigration Service—a guarantee that the pair would spend the end of year holidays with René in Miami. The joy lasted only as long as it took to open the letter, when Olga found that it only contained one "white card," as the exit document was known, and in Irmita's name. Several more days of agony passed before she discovered that the card bearing her name had been sent to an old address where she had lived with her parents, in the Cerro neighborhood.

Christmas passed, the New Year came and went, but the document reached Olga's hands only at the beginning of 1996. Thus it was on January 7 that mother and daughter finally boarded one of the charter flights still permitted by the American government, used mainly by Cuban residents in the United States to visit relatives in Cuba. For Irmita, the first impact of her new life hit while she was still on the plane. When the stewardess offered her a tray of candies, the girl took a handful and asked her mother to save them for later. The woman who was traveling next to them, a Cuban American on her way back to Miami, said with a chuckle:

"You don't have to do that, dear. You're not in Cuba now, you won't have to save food anymore."

"I was taught by my parents always to be polite to everyone," Irmita would remember, more than ten years later, "but I was so angry at that woman that I pretended I didn't hear her—I didn't answer and didn't even give her a smile."

Fifty minutes after takeoff, the Boeing 737 was landing at Miami Airport. They were only able to leave customs after being detained for more than an hour by the Immigration Service, where they were photographed, told to fill in forms and fingerprinted for their ID cards. Holding a doll for his daughter and a bouquet of flowers for his wife, the René who awaited them in a suit and tie was a good deal fatter, with his face covered in a thick gray beard—very different from the image they had kept of him five years earlier, skinny, clean-shaven and almost always dressed in jeans and a T-shirt. Among the people who were with her father at the airport, Irmita barely recognized her great-grandmother Teté, René's grandmother, and Teté's sister Gladys, both of whom had left Cuba when she was still a little girl. In the midst of the turmoil of their arrival, it wasn't the physical appearance of her father, however, that caused the girl greatest astonishment. Irmita's eyes opened wide when she noticed in the large welcome committee the smiling figure of a man she had often seen on the news, on television and in photographs published by the press in her country, always identified as a "terrorist assassin" and "a *gusano* responsible for the death of innocent Cubans"—it was Ramón Saúl Sánchez, the leader of the active anti-Castroist group the Democracy Movement.

After their first few weeks, and with the family installed in René's tiny apartment, Irmita was enrolled in summer school to learn English. Since René's salary at Arrow Air was insufficient to maintain the family, Olguita also had to look for a job. The first one she got was as a carer in a private retirement home, whose clientele was mainly Cubans. As an engineer used to the office environment of Tenerías Habana, Olga didn't adapt well to this new challenge. Apart from the exhausting work, she soon discovered that her duties included the intimate hygiene of very old people on the brink of senility. She resigned even before the first month was up. Her second attempt didn't last long, either. With the help of her husband's friends, she was taken on as a telemarketing operator at a large Miami funeral home. The job consisted of making calls to a list of names previously prepared by the owners—almost all of them elderly people or family members of the terminally ill—offering the services and products sold by the company. The nearly deceased or his relatives had at their disposal anything from simple wakes to ceremonies with cocktails and live chamber music, Catholic, Protestant or Evangelical religious services, caskets of various sizes and prices, cremations, graves and tombs for all tastes and budgets. Makeup gave the appearance of the living to the vainest of the dead, who could be buried wearing European designer clothing —real or false, depending on financial resources. The decision to abandon this job, too, wasn't so much down to the fact that nine out of ten times, Olga's offers were met with obscene language. The problem was that it was a job paid on commission, with an insignificant, almost symbolic, fixed salary—and the majority of people were decidedly uninterested in their future after death.

The only positive side to the brief and unpleasant experience with the undertakers was the familiarity she acquired with the telephone sales system, which made getting her next job easier. She found work in a language school called Inglés Ahora (English Now) owned by a Cuban, where she would remain for the duration of her time in Miami. This time she would be selling English courses by telephone to the Hispanic community. The company's target market, notably recently arrived immigrants, was concentrated along an extensive fringe that runs from Florida to California, passing through Texas, New Mexico and Arizona. Because of the five-hour time difference along this band, her working day started at one o'clock in the afternoon and ended at eleven o'clock at night. Added to her salary of $5 per hour, was the commission on whatever was sold. The products offered by Inglés Ahora went from simple dictionaries to entire lesson packages on cassette tapes or videos. Even when she hadn't sold a single dictionary, and that was a rare ocurrence, at the end of the month Olga received around a thousand dollars net. Added to René's salary at Arrow Air and the odd jobs he did as a pilot for the Democracy Movement, the family was assured of an existence that was modest but without worries—something to which the low cost of living in Miami undoubtedly contributed. The couple's first luxury was to buy a secondhand car. Encouraged by the slight cushion in their domestic budget and, of course, confident that he would come out unscathed from the dangerous mission he found himself in, René suggested to his wife that they might start thinking about making an old dream come true: having a second child.

As mother and daughter would confess many years later, the happiness in the house was darkened only by a ghost about which no one in the family ever said a word: the real activity of the husband and father. In his relationship with the girl, René had to walk on a knife edge. For example, it was inevitable that he would take Irmita along to family gatherings, which usually brought together militants and the leaders of anti-Castroist organizations. And he could see the bewilderment of his teenage daughter, brought up and educated in a communist society, on seeing her father participate in "prayer chains" at the end of which everyone, holding hands, would shout in unison: "Death to Fidel!"

"I wasn't dumb and started to put two and two together," Irmita would remember fifteen years later, now married and planning to give her parents their first grandchild. There were two episodes in particular that made her think. One day René saw a photograph of President Fidel Castro, cut out from some magazine, on the nightstand in her makeshift bedroom. Tactfully, he suggested to the girl that it would be wiser to keep the photograph inside a book. Irmita already had the insight to realize that a true *gusano* would rip the photo to pieces. Or at least would repeat to the daughter that Fidel was "a communist tyrant who had enslaved Cuba," as her father's friends usually referred to the bearded leader. On the other occasion, during a weekend get-together, the wife of one of the big chiefs of the counterrevolution, captivated by the girl's beauty, announced to all present that she was going to arrange her courtship with no less than the grandson of Jorge Mas Canosa, the head of the CANF.

Asked whether he would permit such matchmaking, René kept up the disguise and responded with a smile: "Who wouldn't be proud to see his daughter married to the grandson of the billionaire who'll be the first president of a free Cuba?" In the car, on the way home, Irmita decided to test her father's sincerity and feigned interest in the suggestion to meet, and who knows, to date the grandson of the number one enemy of the Cuban Revolution. René stopped the car and spoke seriously to his daughter.

"Irmita, please," he said, almost whispering, as if he were afraid of being overheard. "You're not seriously thinking of going out with that boy, are you?"

She defused the tension with a laugh. "No, Dad, I don't even want to meet him," she answered. "And I'm very glad to see that you really don't want me to meet him either," she concluded, visibly comforted by what she'd heard. "Without his saying a word to me," Irmita would remember much later, "at that moment a complicity between us was established."

Spared from the play-acting that the disguise imposed upon her husband, Olga was a less frequent presence at these meetings. René's friendship with Juan Pablo Roque helped her get closer to Ana Margarita, mother to a couple of children from her first marriage, both of them around Irmita's age, but even so, the two never came to be friends. Olga strove to conceal the slight dislike she felt for Roque's wife, a feeling that seemed to be mutual. "There was never good chemistry in our relationship," Ana Margarita would confess years later. "Our time together never produced a friendship." In any case, even if the chemistry were good, there wouldn't have been enough time for a friendship to blossom between the two women: when Olga and Irmita set foot in Miami, a silent operation was already in place to send the MiG pilot back to Havana.

Dissatisfied with his performance, and above all, with what was considered Roque's "exhibitionist behavior" in Florida, at the end of 1995 the DSS management had initiated an operation to take him out of the United States safely, which had been given the suggestive name of Operación Vedette (Operation Starlet).

7

JOSÉ BASULTO DEFIES THE WHITE HOUSE AND THE CUBAN MIGS AND DECIDES TO FLY ONCE MORE OVER HAVANA

Compared to the deprivation the Cuban population was enduring during the so-called "special period," Juan Pablo Roque's life in Miami was a bed of roses. However, for him, going back to Havana was far from being a punishment. A report lifted by the FBI from the Wasp Network's files revealed that, months earlier, the serviceman had put in a request to the Main Center for a return to base. Despite what many people think, secret agents are not devoid of sentiment and human emotions. Even so, the reason presented by Roque for his return to Cuba does seem surprising: the fighter pilot was homesick. He missed his home, his wife and his children. The first signs that his relations with Havana were wearing thin appeared in a document sent to the DSS a few months before the major's wedding. Signed by A-4, one of Alberto Ruiz's noms de guerre, who at that time was standing in for Hernández-Viramóntez as commander of the operation, the correspondence made it clear that the marriage to Ana Margarita had not been Roque's idea, but a decree from Havana. On receiving orders to get married the pilot resisted, claiming that "he couldn't do that to Amelita," the wife he had abandoned in Cuba. On that occasion, also according to A-4's report, "Germán [the current alias for Juan Pablo Roque] insisted on his wish to return before the wedding."

For some unknown reason, just eight months after the elegant ceremony at the University Baptist Church, the DSS put Operation Starlet into action. As if they were playing a game of chess, the men from Villa Marista were already preparing their move following Roque's return. They guessed that when the pilot's return became public, the anti-Castroist militants would naturally become mistrustful of René, his best friend in Miami. In order to avoid suspicion falling on him, Havana told René to simulate a split with Roque. René was directed to launch a smear campaign to undermine his friend's reputation in the eyes of the leaders of the organizations frequented by both of them. An outline of how Roque, referred to as Germán, was to go about this was sent to Miami at the end of 1995:

> On the campaign to dishonor or discredit Germán, [Castor] should: look at the possibility of contradicting him in public during meetings and activities; [state] that the book that they published for him was of no value, that in it he expresses his egocentric position, his desire for profit; [observe] that Germán likes to give interviews whether it is radio, newspaper, television, etc. for the purpose of gaining publicity for his personal benefit, but not for the benefit of the organization; [suggest] that he likes to be linked with well-known people, like General del Pino, Basulto, etc., for his personal gain; [complain about] his many [practically unattainable] ideas of actions [such as the story of] a "secret weapon" that was effective during the Second World War [and] that could be introduced in Cuba to be used by counterrevolutionary groups and to promote actions against the government. [Insist on the fact that], if the famous weapon has not been used for fifty years, it puts its validity in doubt.

Juan Pablo Roque felt relieved on knowing he would be returning to Cuba—even though it wasn't exactly a return bathed in glory. Besides the sincere desire to see his family again, time had given him a new certainty: that it would be impossible to keep up his marriage with Ana Margarita. Since the day *Desertor* was launched, she began to carry out a subtle yet rigorous surveillance over her husband. Ana Margarita would become irritated and increasingly suspicious when he gave lame answers to her direct questions. So as not to have to give explanations, Roque alleged that there were "certain things" it was better she didn't know. His wife also found it strange that his personal standard of living had gone up, well above that of their joint life, which continued to be modest. Roque had begun wearing designer clothes and often arrived home with expensive accessories, like his $3,000 Rolex Submariner watch. The dilapidated Toyota Corolla was replaced by an imposing olive green Jeep Cherokee, and in place of his pager he now used a cell phone, which in those days was still considered a luxury. With every new acquisition the pilot was obliged to submit to an interrogation by his wife, who demanded to know where the money was coming from for such extravagances. As always, he would give a confusing answer or repeat that it was better she didn't ask about "certain things." The suspicious atmosphere poisoned the marriage to such an extent that the pair decided to spend a period apart. Months later they were together again, but it was clear that the mistrust that had caused the separation continued to exist within their relationship.

Apart from his decision to rebuild his life in Cuba and the conjugal problems with Ana Margarita, an instinctive intuition seemed to tell Roque that it was time to bring his part in the operation to an end. From one minute to the next he began to fear he was being watched. Not by the FBI—which had indeed been monitoring all the members of the Wasp Network for more than a year now— but by José Basulto. A report sent by Hernández-Viramóntez to Havana describes the climate of mutual distrust into which the Cuban community in Florida had sunk:

[Germán] said that Basulto had called him and had told him that he wanted to talk to him. They agreed to meet on Sunday 4, at the church. And Germán points out that Basulto and Cossío carried out what could be a surveillance measure on him. He says that he arrived in his car and he saw Basulto's van parked there. He drove on and parked his. He got out and didn't see anybody and then he saw that in a Jeep, on another side of the parking lot, from a very good angle,

Basulto and Cossío were observing him, and then they went to meet him.

Germán says that during the conversation, in a way that had never happened before, Basulto and Cossío talked to him using intelligence language, using terms like ["brush pass,"] "mailbox," etc. They explained that some men went to see him and told him that they were members of an organization called (see information, I think it was called "Coalición Patriótica Martiana" [Patriotic Martían Coalition] or something like that) and its main objective was to "eliminate the one" [Fidel Castro] because they have the theory that, if you destroy the summit, the pyramid will collapse. These people asked Basulto to collaborate with money, but he didn't give it to them. Basulto told Germán that he didn't know if these people were from security or what.

On October 10, 1995, when Operation Starlet was in its early planning stages, Miami was agitated by the announcement of the constitution of the Cuban Council, one more group that promised to fight for the end of Cuba's socialist regime. The novelty was that, unlike the dozens of anti-Castroist organizations that proliferated on every corner in Little Havana, the Council did not advocate the overthrow of the government by exiles in Florida, but by dissidents resident on the Island. The role that the Council attributed to itself was to support and organize internal opposition. To prove that their strategy was on the right track, the new counterrevolutionary front announced the existence of no less than 101 "independent organizations" active within Cuban territory. On the list of names in the constellation of "parties," "fronts" and "movements" that made up the Council's founding bodies, the word *democracy* appeared thirty times. Second place went to José Martí—the Cuban apostle worshiped as much by the government as by its opponents—whose name appeared in the denomination of eleven groups. Ten presented themselves as liberal, seven were Christian organizations, seven pacifist, three environmentalist and three feminist. Two of them called themselves "independent news agencies."

Of the 101 names that undersigned the document launching the Council, at least four were already known to the international press as dissidents who lived in Cuba: Raúl Rivero, representing the Cuba Press News Agency, Elizardo Sánchez (Cuban Commission of Human Rights and National Reconciliation), Oswaldo Payá (Christian Liberation Movement) and Vladimiro Roca (Democratic Socialist Current). Roca had acquired notoriety less for his activism than for being the son of the historic union leader and member of the central committee of the Cuban Communist Party Blas Roca, who had died in 1987 at the age of seventy-eight. The most important annoucement was kept until last: the new organization had made a formal request to President Castro to authorize their first assembly in Havana, from February 24 to 27 of the following year. Taking part in the meeting would be representatives from the 101 founding bodies, "representatives of the Catholic Church and international observers from the United Nations." As night fell, on that cool Tuesday in October, there was a sense of impending confrontation.

From then on, the anti-Castroist groups started a noisy countdown of the 137 days that separated them from their highly anticipated February gathering. The date of February 24 had been chosen because it was the 101st anniversary of the Battle Cry of Baire, the fuse that set off the war that would free Cuba from the Spanish yoke. While Cuba simply seemed to ignore the request delivered to the Cuban embassy at the United Nations, the White House openly supported the Council. In one of his speeches to anti-Castroist leaders in Florida, the special adviser on Cuba, Richard Nuccio, made clear what President Clinton's position was on the "Cuban question." "You place too much emphasis on Fidel, and the solution is not in his hands, but in the hands of the human rights communities within the Island," the official said. "If the Cuban exiles helped entities like the Council on a massive scale, it could bring enormous benefits for Cuba and give a positive role to the Cuban community abroad in the solution to the crisis."

The temperature started to rise shortly after the Council came into being, when José Basulto announced on the following Saturday, October 21, that Brothers to the Rescue airplanes would be making incursions into Cuban airspace to drop plastic bags full of pamphlets over Havana summoning the population to February's assembly. At the same time, a flotilla of the Democracy Movement, under the command of Ramón Saúl Sánchez, would sail along the twelve-mile limit of Cuban territorial waters—a high-risk adventure, since on the other side of the invisible border would be the well-armed boats of the Cuban Coast Guard. The widespread publicizing of the plan that Basulto and Sánchez had outlined set off alarm bells in Washington—or more precisely in the office of Cecilia Capestany, director of the Federal Aviation Administration (FAA), the federal government department responsible for ensuring compliance with the air laws of the United States. Three days before the promised pamphlet drop, Capestany circulated a memorandum on the subject among the directors of other areas involved with the problem:

An event with a flotilla seems to have been planned by the Cuban-American leadership of the Democracy Movement for October 21st. For the time being all we know is that they plan to use large boats and make radio transmissions to Cuba from international waters. We do not know if the Brothers will be taking part with planes. During a contingency planning meeting called by the State Department last Friday, the FAA was asked to issue warnings with a view to deterring possible violations of Cuban air space. The Cuban government has not abandoned its decision to take serious measures to defend its national sovereignty. To make matters worse, Fidel Castro should be in New York for United Nations activities on the day the flotilla is planned, which could exacerbate the Cuban government's reaction in the face of possible violations. As part of the efforts between various government agencies to prepare themselves for the events of October 21st, we will issue a Notam [notice to airmen] warning to United States pilots and operators not to enter Cuban air space without authorization. The Notam will coincide with a similar warning made to sailors by the Coast Guard and with an Official Note from the State Department. Apart from that, we will instruct FAA inspectors to meet with Brothers pilots, before the event, to remind them that we will investigate thoroughly any possible violation of American or international regulations.

Signed: Cecilia Capestany.

Issued by Capestany in an attempt to prevent a serious diplomatic incident, the said Notam arrived hours later at all American airports:

> Notam—Cuba: Special notice
> Attention US airmen and operators: due to a potential increase in air traffic associated with a waterborne event in the Florida Straits on October 21, 1995, the FAA recommends that any operators conducting flights in the area remain vigilant for other air traffic in the area and strictly abide by international and FAA federal aviation regulations. The government of Cuba has repeatedly asserted its determination to take actions against aircraft violations of Cuban airspace. These measures are aimed at defending and preserving Cuban national sovereignty and preventing overflight by unauthorized aircraft. Operators entering Cuban space without authorization may be subject to arrest and may place themselves and others at serious personal risk. All aircraft should conform to international regulations and existing guidelines, as well as all applicable Cuban laws, rules and regulations concerning operations into Cuban airspace. (FAA/AIA-120, 10/95)

The feared weekend ended up going by without incident. Although both Basulto and Sánchez had done exactly what they had promised, there was no reaction from the Cuban government—except the predictable diplomatic notes denouncing the aggressions and requesting steps be taken by Washington. But the incursions over Cuba seemed to have no end. On Saturday, December 9, Billy Schuss summoned Juan Pablo Roque for yet another flight aboard a Piper Aztec, prefix N58KM. Despite being shadowed by Cuban MiGs, the plane flew two nautical miles into Cuban territorial waters and scattered pamphlets over Havana, as well as Brothers bumper stickers and small aluminum medallions of the Virgin of Charity of Cobre. On January 13, it was the turn of Basulto and René to fill the skies over the Cuban capital with leaflets encouraging internal dissidents to show up en masse at the action planned for the following month. At the end of the month Cecilia Capestany sent a memorandum reiterating her earlier concerns to her superiors in the FAA, Michael Thomas and Charles Smith Jr. Commenting on the latest incursion by Basulto, the official affirmed that these overflights "can only be seen as further taunting of the Cuban government." According to her, the State Department was becoming increasingly worried about Cuba's possible reaction to "these flagrant violations," to the point where Under Secretary of State Nuccio had checked on the progress of the proceedings opened by the FAA against Basulto for infringement of aviation legislation. "Worst case scenario is that one of these days the Cubans will shoot down one of these planes," she concluded, "and the FAA better have all its ducks in a row." In fact the FAA had already suspended Basulto's pilot's license for four months—during which period he continued to take part in overflights as a passenger.

The wide media coverage in Florida, and the support for the Cuban Council from international political leaders like Prime Minister Margaret Thatcher of the United Kingdom, and presidents José María Aznar of Spain and Václav Havel of the Czech Republic, had the effect of an adrenaline injection into the veins of the Miami anti-Castroist organizations. The majority of these were planning to offer "political and moral" support to the inauguration of the Council anticipated in Havana—whether it was authorized or not—by making flights over the Malecón and taking a large flotilla into territorial waters. An $11,000 suite at the Hyatt Regency Hotel in Coral Gables was reserved from February 24 to 27, for leaders who might prefer to stay on solid ground "monitoring the events" than to embark on planes and boats. Ten days before the assembly, Basulto gave a rapid and provocative interview to journalists David Hall and Pepe Vives, from *Cuba in the News*, a program broadcast by the Voice of America, the radio station sponsored by the State Department. The Brothers leader celebrated one more weekend of incursions into Cuban air space:

DAVID HALL: On the line is José Basulto, from the humanitarian organization Brothers to the Rescue, who for years has dedicated himself to rescuing rafters fleeing from Cuba in search of freedom. Unfortunately, since the United States and Cuba signed the new migratory accords, these escapes have ceased. But that's not what we're going to talk about. It seems that this Saturday it rained a lot in Cuba, didn't it, Pepe?

PEPE VIVES: Yes! And it wasn't water that fell from the skies.

HALL: It was a shower of leaflets with protests against the Castro government. It seems that Basulto has assumed responsibility for this. Welcome to our program, Basulto. It's a pleasure to have you with us.

VIVES: Basulto, over which parts of Cuba did you drop the leaflets?

JOSÉ BASULTO: I can't give details but practically all over the city of Havana. As it was really windy, the leaflets spread out over areas in the vicinity of the capital.

HALL: To what do you attribute the lack of a military response by the Cuban government against you? Disorganization? Surprise?

BASULTO: This regime is not invulnerable. Castro is not impenetrable. Our compatriots on the Island should know that we have assumed personal risks to do what we do. They should do the same. We have to rid ourselves, once and for all, of this internal police we carry around inside of ourselves that makes us think they are always watching us. What we are asking of our people is that they consider the possibility of doing the things that it's possible to do.

VIVES: What has been the reaction of the United States government in the cases of flights like Saturday's?

BASULTO: To our good fortune, it seems that the United States government is always on holiday …

The excitement grew when the *radio bemba* grapevine propagated the rumor that the United States was inclined to intervene should the Cuban government suppress the Council's assembly. Watchful of the commotion, the Wasp Network's agents redoubled their vigilance, sending daily reports to Cuba on the movements in the organizations under their watch. The bulletin transmitted to Hernández-Viramóntez by René reflects the euphoric climate that took hold at the meeting on February 18 of one of the groups supporting the Council:

> Evidently all of these people have great expectations that the *Concilio* [Council] meeting could create a situation that would spoil the Revolution. … [They] expressed a hope that the *Concilio* meeting would

provoke [disturbances]. In my opinion, the view that [they] have on the situation in Cuba is pretty jubilant and they overestimate the difficulties that the country is going through. For them—perhaps they have a reason—*El Concilio* puts us between a rock and a hard place. If we allow the meeting, we lose ground making such a concession, and if we impede it we cloud our image before the international community. Perhaps the weakest point of this reasoning is that they attribute to *El Concilio* an international resonance comparable to the one they have given it in Miami.

On the other hand [they] were asked to make up a list of pilots and planes that in conjunction with the State Department will be authorized to travel immediately to Cuba with assistance once an abrupt change in government takes place. Among the pilots there is me, Freddy Flaker and Jorge Bringuier. [They were] hopeful that the State Department has some information that indicates some rapid change in Cuba and that is why they are preparing these lists. ... I already gave [them] a copy of my passport and my personal information to be sent to the State Department.

The frantic mobilization of the exiles led the Cuban intelligence services to launch Operation Scorpion, designed to "refine the confrontation with the counterrevolutionary organizations" involved in supporting the Council and its intended assembly. The plan foresaw the immediate execution of Operation Starlet, to ensure that Juan Pablo Roque would already be on Cuban soil on February 24. When the air and naval demonstrations in solidarity with the Council began, the pilot would call an international press conference in Havana where he would denounce "the terrorist character" of the anti-Castroist organizations—mainly the one he knew up close, the Brothers. The original idea—whereby Roque would steal one of Basulto's planes and triumphantly come down in Cuba—had to be aborted, because the agent had broken his left arm in an accident and had been barred from flying. Because of this, it was decided that on Friday, February 23, he would begin the journey back. Accompanied all the time by Hernández-Viramóntez and carrying false documents, Roque would go by bus to neighboring Fort Lauderdale and from there get a plane to Tampa, 400 kilometers away in northwestern Florida. There he would be met by Alberto Ruiz, agent A-4, who would hand him a ticket for Northwest flight 478, which would leave at midday for Cancún, Mexico, from where he would take a direct flight to Havana. The direction given to René was "to react first with disbelief and then with condemnation" as soon as Roque's return became public. The Main Center recommended that as soon as he heard the news he should telephone FBI agent Oscar Montoto, "to verify that it was true."

On the night of Wednesday, February 21, on arriving home, Ana Margarita noticed that the half of the wardrobe where her husband kept his suits, jackets, pants and dress shirts was empty. When she asked him about it, he answered that the clothes had gone to be dry-cleaned, since all of them had been spattered with paint when the couple's bedroom had been decorated a few days earlier. Roque also told her that he had managed to get some extra work for the weekend, which would mean being away from Miami from early Friday morning through Sunday. The following night he seemed depressed, hardly touched the dinner that Ana Margarita had prepared, and suggested that they go to bed early that Thursday night. "Remember that tomorrow I have to wake up at three," he said. She wanted to know how she would be able to get in touch during the weekend, in case there was an emergency, and Roque promised to leave his cell phone switched on. Even fourteen years later, Ana Margarita could still reconstruct in precise detail her last moments by her husband's side:

I remember, as if it were yesterday, when Roque left. He told me he was going to do an odd job that weekend ferrying a boat. He would have to wake up in the middle of the night and that evening, before going to sleep, we made love with tender caresses, almost painful. After enduring a previous disastrous and abusive marriage, this time I felt loved, protected, safe. "I'm your bodyguard," he would tell me, like in the title of the film with Kevin Costner and Whitney Houston which we had seen together. This time, yes, I thought that night, my turn had come to have a mature and solid true-love, to protect me and my children from the hardships of life in the United States. "Never forget that you are my wife," Juan Pablo whispered in my ear as he kissed me before going to sleep. At that moment, as he had already asked me sometimes, I considered the possibility of having a child. I thought it better to give him a surprise and let him know of my decision only on Sunday night when he got back.

As Ana Margarita would find out the next day, Roque would never come back. In the middle of the night he disappeared without trace, never to return. Leaving for work on Friday morning, she thought it strange that the battery charger of her husband's cell phone was on the living room table—rare forgetfulness for someone as methodical as Roque. She called his number all day, but the recording she heard was always the same: "This cell phone is switched off." Once home, at the end of the day, Ana Margarita rummaged through drawers and cupboards and discovered that he had taken everything with him, except the wallet with his documents, checkbook and credit cards. The confusion in her head only got worse when she switched on the television and heard the news that the Cuban government had just arrested about a hundred dissidents and prohibited the assembly set for the following day. In intense anxiety and trying to find some link between the news from Cuba and her husband's strange behavior, Ana Margarita decided to go to the building where her mother lived and where Roque parked the Cherokee when he was out of town. The hope was that he had left some message in the car, some sign or indication that might explain what was going on. With her legs shaking, she opened the car door with the spare key she'd brought from home. There on the seat was her husband's cell phone, his key chain with the house and car keys, and there was the dark red bag he'd packed with clothes for the three days that he was to be away from home. Common sense suggested some connection between what was happening in Cuba and Roque's mysterious trip, but Ana Margarita could not figure out what it might be. With her heart pounding, she went home, took an extra dose of sleeping tablets and collapsed on the bed.

Ten kilometers north of Miami Beach, the airport of Opa-Locka was buzzing with activity that Saturday morning. Awaited by television news teams and reporters from Florida's main media outlets, pilots, militants and leaders from the anti-Castroist organizations began arriving along with the first rays of sunshine. As the morning wore on, no one seemed ready to take off. All they could talk about was the events from the previous night in Havana. Opinions were divided on how to react to the imprisonments and to the prohibition by the Cuban government of the Council's assembly. Basulto advised sticking to the plan, and announced that after lunch some Brothers planes would scatter leaflets over Havana condemning the government for its actions. Half an hour away, in Kendall, after a night of lethargic sleep, Ana Margarita was awakened by the insistent ringing of the phone on her nightstand. At the other end of the line a deep male voice asked to talk to Juan Pablo Roque. With surprising agility for someone who seconds before was fast asleep, Ana Margarita jumped out of bed and demanded to know, almost hysterical now, who was calling. It was an FBI agent. She begged: "What do you know about my husband? Where is he?" The man at the other end was abrupt—"I can't discuss that with you right now"—and hung up.

If Margarita had managed to sleep that night, though with the aid of pills, Richard Nuccio had not had the same luck. The bald and affable American special advisor on Cuba had been up all night in his house in Washington, tormented by a somber premonition: something very serious was about to happen. "I hardly slept that night," he would remember later. "I was worried, I thought there was going to be some incident." As he explained many years later, his fears did not come from clairvoyance, but from the logical deductions anyone could make who had witnessed the extreme tension to which the Cuban government had been led by the audacity of the anti-Castroist organizations, particulary the Brothers. In Clinton's advisor's opinion, the migration agreements had moved Basulto to redefine the Brothers' course. "From then on, they put into practice a political agenda of hostility and menace towards the Cuban government, making overflights and throwing leaflets over Cuba," Nuccio recalled. Invariably, the White House's attempts to curb Basulto's provocations came up against the powerful Cuban lobby in Washington. "When we reiterated our warnings to the Brothers, they used to run to Congress to complain to their representatives," the under secretary of state would reveal. "That was all it took for the Cuban American congressmen to accuse the government of persecuting exiles." Despite knowing that he could become a target for the anti-Castroist lobby in Congress, that Saturday morning the sleepless Nuccio succeeded in getting the FAA to suspend Basulto's pilot license indefinitely, a sanction that would, at least in theory, stop him from flying his Cessna N2506 during the fly-by planned for the afternoon. Ten years later, Nuccio would make an emotional mea culpa on remembering the events of that February day in 1996:

"I did everything I could, but I wish I had done more than just write memos, send faxes, make phone calls, sound alarms. I should have jumped up and down, screamed, shouted, invaded the president's office."

The American officials had more than enough reason to be concerned. The State Department had reaffirmed that it was treating "seriously" the warning made by the Cuban government that any boat coming from abroad could be sunk and any airplane shot down. In an official note, the government tried to discourage any adventure by the anti-Castroist organizations: "The freedom to travel, recognized by international accord, gives no one the right to enter a particular country, including Cuba, without previous authorization. All travelers are subject to the customs and immigration authorities and to other applicable laws of the country in question." None of this however seemed to produce any effect. Even though he had been notified that his pilot's license was suspended, a little after one o'clock in the afternoon Basulto took off at the commands of his Cessna, a transgression that would come to cost him the permanent revocation of his license. On board with him was co-pilot Arnaldo Iglesias and the couple Silvia and Andrés Iriondo, he a businesman and she the leader of Mujeres Anti-Represión (Women Against Repression) or MAR. Following one minute behind, two more Cessna 337s identical to Basulto's took off: the *Spirit of Miami* and the *Habana DC*, the latter baptized with the name of a song by the plane's donor, Cuban exile Willy Chirino. The "DC" naturally meant "Después de Castro" (After Castro). On the first plane were Carlos Costa and Pablo Morales, and on the second, Mario de la Peña and Armando Alejandre. Crossing the 24th Parallel, at twenty-one minutes to three in the afternoon, Basulto addressed the Cuban control tower with the usual message: "Good afternoon, Havana Center. This is November-two-five-zero-six, crossing the 24th Parallel. Today our area of operations will be the region north of Havana. Accept the cordial greetings of Brothers to the Rescue and its president, José Basulto, who is speaking." A flight controller from the Havana tower warned that the airspace to the north of the city was "activated" and that any intrusion below the 24th Parallel was subject to risk. Basulto was not deterred. "As free Cubans," he replied, "we have the right to be here."

It was five minutes to three in the afternoon when the Brothers planes, in the shape of three little black dots, appeared on the Cuban Anti-Aircraft Defense radar screens. At that very moment a MiG-29UB Fulcrum fighter-bomber took off from the military base at San Antonio de los Baños, a quiet village half an hour from Havana, where the International Film and TV School created by Gabriel García Márquez was also located. The jet was under the command of twin brothers, Lieutenant Colonels Lorenzo and Francisco Pérez-Pérez, both forty-four-year-old veterans of Angola, the first with one thousand flying hours in that type of aircraft and the second with two thousand. Right after them, a MiG-23 took off piloted by thirty-five-year-old Major Emilio Palacios. The fighters' movements were detected 4,000 kilometers away by Major Jeffrey Houlihan, responsible for watching the radar at the Riverdale airbase in California. Houlihan transmitted the information to the Air Force base at Tyndall, Florida, but was assured by the officer who took his call: "Don't worry, we're aware of the situation." Dissatisfied with what he'd heard, the major called the officer on duty at the Homestead base, also in Florida. According to what Houlihan would reveal in an interview given to CBS, a squadron of F-15 and F-16 fighters was already parked at the end of the runway at Homestead, ready for action, but "superior orders" had forbidden the American bombers from taking off. "The official who answered me was literally pounding the table, demanding the planes be allowed to leave," reported Houlihan, "but there were express orders that no plane should take off." If Havana's patience had come to an end, the American government didn't seem interested in saving Basulto's skin.

8

THE CUBAN CONTROL TOWER AUTHORIZES THE MIG FIGHTERS TO SHOOT: SECONDS LATER, TWO CESSNAS ARE REDUCED TO DUST OVER THE FLORIDA STRAITS

The flames spat out by the supersonic fighter's two engines left a trail of fire in the air, as if a comet had cut through the blue of the sky in broad daylight. Weighing ten tons, the dark gray MiG-29 was armed with four air-to-air missiles, six air-to-ground missiles, a supply of laser-guided bombs and a thirty-millimeter gun with a capability of 150 rounds per minute. At one point, one of the Pérez-Pérez brothers informed Major Palacios, the MiG-23 pilot, that his radar had detected the presence of "a very large boat" sailing below the planes. "It's under me," the major replied. "It looks like a cruise ship." The servicemen were referring to the *Majesty of the Seas*, a 300-meter-long luxury transatlantic liner, weighing seventy thousand tons. That afternoon, with more than 2,000 passengers on board, the *Majesty* was returning from a three-day mini-cruise from Miami through Key West, Nassau, Coco Cay and back via Key West to Miami. Both on the way out and on the way back, while sailing between Key West and Coco Cay, a small island measuring seven by ten kilometers, the ship wound round the entire north coast of Cuba, always avoiding crossing over the demarcation line of Cuban territorial waters. Picked up by nine radar devices—seven in the United States and two in Cuba—communication between the Havana control tower and the two planes took on dramatic tones shortly after three o'clock in the afternoon:

TOWER TO MIG-29: What's your altitude?

MIG-29 TO TOWER: One thousand seven hundred meters. We are observing three planes in the air, sometimes flying together, sometimes apart.

MIG-23 TO TOWER: I'm doing a search to the left and can see one of them, coming from the north.

TOWER TO MIG-23: What's your altitude?

MIG-23 TO TOWER: Two hundred meters.

TOWER TO MIG-29 AND MIG-23: Switch on your radars.

MIG-29 TO TOWER: Switched on.

MIG-23 TO TOWER: Switched on.

MIG-29 TO TOWER: The target is in sight. It's a small plane.

MIG-23 TO MIG-29: I'm going up to two thousand meters.

TOWER TO MIG-23: What color is it?

MIG-23 TO TOWER: It's a blue and white Cessna 337, flying at low altitude.

It was the *Spirit of Miami*, the second to take off from Opa-Locka two hours before. With a history of almost 150 flights on behalf of the Brothers, Carlos Costa seemed unfazed by the presence of Cuban warplanes. Confident that Cuba would not have the nerve to bring down North American civil aircraft, the pilot's only fear was encountering the air maneuver known as "forced landing interception." In these cases, a craft was surrounded by military helicopters that forced it to fly in circles until, without sufficient fuel to return to the United States, the pilot had no alternative but to land on Cuban soil—with all the associated risks. So, seeing the the MiG-29 maneuvering in the air in front of him, Carlos Costa's only comment to his co-pilot Pablo Morales was: "We've got a MiG for company. There's a MiG flying around us …" Richard Nuccio's terrible premonition, however, seemed fated to come true. The recording of the radio dialogue between the Havana control tower and the two planes reveals that at twenty minutes past three in the afternoon, the MiG-29 came face to face with Costa's and Morales's Cessna:

MIG-29 TO TOWER: He's in my sights.

MIG-23 TO TOWER: We need permission.

TOWER TO MIG-29: Permission to destroy.

MIG-29 TO TOWER: I'm going to fire.

TOWER TO MIG-29: Permission to fire.

MIG-29 TO TOWER: Here I go, dammit!

TOWER TO MIG-29: Did you fire?

MIG-29 TO TOWER: We goddam hit him! We hit him!

MIG-29 TO MIG-23: We ripped his *cojones* [balls] apart!

MIG-23 TO MIG-29: Wait! Wait to see where he went down!

MIG-29 TO MIG-23: Mark the spot where we dumped him.

MIG-23 TO MIG-29: This one's not going to fuck with us again.

MIG-29 TO TOWER: We're going up. We're coming back.

TOWER TO MIG-29: Stay there, flying in circles.

MIG-29 TO TOWER: Above the target?

TOWER TO MIG-29: Correct.

TOWER TO MIG-29 AND MIG-23: Climb to four thousand meters. Remain above the destroyed target and maintain low speed.

Six minutes later the MiG-29's radar detected the presence of *Habana DC*, the third Hermanos plane. It was a Cessna, prefix N5485S, piloted by the eldest in the group, the experienced, forty-five-year-old ex-marine Armando Alejandre Jr., who had spent two years as a voluntary combatant in the Vietnam War. His co-pilot was Mario de la Peña, at twenty-five years old the youngest of those flying that Saturday. At twenty-six minutes past three, the Cuban pilot's voice came on the radio again:

MIG-29 TO TOWER: We have another plane ahead.

TOWER TO MIG-29 AND MIG-23: Don't lose sight of him.

MIG-29 TO TOWER: He's in the same area where the first one went down.

TOWER TO MIG-29 AND MIG-23: Stay there, above him.

TOWER TO MIG-29: Is he still in sight?

MIG-29 TO TOWER: We're on top of him.

TOWER TO MIG-29: Permission to fire.

MIG-29 TO TOWER: He's destroyed! Homeland or death, dammit!

A few dozen meters away in the N2506, José Basulto reacted with an uncontrolled burst of laughter and a shout at the downing he'd just witnessed: "MiGs! They're about to fire at us!" In the back seat of the twin-engine plane, the terrified Silvia Iriondo grabbed a rosary from her handbag and began to pray. In panic at the danger of having his plane too reduced to dust by a missile strike, Basulto shut down all of the Cessna's communication systems to avoid identification by the MiGs' radars, veered northwards and made his getaway, flying a few meters above the surface of the sea.

The news of the downing of the two planes and the death of the four pilots hit Florida like a hurricane. Ana Margarita only found out what had happened at the end of the afternoon, when the Argentinian Brothers pilot Guillermo Lares phoned to summon Roque to a press conference that Basulto had called for early evening at the Opa-Locka hangar. Not very convincingly, she explained that her husband was busy on a job outside Miami and had forgotten his cell phone at home. Once radio and TV stations began breaking news of the incident, her phone didn't stop ringing—friends and family were worried in case Juan Pablo had been in one of the doomed planes. She repeated the same answer to all of them: "No, thank God, Roque wasn't in either of the planes." Inexplicably, however, she had received no news from her husband—not even a collect call to say he was OK. Nothing, nothing at all. Unable to eat or sleep, Ana Margarita stayed up all night and spent Sunday glued to the television, waiting for any information that could help her find answers to Juan Pablo's mysterious behavior.

The only fresh news was the disagreement between the American and Cuban governments with respect to the location where the two planes had been shot down. In a threatening official briefing, Secretary of State Warren Christopher characterized the act as "a blatant violation of international law and a violation of the norms of civilized behavior." He affirmed that the United States had "reached the conclusion" that the attack had taken place over international waters, and he ended with a promise: "prompt and appropriate" measures would be adopted by President Clinton in response to what had happened. "We will not limit ourselves to a multilateral action," growled the secretary. "We'll be considering actions the United States can take on its own." The Cuban foreign ministry responded by accusing Christopher of "lying in a cynical fashion," asserting that they had "unequivocal proof" that the two craft—dubbed "pirate planes"—were flying over Cuba's territorial waters. Havana placed at the American authorities' disposal maps that showed, minute-by-minute, everything that had been picked up by Cuban radar, recordings of the communications between the control tower and the two fighters, and even the personal belongings of one of the dead pilots that had been retrieved by the Coast Guard in Cuban waters north of the capital. Clinging to God knows what hopes, Ana Margarita didn't notice when a TV news anchor read out the last paragraph of the Cuban official note, in which lay the key for her to understand what had happened with her husband:

> Finally, to leave in no doubt that Mr. Christopher is telling shameless lies, we inform you that there is among us a pilot from one of these groups that carried out so many actions against our country. He was with them until a few hours ago. This pilot knows a lot. There is irrefutable evidence that these groups are far from performing humanitarian actions, as Mr. Christopher so ridiculously alleges. They constitute a terrorist mafia that hatched bloody plots against our people. We are ready to discuss these matters with Mr. Christopher at the United Nations Security Council or wherever he thinks fit.

Everything pointed to the pilot to whom he was referring as being Juan Pablo Roque, but Ana Margarita would only know this hours later. Sunday night came and her husband gave no signs of life. Again, relying on sleeping tablets, she fell into bed only to wake up the next morning to an uproar coming from the street—a rare disturbance in the placid suburb of Hialeah. She looked out the window, frightened, and saw she was besieged by radio and television vehicles with small parabolic antennas stuck on their hoods, reporters brandishing microphones and cameramen pointing threatening cameras toward the doors and windows of her nice yellow house. The telephone rang, and an agitated friend yelled at her to switch on CNN. She pressed the remote and there on the TV screen in the couple's bedroom was the smiling face of her husband. Clean-shaven, hair trimmed, wearing the Rolex but, as Ana Margarita observed, not his wedding ring, Roque was in Havana with the CNN international correspondent Lucia Newman, giving his first interview to foreign media. The false defector, or the repentant defector as he described himself, denied being a spy for Cuba or that he even belonged to the State's intelligence personnel. He claimed that he had, in fact, defected from Cuba, but had regretted it after four years in Miami. He said that he had been recruited by the FBI to spy not only on the Brothers, but on practically all of Florida's important anti-Castroist organizations—and that the real function of agent Oscar Montoto, Mr. Slingman, was to investigate violations of international neutrality law by the anti-Castroist groups of the United States. He also told how Montoto had warned him not to fly with the Brothers on February 24, "because Cuba was determined to shoot down any plane that invaded its airspace," and accused Basulto of smuggling weapons and explosives for the purpose of mounting terrorist attacks on the Island. But Ana Margarita only felt her heart beat faster when the journalist wanted to know about him, what his fondest memory was of the four years he had spent in the United States. Juan Pablo Roque floored his ex-wife on the other side of the Florida Straits when he smilingly affirmed that the thing he would miss most would be "my Jeep." Hours earlier he had given a long interview on Cuban state TV, where he was introduced only as "a member of the counter-revolutionary organization Brothers to the Rescue"—without any information on the circumstances under which he had left Cuba, or how he had returned.

The following week was taken up with a flurry of protests, condemnations and press conferences called by Florida's anti-Castroist organizations. On Monday, the United States ambassador to the UN, Madeleine Albright, who a year later would be appointed secretary of state by Bill Clinton, gave a speech condemning the Cuban government for shooting down the two planes, ending with a retort to the MiG-29 pilot's words after the first shot. The small, energetic ambassador surprised everyone by using language hardly appropriate for an elegant woman on a solemn platform such as this one. "Frankly, this is not *cojones*," Albright said, raising a stern finger. "This is cowardice." On the lips of a respectable grandmother, the vulgar word packed an even stronger punch. The mayor of Miami, the Cuban American Joe Carollo, announced that he would issue a decree to rename four of the city's avenues after the dead pilots. So far, however, the reactions in New York, Miami and Washington remained on the level of rhetoric. The first concrete measure against Cuba would be divulged that night by the White House. Convinced that neither of the two planes had invaded Cuban air space—"and even if they had, to shoot them down would still be a violation of international norms"—President Clinton announced a series of punitive measures against the Island's government, as he recalled in his autobiography:

"I suspended chartered flights to Cuba, restricted travel by Cuban officials in the United States, expanded the reach of Radio Martí … and asked Congress to authorize compensation out of Cuba's blocked assets in the United States to the families of the men who were killed."

The entrance of the American president onto the scene forced Fidel Castro to deal publicly with the matter. During a ceremony for the masses in the province of Matanzas, the Cuban leader referred to the downing of the planes as an incident that could have been avoided:

"We foresaw this outcome, and we repeatedly warned the United States of the danger. But you saw the violations of our airspace, you saw the increasingly audacious adventures above our capital, something that no country in the world would stand for. Now they've invented that the planes were civilian craft and that they were flying over international waters … They were warplanes, used by the United States in the Vietnam War."

Sure enough, two months later, the United Nations' International Civil Aviation Organization (ICAO) recognized that at least one of the planes that belonged to the Brothers, still had United States Air Force insignia painted on its fuselage. None of that cut any ice with the American government. At that moment, Washington seemed interested only in settling scores with Havana. Ten days after the shoot-down, live on national television, Bill Clinton ratified the Cuban Liberty and Democratic Solidarity Act, aka the "Helms-Burton bill," which had been lying around in the drawers of the White House since its approval four months earlier. In doing so, Clinton, as he would acknowledge in his memoirs, was not moved solely by the desire to provoke internal changes in Cuba, but also by his electoral interests. "Supporting the bill was good election-year politics in Florida," recalls the president, recognizing that the decision "undermined whatever chance I might have if I won a second term to lift the embargo in return for positive changes within Cuba." Intended to tighten even further the economic stranglehold on the Island and to restrict the authority of the US president to suspend the embargo without congressional approval, the law had been drafted by Republican Senator Jesse Helms, from North Carolina, and Democratic Congressman Dan Burton of Indiana, both known for their attachment to the most conservative sectors of Congress and to the Cuban community in exile. Thanks to the Republican opposition, which won a majority in Congress in the 1994 midterm elections, the law had been approved in October 1995 with two thirds of the votes, rendering a future presidential veto unfeasible.

Besides incorporating all the restrictions imposed on Cuba since 1962, the bill sanctioned by Clinton in 1996 was an explicit way of coercing the international community to adhere to the American embargo against the Island. The arsenal of sanctions threatened to deny entry visas to the United States to directors of any foreign company doing business—the verb used in the law is *trafficking*—with the Cuban government, and stipulated fines that could reach, as in fact some did, hundreds of millions of dollars. Merchant ships, no matter under what flag, that moored at Cuban ports were subjected to a quarantine prohibiting them from using American ports for a period of six months. Foreign investors and companies that exploited the assets or occupied the properties of American citizens expropriated by Cuba would be sued in US civil courts. On paper, the prescriptions seemed made-to-measure to consummate the economic strangulation of the Island that had begun with the embargo in 1961, and worsened in 1991 with the end of the USSR. If the United States could get it implemented, the act threatened to be the requiem mass of the Cuban Revolution. Before Havana even reacted, however, there was a chorus of condemnation of the extraterritorial character of the Helms-Burton Act: the European Union, the World Trade Organization, Unesco, Unicef and even the Organization of American States (OAS), from which Cuba had been suspended in 1962 and which rarely opposed Washington, harshly criticized Clinton's decision to enact the package of measures—even though he had no constitutional alternative. As far as these organizations were concerned, in practice the Helms-Burton Act forced the world to choose between doing business with Cuba and doing business with the United States, in blatant violation of international laws and treaties. Even a former Clinton ally would deplore the decision to enact such a draconian law: "In my opinion, signing the Helms-Burton Act was a serious error of Clinton's," ex-president Jimmy Carter would say later.

The law's first clash with reality occurred when a letter from the American government arrived at the offices of Sol Meliá Hotels and Resorts. Six years previous, the largest hotel company in Spain had become Cuba's main business partner. It was to be expected that the majority of the dozens of hotels built on the Island by the Spanish giant stood on properties expropriated by the Revolution, but the company didn't seem to be intimidated by Washington's threats. "None of our executives are all that interested in visiting Disney World," mocked Meliá's spokesman. "And, if forced to choose between the two countries, the group would not hesitate to close its network of hotels in Florida." Anybody engaged in business—or in trafficking, as the American government put it—with Cuba would be notified of the risks. Not even the big multinational conglomerates were immune, like Sherritt International, the largest Canadian mining company, which was exploiting nickel deposits in Moa in eastern Cuba, or the French firm Pernod Ricard, distributors of Havana Club rum in Europe.

In Brazil, the State Department tried to put pressure on the Souza Cruz, a cigarette company controlled by British American Tobacco (BAT). One of the biggest taxpayers in the country and holding 80 percent of the Brazilian cigarette market, with an annual production of 4 billion units, Souza Cruz had built a modern factory in Cuba as a joint venture in equal ownership with the State of Cuba. In their first notification, the American government called the company's attention to the fact that the property it used in Havana had belonged to the American firm Henry Clay & Co.—producing famous brands like Lucky Strike and Pall Mall in Cuba, until it was confiscated in 1960 by the communist government—which constituted a violation of American law and exposed the transgressor to sanctions imposed by the United States. The next step was a visit by the American consul to the Souza Cruz headquarters in Rio de Janeiro. Received by the company vice president, Milton Cabral, the diplomat took almost two hours to enumerate the articles of the Helms-Burton Act infringed by Souza Cruz's "trafficking" with Castro's government. Just like his colleague at Sol Meliá, the Brazilian executive refused to be bossed around. "Our association with Cuba is an initiative by Souza Cruz, a Brazilian company that conforms to Brazilian law. Our majority shareholder is British, and answers to the laws of the United Kingdom," Cabral replied, politely but conclusively. "As such, American laws, with all due respect, have no effect on our business." The consul did not know that such self-assurance was actually based on a fact missed by the State Department's research. Months before the enactment of Helms-Burton, Henry Clay & Co. had been acquired by BAT—which meant that Souza Cruz in Cuba was operating on its own property.

Although it failed to break the back of the Cuban Revolution, Helms-Burton would continue to do damage throughout the presidencies of George W. Bush and Barack Obama. The ammunition used by the State Department, acting in conjunction with the trade, defense and treasury departments, hit targets of all sizes. The victim could equally be a giant like the Credit Suisse Bank—fined $536 million by the US attorney general for having performed thirty operations transferring funds to Cuba—or any American citizen who made an innocent tourist trip to the Island. Not even White House officials would escape the long arm of this anti-Castroist plunder, as testified by the case of Fred Burks, Clinton's official translator. Three years after the law came into force, Burks traveled to Havana with his girlfriend, via Cancún, for a concert by the Buena Vista Social Club, a very popular band at that time. Monitored by the Department of the Treasury, on returning to Washington Burks and his girlfriend were fined $15,000 as a punishment for their night out with the musicians Ibrahim Ferrer and Compay Segundo. From the diplomatic and political points of view, it was not just a question of going back to square one. It was worse. From February 24, 1996, onwards, relations between Cuba and the United States became increasingly somber, hostile and aggressive. Of all the advances made since Jimmy Carter's administration, the only ones to remain standing were the agreements that had ended the migration crisis two years earlier.

The events of that fateful Saturday had devastating effects on Florida's Cuban community. Following Juan Pablo Roque's revelations on television, Miami's atmosphere had become stifling. The first casualty would be a member of FBI staff: publicly exposed by the Cuban, who had even given out his phone and pager numbers, agent Oscar Montoto was taken out of circulation and put temporarily on ice. The climate of distrust and suspicion poisoned the anti-Castroist organizations even more. The organizations in which Roque had operated or those with which he'd been friendly, like the Cuban American National Foundation, the Brothers and the Democracy Movement, tried to reconstruct the pilot's steps in the weeks leading up to the escape and undertook internal investigations looking for answers to the worrying questions they were asking. Was Roque already an agent of the Cuban government when he arrived in the United States, or had he been recruited in Miami? Had he acted alone, or had he left accomplices planted among the exiles? Had the FBI sneaked other informants into the exile groups?

Protected by the pretense of having severed relations with Roque months before his return to Cuba, René managed to wriggle unscathed through the jungle of suspicion which Miami had become. When the dust of distrust had settled, Olga's husband was contacted by Alex Barbeito and Al Alonso, the FBI agents who, thanks to information passed on by him, had broken open the gang of drug traffickers hiding within the PUND and imprisoned the leader of that anti-Castroist organization, Héctor "El Tigre" Viamonte. The FBI had come out of the incidents of February 24 with a doubly tarnished image. On the one hand, public opinion in general had turned against it once it became known that the FBI had recruited an agent without knowing he was an intelligence officer of the Cuban government. On the other hand, the groups of Cubans in exile and their powerful lobby in Congress were furious when Roque revealed that he was paid by the FBI to spy on the CANF, the Brothers and the Democracy Movement. The proposal Barbeito and Alonso made to René was sensitive: to replace Juan Pablo Roque as an informant in the anti-Castroist organizations in which he was active. The invitation apparently showed that the suspicions that the FBI had other informants planted in the exile groups were unfounded. The Cuban asked for a few days to consider—in reality, he needed the time to consult Havana about how to react. In a letter to Cuba, René drew a rough portrait of the two policemen. He said that Barbeito was a young man between twenty-five and thirty, with brown hair, and of medium build, "apparently" of Cuban origin. "He speaks Spanish well with light English interjections. He is dynamic and spontaneous in his speech. He does not have any visible marks." His description of Alonso was more detailed:

Alonso is about forty-five years old with lightly tanned fair skin. He is tall and looks strong but not to the point of being athletic. His hair is slightly wavy and he speaks slowly and with a slight effeminate tendency. He is slightly graying. His facial characteristics are very similar to our comrade Miguel. He seems to be quite methodical and capable. In contrast to Alex who always seems ready for action, Alonso seems analytical above all else.

According to the summary sent by René, the two policemen had told him that the need to keep the Cuban community's political activities under strict control had become fundamental, after the downing of the planes. As they put it, the American government feared being dragged into a military conflict "all because of a little game being played by the provocateurs in Miami." As for working for the FBI, the Cuban suggested to Havana that the proposal be refused. "It is not logical to lend support to a group with which one supposedly has similar ideas and objectives and from one day to the next offer to spy on that group," René argued. "To me this seems to be so vile that even these people would be crazy to trust me after I did that." The Main Center agreed with him. Apart from the risks cited, Cuba had reasons to reinforce the surveillance of the Wasp Network agents over the anti-Castroist groups. The belligerence of the American government raised their spirits and egged on the most radical sectors of the exiles. Smuggling of explosives into Cuban territory and attacks on tourist targets went ahead with increasing intensity. Not even the dramatic death of the four Brothers pilots seemed to have inhibited the anti-Castroist groups' aggressiveness, since the invasions of Cuban airspace and territorial waters carried on as if nothing had happened. In the twelve months following the destruction of the planes, Cuba was the victim of dozens of aggressions planned and financed in Florida. Thanks to reports sent by the Wasp Network agents, in August Cuban security forces arrested an American citizen who was trying to enter the country with a load of explosives, and in September, a Cuban from Miami was caught landing at Punta Alegre beach, in Ciego de Ávila province, in a vessel loaded with weapons. Information supplied by the two prisoners allowed Cuba to thwart various attacks, but did not put an end to the wave of terrorism. At the end of the year, in an interview with Univisión TV in Miami, Luis Posada Carriles and Orlando Bosch reaffirmed their determination to continue sponsoring terrorist activities against the Island.

The impunity and cheek with which the confessed masterminds of crimes that had cost dozens of innocent lives moved freely around the United States was exasperating for the Cuban authorities, but there was strictly nothing to be done—except what was already being done by the Wasp Network agents. Fidel believed that, like Jimmy Carter, Clinton was no buffoon. And he felt sure that, were the American president to know more about the past record and extreme dangerousness of these people, he wouldn't hesitate to put a stop to the provocations originating in or sponsored by Miami. The Comandante had compiled a dossier for Clinton on the topic, but didn't have trustworthy channels for conveying the document directly to the American president, without risk of it passing through the hands—and under the eyes—of the CIA and the FBI. The solution appeared at the end of April, when a private jet landed at Havana Airport carrying the ex-senator and Democratic ex-candidate for the presidency of the United States, Gary Hart. Besides his political savvy, Hart possessed a privilege of particularly interest to the Cuban president: direct access to Bill Clinton. It remains unclear what could have led a politician of Hart's importance to make a private trip to Cuba in the midst of the witch-hunt unleashed by Washington against everything that might smack of Castroism. What is known, however, is that on his return to the United States he was carrying in his luggage 200 pages and various videos and cassette tapes, all material prepared under the personal supervision of Fidel Castro. Based largely on the thousands of reports sent in by the Wasp Network to Cuba, the dossier listed, one by one, all of the attacks carried out against the Island since the early 1990s. Each crime came with the details of who had committed it, who had planned it and who had paid for it—all proven by telephone recordings and secretly filmed videos.

Three weeks after Hart received the documentation from Fidel's hands, on May 24, 1997, a bomb destroyed the premises of the Cuban tourist agency Cubanacán, in Mexico City. The initial investigations showed that the modus operandi and the type of explosives used in the attack were very similar to those used against tourist targets in Cuban territory. The details supplied to the police by the immigration services, when cross-checked with those of hotels in the Mexican capital, pointed to the instigator—or instigators—of the attack being from a country in Central America.

The clues coincided with investigations being undertaken by the Wasp Network in Miami. For quite some time the group headed by Hernández-Viramóntez had suspected that mercenaries from Guatemala and El Salvador were being contracted by exiles in Miami to carry out bomb attacks in Cuba and elsewhere. But there was still a piece missing from the puzzle that had yet to fall into place.

9

THE MERCENARY CRUZ LEÓN DIDN'T WANT TO KILL ANYONE. HIS DREAM WAS TO BE JUST LIKE SYLVESTER STALLONE

It would still take some time, but the clues uncovered by the Cuban agents would eventually lead to a young Central American who lived 2,000 kilometers from Miami, knew almost nothing about Cuba and never even imagined that the second man in the revolutionary hierarchy, Raúl Castro, had the same first name as he did. What the twenty-six-year-old Salvadoran Raúl Ernesto Cruz León really liked was rock n' roll, sports and target practice at private shooting ranges in El Salvador's capital, San Salvador. With no interest in politics, his idol was the hulk Sylvester Stallone: he'd seen all his movies, some of them several times. In 1995 he was working as a bodyguard at Two Shows, a company that offered personal security to foreign personalities and artistes visiting El Salvador. Cruz León had always liked guns, and his familiarity with them stemmed partly from his father's activities as an army soldier, and also from the fact that throughout most of his youth, El Salvador had been immersed in a brutal civil war. During that period it was as easy to buy a machine gun as a pair of shoes. When Cruz León was fifteen, he and his mother, brother and two sisters were shattered by the news that their father, stationed at the Sensuntepeque barracks, a hundred kilometers from San Salvador, had killed himself with a single shot to the head. Since a group of guerrillas had occupied the road that linked the capital to the barracks, the Cruz Leóns had to wait several days before collecting the corpse from the local morgue and burying it in San Salvador.

Thanks to his mother's unsparing efforts, the boy managed to reach ninth grade at the Colegio Salesiano, which he left as a fluent English-speaker. At seventeen, his favorite toys were a Russian Makarov pistol, an Italian nine-millimeter Beretta and a Smith & Wesson with a laser sight. His passion for firearms would lead him to take the Army cadet course, but despite twice coming second at its shooting championships, he didn't adapt to the rigid discipline of the barracks and lasted only a year at the military academy. He didn't smoke, didn't drink and had never tried drugs—not even marijuana, which was usually consumed openly by his showbiz clients. His only addictions were guns and extreme sports, like climbing, rafting and surfing. He was not much given to reading and could remember only two books that had made an impression on him: *The Old Man and the Sea*, by Ernest Hemingway, and *Manual of the Warrior of the Light*, by the Brazilian Paulo Coelho.

The young Salvadoran's heroes were not, in fact, Stallone's recurrent characters John Rambo and Rocky Balboa. His ideal of bravery and courage was embodied by Ray Quick, the pitiless bomb and explosives expert portrayed by Stallone in what Cruz León considered a cinema classic, *The Specialist*. And Cruz León often compared himself to Ray, as he felt they shared many characteristics. However, one difference between them was paranoia. Ray was unshakable when facing danger and displayed an enviable coldness. Cruz León was not easily frightened, but he distrusted his own shadow. Yet in Cruz León's eyes both men had good souls. Ray had shown this several times, as in the scene where, alone and unarmed, he beat up four Hispanics who were threatening a young girl on a bus in Miami. And there were other similarities. They both detested blood: Ray never used knives and cringed at the sight of a sharpened blade; Cruz León turned pale when he had to have a blood test. They both liked cats: Ray had a furry Angora that had followed him silently one night for several blocks in Miami Beach until being adopted, with the name of Timer—an instrument they both used in their jobs; Cruz León kept a scruffy cat called Hija (daughter), who got on well with his canary. The two men were the same height, about five foot seven, and although at fifty-one Ray was almost double Cruz León's age, he was a mass of muscle and a disciplined weightlifter. Like Stallone, Cruz León didn't have the perfect Hollywood face: a typical Central American mestizo, he also sported a big chin, an effect of the prognathism that had resisted years of orthodontic braces.

But Ray Quick's unique status also lay in his enviable relationship with the gorgeous May Munro (played by Sharon Stone), who contracts Quick to liquidate the leaders of a Miami mafia gang. Among them are the men who killed her parents, a crime she witnessed when she was ten years old. Convinced that a hired hitman will not be reliable ("Bullets can always go astray," she says), Munro decides to hire an explosives expert. Not just someone who can blow up walls, but someone who can guarantee absolute precision—a specialist. That's Ray Quick. A retired CIA agent living in Miami, Quick provides services to both government and private citizens— so long as they respect his code of ethics: he will perform no act that might involve the risk of death to innocent people or children. By the time the last man in his contract with May Munro has dropped dead, the two protagonists are living under the same roof. Cruz León thought the prize was deserved: after all, Ray wasn't just a specialist, but a victorious hero. The Salvadoran was still a beginner, but he felt the day would come when he too would complete a contract and take a May Munro to bed.

Cruz León was awakened from his daydream by the turbulence experienced on the Taca Airlines Boeing 737, which had taken off from El Salvador on the morning of July 9, 1997. He would still have to face a stopover of at least three hours in San Juan, Costa Rica, where he would then embark on the final leg of his journey: a flight to Havana, Cuba. What was a two-hour direct flight could often take up to eight hours, such was the length of time lost in stopovers and connections. How had a person like him learnt so much about Ray Quick? The encyclopedic knowledge was due to the fact that he had watched *The Specialist* dozens of times. It didn't matter that Ray and May were characters invented by a Hollywood scriptwriter, they were nevertheless the model couple for Cruz León. The Salvadoran knew he had a long way to go to reach the level of a Ray Quick, but he was taking his first steps in his career as a specialist: after all, here he was on his first mission, armed to the teeth. Or, to be more precise, to the feet.

Although he wore size nine shoes, on that day Cruz León wore a pair of Timberland boots that were size twelve and a half. The empty space between the tip of each boot and his toes was filled with 250 grams of C-4, the preferred explosive of terrorists and action film heroes alike. With a detonation velocity of nine kilometers per second, more than 30,000 kilometers an hour, a handful of C-4, the size of a tennis ball, is sufficient to knock down concrete walls and steel girders. What gave Cruz León a feeling of safety, despite the lethal material at his feet, was knowing that without the aid of a detonator, that gunk was as lethal as plasticine. His detonators, wires and timers were sensibly stored away in the blue nylon Tommy Hilfiger backpack that he'd placed in the overhead baggage compartment. Except for an unforeseen delay of several hours, the stopover in Costa Rica went by without incident and it was already night when the passengers were called to board the plane that would take them to Cuba.

In reality, Cruz León's stressful adventure had begun a month before. His recruitment by Francisco Chávez Abarca happened at the end of May, six weeks before that trip. In fact the initiative had been his. Cruz León wanted to sell his sister's van and someone recommended he look up Abarca, the owner of a used car lot and a small rental firm called Geo Rent-a-Car, both installed in a garage in San Salvador. A lot of people said that both the store and the rental firm were a front used by Central American carjacking gangs, but since he wanted to sell and not buy, Cruz León had nothing to fear. He had already heard about Abarca, who was young like him, gruff, suspicious, reserved and the owner of a belly of monumental proportions—whence his nickname Panzón ("Big Paunch"). During the negotiation for the van they discovered their common taste for guns and arranged to meet one day at the Xangai shooting range, near the capital. The deal was finally closed—in cash, because the enigmatic Abarca never used checks or credit cards. A few days later he showed up one late afternoon at Two Shows for a coffee, and as he was leaving beckoned Cruz León to his car, a shining white Nissan Pathfinder. From the glove compartment he took out a misshapen ball that looked like pizza dough, and asked, kneading it with his fingers:

"Do you know what this is?"

"I've seen it in movies. It's C-4, isn't it?"

Keeping up an air of mystery, Abarca was throwing the ball from hand to hand:

"Yes, there's no better explosive than this. You can whack this ball with a hammer or play baseball with it and nothing happens. You can put it in an oven at temperatures as high as 300 degrees centigrade and it doesn't explode. But all it takes is a nine-volt electric pulse, the energy from an ordinary battery, like the ones in children's toys, for this little ball to sink a ship or blow a thirty-ton tank off the ground."

He started the car and invited Cruz León to a demonstration:

"Come on, I'll show you how this shit works."

He sped through the streets of San Salvador towards the coast. On the way he extolled the virtues of C-4. Apart from its superior explosive capacity when compared to military dynamite, it had a unique characteristic: its plasticity. "With C-4 you can rip the cover off the glove compartment of this car without scratching the dashboard or hurting anyone," he explained as they left local traffic behind, "but it can also produce an expansion wave enough to turn a ten-story building into a mountain of rubble." Cruz León knew what Abarca was talking about: making explosions with surgical precision was exactly what made Ray Quick a specialist. Minutes later the car pulled up on the sands of La Perla, a rocky outcrop rarely visited by seaside tourists. Abarca took some objects out of a bag and got out of the car. Walking between the rocks, he was followed closely by Cruz León. He chose a rock, crouched down on the ground and laid out what he had been carrying: a miniature screwdriver, a portable calculator-alarm clock, a detonator—a metal cylinder similar to a big nail with no head—and two pieces of wire in different colors. With the screwdriver he opened up the calculator and took out the bell, the size of a coin, then attached the loose wires to one end of the detonator. The other end of it was inserted into a little ball of C-4 the size of a chewed-up piece of gum. He set the clock to go off in five minutes, tied it all up with a piece of insulation tape and stuck the package behind a rock the size of a car. Cruz León hurried to take shelter behind another pile of rocks, but Abarca calmed him down. "Don't worry, it's only going to explode in five minutes," he explained as he walked along the sand. "And even if we were there, we'd be safe because I placed the explosive so as to make the rock explode on the opposite side to where we were." Just in case, Cruz León preferred to wait behind the trunk of a palm tree, but the confident Abarca stayed on the beach, without protection. Five minutes later a loud thud blew half the rock into the air—exactly on the side chosen by Big Paunch.

Weeks later, Abarca reappeared at Two Shows and took Cruz León out to a half-empty Italian restaurant. Speaking even more quietly than usual, he went straight to the point, without mincing his words:

"Want to place two bombs for me? You saw how easy it is to set one up."

On hearing that, Cruz León's jaw dropped even further:

"Bombs? Where? For you?"

"It's not for me, it's for some friends in Miami."

Ray Quick's humanitarian spirit seemed to take him over:

"Place bombs to kill people? Count me out."

"No, it's not to kill anyone; it's just to scare them. We only want to make *bulla*, a lot of noise."

"Here in El Salvador?"

"No. It's in another country."

"Which country?"

"I can't tell you. If you accept, I'll say where it is. I pay 15,000 *colones* per bomb, plus travel expenses, accommodation and food."

The "friends in Miami," as would become clear later, were Luis Posada Carriles, Guillermo Novo Sampol and Pedro Ramón Crispín—the trio that would be arrested and pardoned in Panama years later—as well as Arnaldo Monzón Placencia and Francisco "Pepe" Hernández, director of the Cuban American National Foundation. The meetings between Big Paunch and the group normally took place at the Mister Don snack bar, in the Salvadoran capital, or in a suite at the Radisson Hotel in Guatemala City. Fifteen thousand *colones* was not exactly a fortune, but it was enough to buy $1,500 on the black market. As there were two bombs, that meant 30,000 *colones*, or $3,000. Or three months' salary at Two Shows. Cruz León wanted to know how many days the job would require—"You know that I have a boss and a schedule to keep to," he said—and was reassured. Between leaving El Salvador and returning, the mission would take a week at most. Cruz León had a day to decide. As if he were doing the most natural thing in the world, Chávez Abarca devoured a bowl of spaghetti and another of meatballs and drank a bottle of wine, while his dining companion was almost too excited to touch a bite. Years later Cruz León would remember the ecstasy that had seized him that night:

"I know it sounds ridiculous, but right there I imagined I was Ray Quick. What I felt at that moment was this: I was Ray Quick. I was Sylvester Stallone. I was going to put bombs in some unnamed country. I'd come home and go to bed with Sharon Stone. I felt like a spy, I felt I was the greatest."

The fascination gave way to paranoia when the next day Chávez Abarca revealed the name of the country where the two bombs would be placed:

"Cuba? Have you gone nuts? They say Cuba's the most militarized country, the most policed in the world. I heard there's even a wall in Havana, like the one in Berlin. There must be cops, cameras and mikes everywhere, even under the hotel beds!"

Once again Big Belly calmed him down, saying that all this famous surveillance was just communist talk:

"I was in Havana less than a month ago. I put two bombs in a hotel and walked out of there without being bothered by anyone.

And if you ever did get caught, which is completely unlikely, we would hire a good lawyer and in a few hours you'd be here again. As you can see, I went over, placed some bombs and here I am, all in one piece."

It wasn't bravado. Abarca had in fact been in Cuba and on the night of April 12 had activated a charge of C-4 explosive in the restroom of Aché, a disco on the ground floor of the Meliá Cohiba, the country's most luxurious hotel, where he was staying. By a miracle the bathrooms were empty at the time of the explosions and there were no casualties. Two weeks later when he was getting ready to check out, he stuck another package with 400 grams of explosive into a flower vase in the corridor of the fifteenth floor of the same hotel, but this time the security services deactivated the bomb before it went off. What Big Belly did not tell him was the difficulty in getting paid. Since the bomb on the fifteenth floor hadn't exploded and the blast at the Aché had occurred in the middle of the night, with the dance floor and the lobby already deserted, the Cuban government had managed to suppress news of the two attacks for weeks. For several days, no information about these explosions was leaked to the international press.

Abarca persisted over the phone with the "friends in Miami," demanding what he was owed, until he got this answer by fax at his car business:

As I already explained to you, if there is no publicity the work is useless. The American newspapers publish nothing that has not been confirmed. I need all the details about the discotheque to be able to check them. If there is no publicity, there is no payment. I'm expecting the news today, I'm leaving tomorrow and will be gone for two days.

Accept the respects of
Solo [an alias of Posada Carriles]

Cruz León took heart and accepted the job. He was then coordinating the security for a rock band that was playing in El Salvador, and it wasn't hard to arrange a week's vacation. Abarca asked for his passport—Cruz León had already made short tourist trips to Mexico and Central America—and on the night of Tuesday, July 8, the eve of Cruz León's departure, Abarca appeared at the modest apartment Cruz León shared with his mother and brothers downtown, in the Cuscatlán neighborhood. Abarca was carrying a suitcase with the boots, a ball of the explosive wrapped in aluminum foil and the rest of the paraphernalia needed to carry out the attacks. He laid out on the dining table the calculators, pieces of wire, detonators, batteries and a voltmeter, a plastic gadget little bigger than a cigarette pack, with a small display and two mini-clips to test whether batteries are producing the voltage necessary for detonation. This time he slowly went through the operation he'd done on the deserted beach, explaining the details step by step. As he couldn't afford another fiasco—for whatever reason, the bomb on the fifteenth floor of the Meliá Cohiba Hotel in Havana didn't explode—he made a rough diagram in Cruz León's diary showing where and how to attach each wire and how the detonator should be adjusted. The batteries and wires would travel hidden inside a General Electric radio-alarm clock, the size of a book, and the voltmeter and a small roll of insulation tape would be packed at the bottom of his toilet bag together with his toothbrush, toothpaste, shaving cream, razor and a bottle of eau de cologne. The detonators would be carried in the core of two felt-tip markers. Before saying goodbye, Abarca repeated the objective of the explosions:

"The people in Miami don't want to kill anybody, just to show foreigners that going to Cuba as a tourist can mean mortal danger. Here are some of their suggested targets, for you to choose the two where you'll place the bombs."

As Abarca dictated, Cruz León wrote down the names of the hotels in his pocket diary—the Meliá Cohiba, Nacional, Capri, Comodoro, Santa Isabel and Tritón (which he mistakenly noted as "Plutón"). Apart from these, the "pals in Miami" had included the two most visited tourist spots in the Cuban capital: the bar and restaurant La Bodeguita del Medio, Ernest Hemingway's favorite venue for his infamous drinking sessions, and the Tropicana, the country's most traditional cabaret and nightclub. On leaving, Abarca gave

Cruz León $500 in cash and a plastic briefcase from the Joanessa travel agency where his package tour had been acquired, containing the air tickets and two vouchers, one for the airport transfer and the other to cover his daily expenses at the Ambos Mundos hotel, with full board included. The choice of the hotel was Cruz León's only request to Abarca. He could have chosen a luxury place like the Nacional or the Cohiba, both located in Vedado, the chic part of Havana, but Cruz León preferred the romantic three-star hotel in Old Havana for a special reason, as he would reveal years later:

"I'd read in a tourist brochure that it was at the Ambos Mundos that Hemingway wrote *For Whom the Bell Tolls*. By coincidence, they reserved a room for me on the fifth floor, next door to the room where the writer lived, which had been transformed into a museum."

On the morning of July 9, in the taxi that would take him to the San Salvador airport, Cruz León felt paranoia set in again. No matter how convincing Abarca's reassurances that there was no risk whatsoever in carrying the explosive inside the boots, his feet were sweating profusely. He stopped at a drugstore, bought a small tin of antiseptic talcum powder and poured half the contents inside each boot. There were no unforeseen events on leaving the country. Used to welcoming and seeing off personalities for Two Shows, Cruz León knew everybody at the airport and was ushered through without a hitch.

It was already past eleven at night when the flight attendant announced that the plane was about to land at José Martí Airport in Havana. Abarca had chosen him a flight that would arrive late in Cuba, because he believed that at the end of the night, the police and immigration agents are usually tired and security checks are laxer. He was wrong. The passengers had already shown their passports at the entrance gates when two young men in uniform approached Cruz León, scowling, and ordered:

"Empty the backpack on the counter and open the case."

He thought he was going to have a heart attack, but the officials seemed more interested in locating some smuggled article. They ran their fingers between the clothes, looking for some hidden object, but they were doing it slowly, as if they wanted to delay him on purpose. They fumbled around, rummaged here and there, looked at the passport and the vouchers without finding anything suspicious. Feeling certain that he was in the clear, Cruz León decided to play the tough guy. He turned to one of the officials and asked the fatal question:

"Don't you want to see if you can find some contraband hidden between my teeth?"

The answer was immediate:

"Put your things back in the backpack, close the case and come with us."

At the end of a corridor the three of them went into a small room, where the door was then locked. One of the policemen rapped:

"Take off your cap and your shirt and pull down your pants and underpants."

Bare-chested and without his cap, Cruz León lowered his head to unbuckle his belt and loosen his pants, when he noticed that some of the talc he'd used to powder his feet had come out between his laces, with a dusting of white all over the tips of his boots. "At that moment, I felt that because of my cowardice, my stupid nerves, I had just signed my own death sentence," he would remember afterwards. "Even a child would have suspected that I was carrying cocaine in my boots. I was totally fucked." By luck, however, when he undid his belt, the pants and underwear fell on top of his boots, preventing the policemen from seeing the white powder. They made him lift up his testicles and separate his buttocks with his hands, leaving him semi-nude for some more minutes while they flicked through his passport and the rest of his paperwork again, and only then did they give the final order:

"Get dressed. You're free to go."

In the van that took him to the hotel, surrounded by noisy tourists, he felt born again, like Lazarus. And he repeated to himself in silence:

"I'm Ray Quick. I'm Ray Quick. I'm Ray Quick."

Half an hour after the scare, Cruz León walked into the pink, five-story Ambos Mundos Hotel on the corner of Obispo and

Mercaderes, halfway between the Plaza de Armas and the Bodeguita del Medio. Once installed in room 521, two doors away from 511, Hemingway's museum-bedroom, Cruz León had doubts about the security of the digital safe screwed to the inside of his wardrobe. He chose to hide his electronic gadgetry in nooks and crannies in the furniture, like the empty space behind the drawers of the two nightstands and the pulley casing of the wooden blinds—always being careful to keep the detonators and the batteries separate from the C-4 paste which he had cautiously removed from his boots. He took a shower, fell into bed and sank into a deep sleep.

He woke up next morning and went down to the self-service cafeteria on the ground floor of the hotel wearing shorts, T-shirt and sandals. Perhaps because it was very early, there were no other guests there. He filled his plate with omelet and rounds of sausage, took a piece of toast, butter, a cup of coffee, and chose a table at random. As he began to eat, he saw a young couple come out of the elevator and serve themselves at the buffet. To his surprise, although all the other tables were empty, the pair crossed the room and went up to him. It was the young guy who asked him politely, again setting off his paranoia:

"Mind if we join you?"

With his heart pounding at record-breaking speed, he feigned spontaneity and answered, smiling:

"Yes, of course, with pleasure."

The girl wanted to know where he was from and he thought it best to lie:

"I'm from Honduras. How about you?"

Cruz León didn't like the answer:

"We're from right here. We're Cubans."

He had heard that it was common for Cuban couples to spend their wedding night in tourist hotels, and added:

"Are you on honeymoon?"

The man replied, smiling, between spoonfuls of yogurt:

"No, we're not even married. We're from the police."

Cruz León felt the omelet turn over in his stomach, his hands and feet began to sweat, but he kept his cool and joked:

"So that means I'm a suspect?"

The Cuban gave a laugh:

"No, of course not! As we're responsible for internal security here at the hotel, we have our meals here. When we saw you eating alone, we decided to keep you company."

Hunger gave way to fear and Cruz León thought it best to get out of there as quickly as possible. But go where? He thought about going out onto the street, but feared the exits might already be guarded by other cops. He made an excuse, got up and walked towards the elevators, looking out of the corner of his eye to see if the couple were following him, but they stayed at their table, eating breakfast. He went up to his room with shaking hands and sat on the edge of the bed, deciding what to do. He was sure he'd been rumbled, those policemen must just be waiting for the right moment to arrest him. After thinking for a few minutes, unable to calm down, he picked up his backpack, put on his cap and decided to go out. It would be no surprise if he were to open the door and run into this couple waiting for him, guns in hand, but the corridor was just as empty as before. When the elevator got to the first floor, he noticed that the couple was no longer in the cafeteria. The street was already busy with people—tourists, taxi drivers and street vendors offering souvenirs and loose cigars—and he used the opportunity to mix in with the bystanders, always squinting his eyes to see if anyone was following him. He saw a bici-taxi going by—a sort of Cuban rickshaw—and flagged it. He asked the rider to take him to the Vedado neighborhood, four kilometers away. The driver suggested they go via the Malecón, the seaside boulevard, but he preferred to go through the narrow streets of Old Havana, a longer route and not as nice but it would allow him to check with more certainty if he were being followed. Forty minutes later he got off near the Hotel Nacional, convinced that his jitters had been nothing more than just another paranoia attack.

During the next two days Cruz León explored the Cuban capital by taxi, on foot and by bici-taxi. He visited the eight targets suggested by Abarca, some of them more than once, until deciding on the Capri and the Nacional. A hundred meters apart, both of these hotels were part of Cuban history. Opened in 1955, two years after Batista's Hotel Law gave tax breaks to large hotels and casinos, the modernist, twenty-five-story Capri was owned before the Revolution by a trio of Americans famous in the crime world: the actor George Raft and the gangsters Santo Trafficante and Meyer Lansky, the latter immortalized by Lee Strasberg in Francis Ford Coppola's *The Godfather Part II*. Built in Spanish Neoclassical style and set in enormous gardens, the seven-story Hotel Nacional dates from 1930. Considered for decades the most luxurious hotel in the Caribbean, it was the favorite of celebrities like Winston Churchill and the Duke and Duchess of Windsor, as well as Tyrone Power, Errol Flynn, Marlon Brando and Orson Welles. In 1951 its presidential suite was covered in flowers to welcome the newlyweds Frank Sinatra and Ava Gardner.

Cruz León had picked the night of Friday, July 11, to prepare the bombs. He had dinner early, went up to his room at the Ambos Mundos, closed the window that looked onto a small interior garden, pulled the drapes, and spread his material over the bed. Squatting on the floor, he opened the diary to the page where Chávez Abarca had drawn the diagram and unscrewed the covers of the two calculators. He attached one end of the wires to the bell and the detonator pin, and the other end to the two battery terminals, not without first checking with the help of the voltmeter that the power generated was nine volts. He closed both mechanisms with a piece of insulation tape and divided the C-4 paste into two equal balls, putting them inside an opaque plastic bag. He put everything in the backpack, taking care to keep the calculators, batteries and detonators in one compartment and the explosive in another. He gathered up the pieces of wire that had fallen on the bedspread, flushed them down the toilet and went to sleep.

Cruz León woke up next day at nine o'clock, took a shower, put on his tourist gear—shorts, T-shirt, sandals, cap and sunglasses—donned the backpack and went down for breakfast, asking God to make sure he would not cross paths with the couple from hotel security. He had a small plate of fruit salad and a yogurt, and went out to look for a taxi. Fifteen minutes later he was sitting in an armchair in the lobby of the Capri Hotel. Apart from the employees at the reception desk, there was only a woman standing behind a table spread with tourism brochures. He was about to go to the first-floor bathroom to stick the detonator into the ball of explosive and activate the timer, when he was approached by a young, slim black man, wearing a white toque and apron:

"Are you a guest of the hotel?"

This was all he needed. Another Cuban chatting him up.

"No, I'm not. I'm waiting for a friend."

"Here's the thing: I'm the hotel cook, and I need to borrow five dollars to buy a bus ticket to visit a sick relative out in the country …"

Cruz León didn't even let him finish. He stuck his hand in his pocket, took out a ten-dollar bill and gave it to the Cuban, who was effusively grateful:

"Thank you so much. Come to the restaurant on Monday and I'll make a special dish for you."

The Salvadoran waved him off irritably:

"That's OK, that's OK, now excuse me, I'm waiting for someone."

He locked himself in one of the restrooms of the reception area, opened his backpack, sank half of the detonator into the ball of C-4, set the clock to go off in ten minutes and went back to the lobby carrying the plastic bag with the bomb inside. He lodged it behind the armchair where he'd been sitting and marched swiftly out to the street. Just as he had already timed it, he took one and a half minutes to cover the distance of one block to the Nacional. In the hotel restroom he fixed the second bomb to go off in seven minutes, put everything into another little plastic bag and went back to reception. He was about to slip the package behind a flower vase, when a smiling young girl in a miniskirt appeared in front of him. He soon realized she was a *jinetera*, a call girl, looking for clients. Before she could open her mouth, he cut her off with a threat:

"I'm not interested in sex. If you don't get out of here right now, I'm calling the police."

The girl turned around, scared, and walked away. Cruz León was able to make his way to the vase at the end of the tiled lobby and discreetly hide the little bag among the foliage before going out onto the street. As he was descending the steps leading to the front gardens, the bomb went off, turning the hotel's enormous front door into thousands of shards of broken glass. A group of European tourists who were getting off a bus stampeded wildly through the trees, and Cruz León took the opportunity to mix with them. In the midst of general panic and confusion, he walked on for a few minutes; when he got to the Malecón, he heard the second bomb explode at the Capri. He wandered for half an hour, took a taxi and asked the driver to take him to the Plaza de Armas. He was perspiring so much that he changed his green shirt for the white spare he was carrying in his backpack. He spent the day cruising around aimlessly among the tourists who filled Old Havana and only at dusk, after making sure there were no police waiting for him, did he return to the Ambos Mundos. On Sunday morning he went to a newsstand and bought copies of *Granma* and *Juventud Rebelde*, the two main newspapers in Cuba, and was surprised to see that not a single word had come out about the two explosions. No photos, no news, nothing, absolutely nothing. On Monday, July 14, when his package tour was over, the van from the agency picked him up at the appointed time and took him to the airport. The departure went off smoothly, and at midday the Taca plane was heading for Costa Rica. The mission had been accomplished.

Thirteen years later, in April 2010, sitting in a prison cell at Villa Marista in Havana, waiting to be led before the firing squad, Cruz León, now fifteen kilos heavier, would remember that far-off sunny Monday morning:

"When the plane flew over Havana, I was thinking of only one thing: I really was Ray Quick. I was a specialist. I deserved to take Sharon Stone to bed."

10

FOR $7,500, THE SALVADORAN RETURNS TO CUBA TO PLANT ANOTHER FIVE BOMBS IN HOTELS AND RESTAURANTS

Although the Cuban press had not published anything about the terrorist attacks on the Capri and Nacional hotels, when Raúl Ernesto Cruz León arrived at the Comalapa Airport he was met by Chávez "Big Paunch" Abarca, who handed over the 30,000 *colones* in cash, as promised. In spite of the Cuban authorities' efforts to cover up what had happened, the explosions had been seen by dozens of witnesses, many of them foreigners, and eventually the news was spread by international agencies. Only then did the Salvadoran begin to realize the consequences of his work in Cuba. Abarca told him that neither of the bombs had caused any fatalities. What the newspapers reported was that the attack on the Capri had resulted only in material damage, estimated at $50,000, but the C-4 charge placed at the Nacional had blasted glass shards throughout the central lobby, leaving a Cuban cook, along with three foreign tourists, injured as they were leaving the elevator at the time of the explosion. One Jamaican and a Mexican had been slightly wounded while a Chilean, Maria Angélica Pinochet, suffered a cut on her leg that meant she had to spend fifteen days under observation in a local hospital. From Abarca's point of view, the operation was a total success:

"The goal was exactly this—to terrorize foreign tourists. My friends in Miami are delighted with your work."

Less than three weeks after Cruz León's return to El Salvador, the flow of tourists to Cuba went into its seasonal decline. When the July vacation ended, thousands of foreigners abandoned the hotels and sights of the capital and the seaside resorts along Cuba's coastline. On the morning of August 4—a Monday—the large travertine marble lobby of the Meliá Cohiba Hotel was crowded with Europeans, Asians and Latin Americans as they lined up at the front desk to check out. The big clock hanging on the wall behind the desk stopped as the hands were pointing to seven thirty—the time when the place shook from the blast of a bomb stowed under a heavy five-seater couch. The expansion wave threw the couch up against the ceiling, opened a crater in the wall, sent glass flying in all directions and left tourists and hotel employees distraught, but miraculously no one was hurt. The real damage would come to light some days later: shortly after news of the explosion was published in the international press, travel agencies from various countries contacted the Sol Meliá to cancel tourist packages to Cuba. In the eight months that followed, the most expensive and luxurious hotel in Havana would remain completely empty. "The image of the Meliá Cohiba and Cuba in general, as secure tourist destinations, has been seriously affected by the event," reported the director of the Spanish company in a letter to the Cuban authorities. "What needs to be considered is that one of Cuba's strong points as a tourist destination was its internal security. Future losses are incalculable."

The laboratory examination of fragments from the scene of the blast revealed that both the explosive and the other materials used in confecting the bomb that went off at the Meliá Cohiba Hotel—Casio calculators equipped with alarms, nine-volt Kodak batteries, detonators and plastic bags—were the same as those used in the July explosion at the Capri and the Nacional hotels. The perpetrator of the attack managed to escape. It was Otto Rodríguez Llerena, a forty-year-old Salvadoran, blue-eyed and sturdy, with sparse gray hair covering his ears. Although they didn't know each other, Llerena and Cruz León had more things in common than their nationality: both were former military men, both were working for private security companies, and both were paid by the same "friends in Miami."

On August 13, one month after Cruz León placed the bombs, the "friends in Miami" spent $30,000 on a full-page advertisement in the *Miami Herald*, in which the Cuban American National Foundation hailed the attacks, attributing them to the internal opposition. Although there was no doubt that it was the work of mercenaries, the "Message to Public Opinion" claimed that the bombs were a "clear message sent to the world by Cubans: the message of a people not resigned to the slavery and poverty to which they have been subjected by the Castroist regime." The ad attributed responsibility for the actions to "highly organized people inside the country, perhaps members of the Cuban Armed Forces." At the end of the text it supported "unequivocally, unconditionally and without reserve, all acts of internal revolt whose objective is the expulsion of Fidel and Raúl Castro from power." Of the twenty-eight members of CANF's Executive Committee who signed the advertisement, thirteen were on the list of "individuals associated with terrorism" that the former senator Gary Hart had received from Fidel Castro. And at least six, as it would transpire later, were directly involved with the operations pulled off by Cruz León in Havana.

Besides the CANF, other organizations had ample cause to worry about what was happening in Cuba. When the Berlin Wall fell in 1989, heralding the collapse of the Soviet Union, tourism revenues were statistically insignificant in the Island's economy. The country's hotel chains offered just over 10,000 rooms, to house an annual flow of less than 300,000 foreign tourists. Moreover the great majority of visitors were industrial workers from countries within the USSR, traveling on partnership agreements ratified between Moscow and Havana, who spent little or no money. During the freezing East European winters, outdated and dangerous Ilyushin airplanes disgorged swarms of worker families from the most far-flung corners of the Iron Curtain onto Cuba's sandy beaches. With all expenses paid in advance—airfare, bed and board—it was possible for them to spend a month under the hot Caribbean sun without putting their hands in their pockets. The country's basic income was still from sugar, with production breaking historic records: the 1989 harvest had exceeded 8 million tons, an amount never before and never again achieved. After sugar, far below, came the revenues from tobacco, rum and nickel exports.

The collapse of the Soviet Union forced the Cuban government to do some juggling, considered as heresy by the old guard of the Sierra Maestra. The first measure taken represented a break with the dogma of complete State control over the economy, and opened the country's doors to big foreign hotel groups owned by private capital. Billions of Canadian dollars, Spanish pesos and French francs were rapidly turned into bricks and mortar in the form of luxury hotels and resorts all over the Island, transforming Cuba's 1,200 kilometers of beach into a building site that seemed to have no end. Five years later, the profile of the Cuban economy had undergone a drastic and salutary transformation. In 1995 the sugar harvest barely surpassed 3 million tons, less than half of the output at the end of the 1980s. The newly born tourist industry moved as rapidly in the other direction: over the same period, it grew a startling 20 percent per year. When Cruz León was hired by Chávez Abarca to place bombs in Cuba, the country's tourist network provided more than 30,000 rooms catering to around 1.5 million foreign visitors— all of them, without exception, from capitalist countries, and therefore with hard cash to spend.

By the time the Cuban diaspora woke up to this development, the dinosaur whose imminent death was celebrated every night in little Havana was giving signs of emerging from its coma. Cuba's quick and radical response to the crisis took by surprise the extreme-right groups that had turned southern Florida into a sanctuary for those planning armed attacks against the Island. If it was tourism that was saving the communist regime, then it was tourism that should be attacked. In the first five years after the sinking of the USSR, 127 aggressions were registered against the country with the sole aim of terrorizing tourists. During this period, the hotel industry in the town of Varadero alone was the target of seven explosions that left six people dead. In February 1996, the sumptuous Las Américas Hotel, a 400-room complex of buildings and bungalows built by the Spanish group Sol Meliá, was machine-gunned by sea by boats from the PUND, or National Democratic Union Party. Months later and with René's help, the PUND was shut down by the FBI for smuggling cocaine between Honduras and the United States. Three passenger ships had been machine-gunned in Cuban territorial waters, and thirteen planes carrying tourists were hijacked mid-flight. On thirty occasions Havana lodged formal protests with Washington and denounced to international bodies the invasion of its airspace by Miami-based organizations, such as the Brothers, who called themselves humanitarian. Blessed by the CANF advertisement that attributed the July and August bombings to "internal revolt," these organizations felt they had the backing to intensify and increase the number of violent acts against Cuba.

Indifferent to the commotion the attacks provoked in Miami, Raúl Ernesto Cruz León had gone back to the routine of his job at the Two Shows security company. In the middle of August, he was sought out by Chávez Abarca who brought him a fresh offer of work. Even before knowing what it was about, he answered that if it meant traveling one more time with explosives in his shoes, Big Belly could look for someone else:

"If the police had ordered me to take my boots off at the airport, by now I'd already have been shot. Don't count on me."

Abarca reiterated that there would be no risks—"If the worst happens, we hire a good lawyer, he pays your bail and a few hours later you're back in El Salvador"—and revealed that this time the job was even better:

"This time there won't be two bombs but five. That's 7,500 dollars, and as a reward for the success of your previous mission, your package will include a trip to Varadero. Not to bomb hotels, just to enjoy yourself."

Chávez Abarca had little trouble persuading Cruz León to accept, but there was a hitch when Abarca told him that the "friends in Miami" needed the job to be executed immediately. At that time Two Shows was taking care of the security of a visiting European circus, a job that would require Cruz León's presence in El Salvador until the end of the month. So it wasn't until the last day of August that the Sylvester Stallone fan could morph once more into the character of Ray Quick. One afternoon Big Paunch arrived at his house with a bag containing five portable calculator-alarm clocks, batteries, wires, detonators, insulation tape, small plastic bags and mini pliers. As well, Chávez Abarca brought a cardboard box carrying a used twenty-seven-inch Sanyo television, inside of which enough explosive was concealed to assemble the five bombs. Cruz León later remembered that while he was closing his suitcase, a television news flash announced that Lady Di had been injured in a car accident in Paris and been taken to the Pitié-Salpêtrière hospital in a coma. Before departing, Big Belly left $500 in cash, the plane ticket and a voucher to cover transport expenses and accommodation, with breakfast and lunch included, for five days in Havana and one in Varadero. To reduce the risk of the mercenary being recognized, this time another hotel was chosen, the four-star Plaza, ten blocks away from the Ambos Mundos where the Salvadoran had stayed in July. Built in 1901, the Plaza had just as much history as the Ambos Mundos: its spacious, high-ceilinged rooms had once received Albert Einstein and the modern dance pioneer Isadora Duncan. Celebrities such as the legendary American baseball player Babe Ruth and the Russian ballerina Anna Pavlova had been known to sit at the roulette and blackjack tables of its glamorous casino. Provided by the same Joanessa agency, Cruz León's travel package cost just under $2,000.

In spite of the tight spot Cruz León had found himself in the previous month, Chávez Abarca again insisted that late at night the airport police would be too tired to perform such rigorous checks. So, the trip began in a Taca Airlines Boeing that departed San Salvador at five o'clock in the afternoon, made a brief stop in Guatemala City and landed at Jose Martí Airport in the first minutes of September 1. When the passengers entered the airport's main hall, the TV screens on the walls were broadcasting the news that Lady Di had passed away in Paris.

The late hour made things no easier for the Salvadoran. As he lifted the well-wrapped television set from the baggage carousel, he was approached by a uniformed female officer wanting to know what was in the box. Cruz León opened up the top and showed the dusty television that he intended "to give as a present to a girl-friend." The woman asked to see a sales receipt. He answered that the equipment was obviously used, and he had lost the receipt long ago. The inspector was not convinced:

"Go to the teller and pay the tax due. Or if you prefer, you can leave the television in storage here at the airport and withdraw it when you embark to return to your country."

Even though it was hard to swallow, Cruz León had no alternative. Although he was carrying a credit card and some spare cash of his own in his wallet, the chunk bitten off by the Cuban customs—which relieved him of an astounding $350—accounted for more than half the money Big Paunch had given him for extra expenses. Once settled in his room at the Plaza, the Salvadoran took advantage of the insomnia brought on by the upsets of his arrival to organize his work. With the help of a Phillips screwdriver he loosened the screws of the TV set's outer casing, inserted his fingers under the rear part of the cathode tube and drew out something similar to a large, peeled banana. It was the mass of C-4 that would be divided into five parts, one for each attack planned for that trip. With the same screwdriver he opened a white plastic General Electric radio-alarm clock that he had brought in his suitcase, and removed the five detonators which any ordinary person could easily mistake for innocent metal pins. Just as he had on his previous trip, he laid out the electronic equipment on the bed, and kneeling down he began testing the batteries: securing the two alligator clips to the positive and negative poles, checking the display on the hand-held voltmeter to make sure they were generating the nine volts necessary for detonation. One of them didn't even reach seven volts. Cruz León tested it several times and got nowhere: the needle never passed the number seven. "With no idea of how to fix the problem, I silently asked myself a question," the mercenary would remember many years later: "What would my hero Ray Quick do in this situation? So, I decided the wisest thing would be to eliminate one of the bombs." He assembled the other four, careful to keep the explosive away from the detonators, and placed each one of them in a small opaque plastic bag. The material that would have been used for the fifth bomb was stored in another small bag and hidden in a corner of the drawer, a place he still thought more secure than the safe installed inside the wardrobe.

He gathered up the remnants and bits of wire and adhesive tape on top of the bed, dropped them in the toilet and flushed, making sure everything was washed away. Then he sat on the edge of the bed and started to examine the list of targets that had been suggested by Big Paunch before the first trip. On the list were still the two hotels that he had attacked in July—the Nacional and the Capri—and seven more targets for him to choose from: the hotels Meliá Cohiba (that he had written as "Melea Coíba"), Comodoro, Santa Isabel and Tritón ("Plutón," according to him), the Tropicana night club, the Ipanema discotheque and the traditional restaurant La Bodeguita del Medio. It was well into the early hours when he finally fell asleep, only to be awakened at eight in the morning by the front desk informing him that the minibus to Varadero was waiting. The trip was pleasant. Had it not been for the paranoia that made him think that some of the other bus passengers were staring at him, Cruz León would have had a relaxing day. He sunbathed, swam among underwater rocks with a snorkel lent by the hotel, and for lunch had a tasty *langosta a la mariposa* accompanied by a can of Bucanero dark beer—all included in the voucher he had received in El Salvador. At the end of the afternoon the group got back on the minibus, arriving at the Plaza after dark. Exhausted by the activity and the previous night's bad sleep, the mercenary threw himself onto the bed with his clothes on and slept for twelve hours.

The next two days were taken up with choosing the four targets. Cruz León read and reread the list in his diary, which was made up of what he knew were only suggestions. For Chávez Abarca and his friends in Miami, the important thing was to place the bombs in tourist locations, whatever they might be. Making his rounds by taxi, on foot and by bus, the Salvadoran examined the routes between the places suggested, and measured the time it would take him on foot from one point to the next when he came to distribute the bombs—which were still hidden in his hotel room. After making the calculations and considering the risks, he decided to stick with only one of the hotels suggested, the Tritón. Inaugurated shortly after the demise of the USSR, the modern, three-star hotel stood in the Miramar neighborhood of Havana beside an identical twenty-story tower, the Neptuno. As the plan was to make the four bombs explode simultaneously, the safest and most rational thing to do was to choose targets close to one another. On his tourist map of Havana he marked the Tritón, its twin the Neptuno, the Chateau and the Copacabana hotels. All on the beach, the four were favorites of foreign diplomats because of their proximity to the dozens of embassies located nearby. Being five minutes away from the Exhibition Pavilion, the Business Center and the Convention Palace, these hotels also attracted businessmen. With his targets chosen, Cruz León was getting ready for bed when the phone rang in his room. It was Chávez Abarca, wanting to how things were going. He answered that everything was going according to plan. He mentioned he'd been forced to pay taxes on the TV set, and wanted to know if there was a way to get the money to him in Havana. Without going into details he told Abarca:

"D-day is the day after tomorrow."

The monosyllabic Big Paunch said "Good luck," and hung up. On the morning of Thursday, September 4, Cruz León donned what seemed to him the proper garb for a typical tourist: shorts, a green T-shirt, huarache sandals, baseball cap, a camera around his neck and sunglasses. "Apart from the camera, a Canon, everything was Tommy Hilfiger, my favorite label," he would remember. He shouldered the same backpack as before, in which were the four bombs and their respective detonators, carefully stored in separate compartments. After breakfast in the hotel dining room, he went out onto the street. A minute later, as he was jostling with a group of tourists looking for a taxi, he felt his blood turn cold as he heard a woman shouting:

"Raúl Ernesto! Raúl Ernesto!"

He looked out the corner of his eye and saw on the other side of the street a call girl with whom he had gone to a disco during the previous trip. He pretended not to hear and walked faster, but the girl caught up with him and took his arm, smiling:

"Raúl Ernesto! Remember me?"

Not knowing how to deal with the situation, he answered with the first thing that came into his head:

"You're mistaken. I'm not called Raúl and I don't know you."

The girl was astonished by his hard tone:

"Excuse me, but a month ago we went out together. You are Raúl Ernesto!"

The Salvadoran abruptly cut short the conversation:

"Miss, I am not called Raúl Ernesto, I've never seen you before and this is my first time in Cuba. Excuse me, I have things to do."

He dived into the first taxi that appeared and asked the driver to take him to Miramar. So as not to arouse suspicion, he got out two blocks before the Hotel Copacabana, the first of his four targets. According to his calculations of the previous days, it would take six minutes on foot to cover the 300 meters that separated the Copacabana from the second target, the Hotel Chateau, and eighteen minutes more from there to the twin towers Tritón and Neptuno, where he planned to plant the other two bombs and which lay one kilometer beyond the Chateau. It was a little after eleven in the morning when the Salvadoran entered the Copacabana, a three-star, four-story hotel, built in the times of Batista and restored when tourism picked up again at the start of the 1990s. He sat at the carved wooden counter of the downstairs bar and had to wait a few minutes, watching news of Lady Di's death on TV, until a waiter finally appeared to serve him a beer and promptly vanished. Cruz León took advantage of the apathy of the place to go into the restroom to activate the bomb. Locked in a cubicle, he sat on the toilet, stuffed the detonator into the mass of explosive, and set the calculator's alarm clock to go off in forty minutes. At ten past midday the first bomb would explode. As he needed only twenty-four minutes to cover the trajectory between the hotels, he would have sixteen minutes to spare, time enough to disappear from the area before the explosions. He left the restroom carrying the activated bomb in a small plastic bag, already counting down. He went back to the bar to pay for the beer, but there was no one to take the money. Desperate to leave quickly, he made for the cashier, pushing the bag into one of the holes on the side of a cylindrical metal ashtray as he went past. He paid for the beer and left. "Again, at that very moment, I was captured by the spirit of Ray Quick," Cruz León would remember years later. "Seeing that lobby empty, I thought: I'm going to carry out my contract without killing anyone. Right there I truly felt like a specialist."

Just as he had planned, six minutes later he was at the entrance of the Chateau, a smarter hotel than the Copacabana, with the extra attraction of a swimming pool with a bar. In the reception area he encountered a huge aquarium full of lobsters and different fish, and thought of putting the second bomb there. "It would be amazing to blast water, fish and shards of glass all over the place," fantasized Cruz León. The idea was discarded when he saw that on the other side of the aquarium a group of women were chatting— he had no plans to kill anyone. While seeking the ideal place to execute the attack, he grabbed the Canon and began to take photos at random, "trying to act like a normal tourist." Suddenly he noticed that far from passing undetected, he was calling attention to himself: every one of the men circulating in the lobby, doubtless foreign executives or businessmen, were wearing jackets and ties. Realizing his blunder, he stopped taking photos and got on with the job. He thought of kicking the plastic bag underneath a case displaying Cuban cigars and souvenirs, but then a hotel employee came and sat in a chair behind the display case. Time was ticking by and he was still undecided: every time he saw an appropriate spot, the place would suddenly be occupied by someone, forcing him to change his plans. He looked to the rear of the large room and saw a set of wicker couches and easy chairs around a coffee table without anyone nearby, and decided that was the place. He sat down on one of the couches, pretending to read a magazine picked from atop the table, and discreetly slid the plastic bag underneath the furniture, concealing it behind a curtain.

Only when he went out onto wide, tree-lined First Avenue, across from the hotel, did he look at his watch and realize that he had lost more time than he meant to at the Chateau. There were only twenty-five minutes left until the bombs would explode. To reach the twin hotels, plant the bombs and escape at least ten minutes before they went off, he would have to cover the 1,000 meters that separated the Chateau from the Tritón-Neptuno complex in eight minutes—a performance worthy of a marathon runner. He thought of hitching a ride from one of the cars on the avenue, but was afraid of giving himself away at such a tense moment. He wasn't an athlete, but he played sports regularly enough to feel he could make it in time. He set off at a gallop under the burning sun with the two balls of C-4 bouncing around in his backpack. He got to the Tritón with his T-shirt soaked in sweat, but the sprint had been worthwhile. If he could plant the bomb within two minutes, there would be time to place one at the Neptuno, too, and disappear before the explosions. The first floor of the Tritón was full of people. Cruz León went into the restroom, set the alarm clock on the Casio calculator for ten past midday, stuck the detonator into the ball of C-4 and swept everything into the plastic bag. Returning to the lobby, he saw there were two rooms at the end of the corridor—one with a noisy group of tourists and the other empty—he selected the empty one right away for this bomb. However, before he could get there, a tourist guide put six teenagers into the room, who by their accents he identified as Spaniards. Only then did he notice the presence of a hotel security guard, a black man in a dark suit and tie plus the unfailing electronic earpiece. At his waist, under his jacket, was the visible contour of a gun. The presence of the security man, the clock ticking, and the impossibility of finding a place where the bomb would explode without causing fatalities, aroused in Cruz León a painful mixture of paranoia and despair. With a strong desire to vomit, he walked around for a few minutes in the lobby until he found the solution, a couch placed up against a glass wall looking out on the hotel garden. From all that he'd seen in the movies and that Big Paunch had taught him, the Salvadoran knew that, on exploding alongside glass, the bomb would produce an expansion wave on the outside, sparing the people that were milling around inside the Tritón's reception area. He stuffed the bag between the couch and the glass wall; only when he got up did he realize that he was running seriously late. With only five minutes to go until the explosions, there was no time to place the Neptuno bomb.

He walked to Fifth Avenue, the same street where René used to do his morning jogging, hailed a taxi and asked the driver to take him to Old Havana. The car was still in Miramar when Cruz León heard in the distance the thud of the first explosion and soon afterwards, those of the other two. Playing innocent, he asked the driver what the noise was, but the guy didn't seem concerned. "They're building a hotel called the Panorama over there by the beach," he answered, "and that must be the sound of the dynamite used for breaking rocks on the site." Afraid of being identified by the gaudy green of his T-shirt, he once again leaned toward the driver:

"Sorry, mister, but I'm feeling very hot. Do you mind if I take my shirt off?"

The driver reacted good-naturedly:

"Mister, you're the tourist. Do whatever you want. If you like you can even take your pants off."

The car had still not reached the tunnel that separated Miramar from Vedado when it stopped in a traffic jam—a rare problem in the Cuban capital. The Salvadoran found it odd that, although the stoplight fifty meters ahead had turned green several times, the cars were not moving. He froze again when he realized that ahead of them was a *pinza*, a police check. Uniformed, helmeted and armed, two men from the militarized PNR, the Revolutionary National Police, had parked their Guzzi motorcycles in the middle of the road and appeared to be inspecting cars and asking for documents. Terrified, he asked the driver what was going on and once more the easy-going Cuban reassured him:

"For sure Fidel must be somewhere around. When the coman-dante's entourage goes by, they usually hold back the traffic on some streets. We'll soon be off again."

This time Cruz León's paranoia was well founded. As the line of cars inched forward, he was able to see that the police were indeed stopping every vehicle, asking drivers and passengers for their documents, and searching inside briefcases, purses and bags. "At that moment I knew I was fucked so I decided to be radical," Cruz León would remember. As he wasn't carrying a gun or a knife, not even a pocket knife, he decided to resort to the weapon he was carrying in his backpack. Using only one hand, to raise no suspicions from the taxi driver, he took out a metal detonator from the interior pocket of his backpack and stuck it into the round mass of C-4. He reached for the calculator-alarm clock, which showed the time as twelve-thirty, and stayed at the ready. When it came to their turn, he would activate the bomb and that would be it: faced with the prospect of arrest, the Salvadoran preferred to commit suicide, taking the driver with him and anyone else close to them in the traffic jam. The line was moving slowly. There were only two cars to be inspected ahead of them when a third policeman appeared. Without getting off his bike he said something to his two colleagues, who immediately released the traffic and zoomed away. Cruz León's heart rate began to return to normal. Again using just one hand, he removed the detonator from the ball of explosive, put it back in the pouch and zippered it shut. On the road to Old Havana they passed several police cars and ambulances racing in the opposite direction with lights flashing and sirens blaring. Passing in front of a flea market in the middle of the Malecón, the mercenary had the idea of blending with the hordes of foreign tourists who were milling around between the brightly colored stalls. He told the taxi to stop, and got out. Soon he realized why he was attracting curious stares: he was the only person in sight not wearing a shirt. He hurriedly bought a plaid cotton shirt at the nearest stall, put it on and disappeared into the crowd.

After walking around for half an hour among the little stalls selling old records, buttons, posters, loose cigars and shirts and berets with pictures of Che Guevara and Fidel Castro, he finally felt safe. It didn't look like he was being followed, nor were there many cops around. He bought a can of Tropi-Cola, the Cuban equivalent of Coca-Cola, and sat down on the low wall that runs along the

Malecón. Sitting facing the sea with his back to the street, to shield from prying eyes, he took the diary out of the backpack and again went over the list of targets suggested by the "friends in Miami" to Chávez Abarca, looking for somewhere to plant the bomb he hadn't been able to detonate at the Neptuno. He ran his finger down the names of three hotels and two nightspots and paused over the last one, the restaurant La Bodeguita del Medio. That's where he'd plant the bomb he still had in his backpack. Tucked in an alleyway in the middle of a labyrinth of narrow bumpy streets in Old Havana, the restaurant would allow for a safer escape should the need arise. Besides, it was less than ten blocks from the Plaza, where he was staying, something that also had to be considered in an emergency. Tossing the empty can into the trash, he took the bicitaxi that would drop him off ten minutes later on the doorstep of the sixty-year-old Bodeguita on Calle Empedrado. A succession of tiny rooms cluttered with dozens of tables, the place gained notoriety in the 1950s. Attracted by the delicacies of its Cuban Creole cuisine, tourists from all over the world lined up to savor what in fact was the day-to-day food of millions of Cubans: black beans and rice, roast suckling pig, cooked manioc, pork crackling and *tostones*—thin slices of plantain fried at a very high temperature. As tradition demanded, that calorie-bomb was to be washed down with the famous drink that had been invented right there in 1942, the *mojito*—made with white rum, sugar, lime and mint leaves. The most illustrious client of all to have passed through, the writer Ernest Hemingway, had his own permanent spot at the bar by the entrance, and used to stumble out of the place in the early hours of the morning, in the direction of the Ambos Mundos, where he lived. He was the first person to sign his name on the wall, soon imitated by another diner, then another until it became a tradition: every ruler, performer or celebrity who visited the country was invited to be immortalized on the walls of the Bodeguita.

Cruz León arrived a little before two in the afternoon. The restaurant was bursting at the seams. The wait was one hour, warned an employee, but he was welcome to have a drink at the bar meanwhile. Although he had already eaten dinner there on the previous trip, the wait would give him the opportunity to choose the best place to put the bomb. He asked for a *mojito*—which from the first sip he found disgusting—and walked around the tables pretending to look for the signatures of well-known people on the walls. He stopped in front of the most important ones, marked in red ink: the Chilean poets Pablo Neruda and Gabriela Mistral, the American actor Errol Flynn, the late Chilean president Salvador Allende and of course, Hemingway's. He walked around a little more and went back to the bar. "When I saw the quantity of people crowded round the tables I thought: if I set off this bomb here, I'm going to kill more than a hundred people, I can't do that," the Salvadoran would say later. "I thought it wiser to get out of that heat a little, get rid of the *mojito* and think more clearly about what to do." He paid for the drink and walked to the square in front of Havana's Cathedral, a few blocks from the restaurant. He spent an hour flicking through old books and magazines in the used book stalls under the shade of the trees, but no new ideas came to his rescue.

When he returned to the Bodeguita, the place was almost empty. They showed him to a table on the second floor, in a room with only one couple dining in it. But at that very moment the paranoia came back, and came back with a vengeance. Convinced that the couple at the neighboring table was from the police, he tried to locate the emergency exits in case he needed them, but found none. He could leave only the way he came in. Absorbed in thought, he was startled by the waiter standing in front of him, waiting for him to order. He asked for the roast pork, a choice he'd regret a few minutes later. The dish arrived and as he took the first bite, he noticed the couple staring fixedly at him. To calm himself down and relieve the paranoia that was already knotting his stomach, he asked for a drink—"anything strong." The waiter put a glass full of a yellow liquid on the table. The Salvadoran slugged it down in one go, Triple Sec, the sweet sticky liquor made from dried orange peel with an extremely high alcohol content. No sooner swallowed than the drink arose in his throat with the fury of an erupting geyser. Covering his mouth with his right hand and grabbing the backpack with his left, he shot off to the washroom where he arrived already vomiting. Feeling better, he washed his face, glancing around, only to realize right away that the room was no good for placing the bomb. Returning to the table, he changed seats, so as to better keep tabs on the neighboring couple's stares. From the chair he was now sitting in, he saw the ideal spot to hide the plastic bag with the explosive: the corner of a horizontal refrigerator used for storing fresh meat and cans of beer. The equipment's position, up against one of the walls and next to the stairs, meant that he could deposit the bomb on his way out without being seen. Pretending to be feeling sick again, the mercenary went into the restroom with the backpack in his hand and sat on the toilet to activate the bomb. When he was about to set the timer, he noticed that the calculator's dial was defective: the alarm could only be set for the moment when the indicator changed from "pm" to "am," in other words at midnight. "What seemed to be a problem was in fact a solution for me," Cruz León would say later. "The Bodeguita would probably be closed at that time, and the bomb wouldn't claim any victims." He set the explosion for midnight, paid the bill, got up and as he was leaving, discreetly stuffed the plastic bag behind the fridge. He hurried down the stairs and into the street.

For a half hour he zigzagged between the peeling colonial mansions of Old Havana, until he was certain he was not being followed. Halfway through his walk he sat on a bench under a tree in the Parque Cervantes and began to divest himself of anything in the backpack that could compromise him. The calculator that would have been used to detonate the fifth bomb, a roll of insulation tape, some pieces of wire and two empty plastic bags, identical to those he had used to hide the bombs, all went into a garbage can. He walked on to the San Carlos de la Cabaña fortress, famous as Commander Che Guevara's headquarters after the overthrow of Batista, which was now a museum. Out of sight of tourists and officials, he leaned over the low stone wall surrounding a well, at the bottom of which, dozens of meters below, seawater could be seen. Here he dropped the useless batteries, a small pair of electrician's pliers for cutting wires and a yellow plastic voltmeter. Free of anything that could associate him with the bombs, he strolled, relieved, towards the Plaza hotel. As his package trip lasted until Saturday at noon, he would have the whole of Friday to relax a bit and wander around the Cuban capital with no commitments. Before going into the hotel, he took a turn around the entire block to identify anybody on the lookout or with a suspicious demeanor, but from what he could see there was nothing and no one to justify taking any particular precautions.

He fell into bed fully dressed, but was awakened a few minutes later by the telephone ringing. At the other end of the line he heard the unmistakable, deep, laconic voice of Chávez Abarca, calling from San Salvador:

"I just heard the news on the radio. Congratulations."

Cruz León answered abruptly:

"I don't want to know about that. What I want to know about is the money you were going to send me. Now I don't even have enough for a taxi ride."

"Your money is already in Havana."

"Did you send it to a bank?"

"No. Go to the reception at the Capri Hotel and pick up a sealed envelope that was left there in your name. There are 500 dollars inside."

Stunned by the news that he would have to go back to the place where he had planted a bomb the month before, Cruz León lost his temper:

"Son of a bitch! There are dozens of hotels in Havana and you had to pick precisely that one, the Capri?"

"It wasn't me who chose it, it was our messenger. Have a nice trip and I'll see you on Saturday."

The Salvadoran put on his sandals, slung his pack over his back, went down to the street and took a taxi to the Capri. At the hotel entrance he asked the driver to wait, because he'd be back in a couple of minutes. There was a lot of activity in the lobby and at the reception desk. While awaiting his turn he noticed a mulatto at the entrance, wearing a blue shirt, whom he could swear he'd seen earlier, maybe on the visit to the La Cabaña fortress; but then attributed the suspicion to his own eternal paranoia. When it came to his turn, he asked the receptionist if someone had left an envelope in his name. The clerk rapidly checked the pigeonholes, opened some drawers and returned empty-handed:

"I'm sorry, sir, but there is nothing addressed to you."

Devastated and furious, he headed for the street. The moment he stepped onto the sidewalk he was surrounded by six men in ordinary clothes, including the dark man with the blue shirt. Visibly concerned not to attract the attention of the tourists going in and out, one of them, with long hair and dark glasses, spoke softly, almost in a whisper:

"We're from the Ministry of the Interior. You're under arrest. Don't try to resist because we're armed."

Half an hour later, in a cell at the Villa Marista prison wearing only his underpants, Cruz León understood the true seriousness of his situation. He found out that the explosions at the Chateau and Tritón hotels had caused only material damage and minor injuries, but not the one at the Copacabana. The cylindrical metal ashtray where he chose to deposit the plastic bag had been transformed into a half-meter-long grenade, shooting blades of aluminum throughout the entire hotel lobby. One of them hit thirty-two-year-old Italian tourist Fabio di Celmo in the throat, severing his carotid artery and killing him instantly. Cruz León did not have to be a specialist in Cuban matters to know that on the island a crime like this would be punished by the severest of sentences: death by firing squad. Minutes after he arrived at the prison, the interrogations began. Three officers from the counterintelligence office at the Ministry of the Interior, dressed in plain clothes—Lieutenant-Colonels Roberto Caballero and Francisco Estrada, and Colonel Alberto Rabeiro—took turns at reconstructing, minute by minute and step by step, the prisoner's movements since his arrival in Havana. The presence of Rabeiro, the top man at the Directorate of Investigation and Operations, gave an indication of the importance that the Cuban intelligence services attributed to the prisoner. Judging by the interrogators' questions, Cruz León concluded that he must have been followed at least from the moment he had thrown away the calculator, the tape, the wires and the plastic bags in the garbage can in Parque Cervantes. If this were true, there was no doubt that his hotel-room phone had already been tapped when Big Paunch called. Pressurizing him to take responsibilty for the attacks, the officers told him that the internal stitching of his backpack bore minuscule particles of the kind of wires used to detonate the three bombs. In spite of such evidence, the mercenary obstinately denied everything, clinging to a single hope: at midnight the bomb planted at La Bodeguita would explode, offering him a powerful alibi. If he was in custody at the time of the explosion, then it must be somebody else carrying out the attacks.

The interrogations continued, without a moment's interruption. From what little Cruz León would remember of that night, the moment of greatest paranoia occurred when one of the officers came into the cell and asked him to put his hands face down on the table, seemingly announcing that the torture would begin:

"We shall have to remove part of your fingernails. I'm going to call a technician to do this."

While waiting for the "technician" to arrive, the prisoner made up his mind. "I almost freaked out just thinking that someone was going to rip out my fingernails with pliers or pincers," he would remember years later. "But I decided that even so I would keep on denying everything until midnight, when the Bodeguita bomb would explode. It was the fingernails or the death penalty." The state of panic he was in receded only when a man appeared with a harmless nail cutter: he was indeed a technician, there to collect nail clippings for a laboratory examination. These clippings would be used by sniffer dogs specializing in the inspection of places where explosions had occurred. At eleven o'clock that night, one hour ahead of time, the bomb at the Bodeguita exploded. The icebox was thrown up into the air, knocking a wall down and opening a hole in the floor. The restaurant was still open, but there were no clients on the upper floor and the only casualty was a waiter who lost some of his hearing in one ear. On learning the news, Cruz León played what he imagined to be his trump card:

"You've been wasting your time for several hours on an innocent man while the real terrorist is free, planting more bombs."

The argument seemed to stand up, but the die had been cast. The Cuban police had more than stray clues in their possession; they were already certain that he was the person who planted the four bombs that day, and suspected that he had also bombed the Nacional and the Capri weeks before. Being a rank amateur, Cruz León had not taken the trouble to erase his fingerprints from glasses, bar counters, cutlery and faucets at all the places where he'd been that day. This carelessness allowed the police, after comparing the prisoner's fingerprints with those collected at the scene of the explosions, to conclude that on that day he had been in the Chateau, Copacabana and Tritón hotels and at the Bodeguita. Another fatal mistake had been to throw the calculator into a garbage can. In the debris resulting from the bomb at Bodeguita, the police had found two calculator keys—the number 1 key and the √ key, the square root sign. Comparing them with those of the calculator found in the trash in Cervantes park, it was discovered that both were Casios, model QA-100, and identical to each other. There was no way that Cruz Léon could keep denying it. Before midnight, he threw in the towel and confessed responsibility for all the attacks, the four on that day and the two the month before. "Realizing there was no way out, I was able to think of only one thing," the Salvadoran would reveal. "Sylvester Stallone ended his movie in bed with Sharon Stone, and I would end mine in front of a firing squad."

11

THE CUBAN INTELLIGENCE SERVICES SET TWO TRAPS, BUT FAIL TO CATCH BIG PAUNCH, THE RECRUITER OF MERCENARIES HIRED BY MIAMI

The news of Cruz León's imprisonment was treated as a state secret for six days, time enough for the Cuban intelligence services to join the links of a chain that started in the organizations monitored by the Wasp Network in Miami, went through Guatemala and El Salvador and ended in the Cuban hotels as C-4 bombs. Knowing that he had done the most stupid thing of his life and that his days were numbered, the Salvadoran decided to cooperate with the Cubans. As well as owning up to the six attacks, he detailed his relationship with Chávez Abarca and revealed that Big Paunch was just a go-between acting under the orders of someone in Miami known as Solo. Cruz León did not do that by virtue of any ideology, for he had none, as he would admit later. What moved him was a glimmer of hope that his death sentence might be commuted to thirty years in prison, or even to life. So, on Friday morning the prisoner entered a room at Villa Marista where the three officers who had interrogated him the previous day and a woman, also dressed in an olive-green uniform, were waiting for him. There the group remained on duty for the next four days, while Cruz León tried dozens of times to phone Chávez Abarca. He called him at home, at the Geo Rent-a-Car office, and at Big Paunch's brother's home, and he kept trying for hours but the answer was always the same: he wasn't there. At the end of each call the mercenary begged for Abarca to call him back—and he would always leave the number of a "neighbor near the house where he was staying in Havana, a lady called Odalys." Any call made to that number would come through to the desk in that room at Villa Marista. Every call was recorded and monitored with earphones by the four intelligence officers around him. The presence of the woman could be explained by the fact that in the event of Chávez Abarca's calling back, the call should be answered by "Odalys," the supposed owner of the house and the phone. Between attempts to get Abarca on the phone, Cruz León was further interrogated.

This exercise in patience lasted until half past midnight on Tuesday, September 9, when the phone finally rang. Awakened from a nap by the noise, the woman in uniform jumped up and picked up the phone, automatically switching on a tape recorder, and went into character as Odalys:

ODALYS: Hello? Hello?
WOMAN'S VOICE: Good evening, may I speak to Odalys?
ODALYS: Speaking.
WOMAN'S VOICE: This is a call from Guatemala to Odalys. Hello? Hello!
ODALYS: Hello, go ahead.
WOMAN'S VOICE: Hello, this is from Guatemala for Odalys. Is that her speaking?
ODALYS: Yes, it's me.
WOMAN'S VOICE: One moment, please.
CHÁVEZ ABARCA: I need to speak to Raúl, please.
ODALYS: With whom? Hello, I don't understand. Can you hear me?
CHÁVEZ ABARCA: Yes, I can. I'd like to speak to Raúl, please.
ODALYS: Please hold, he is two houses away from here.
CHÁVEZ ABARCA: Yes, thank you, I'll wait.

The woman got up and called in the three soldiers who had been taking part in the interrogation sessions and, of course, Cruz León. A few minutes later, she picked up the phone again:

ODALYS: Hello?

CHÁVEZ ABARCA: Yes.

ODALYS: He's coming.

CHÁVEZ ABARCA: Thank you.

The prisoner sat down at the table and started a tense dialogue, full of swear words, while the three officers listened in on their headphones:

CRUZ LEÓN: Hello?

CHÁVEZ ABARCA: Hello!

CRUZ LEÓN: What's up? What happened?

CHÁVEZ ABARCA: How are you?

CRUZ LEÓN: I'm in deep shit, you sonofabitch!

CHÁVEZ ABARCA: Cool down…

CRUZ LEÓN: Don't fuck me around, you hear? Don't fuck with me! What happened, asshole? I've been trying to talk to you for days and you don't pick up! What's the fucking matter?

CHÁVEZ ABARCA: I sent you the money and waited for you to call me, but I guess the lines got crossed somewhere.

CRUZ LEÓN: What money? There was nothing for me at the Capri! Nothing!

CHÁVEZ ABARCA: That sonofabitch!

CRUZ LEÓN: Yeah! This has fucked everything up. All the hotels are under close surveillance. That's why I didn't leave on Saturday. Just imagine the state I'm in.

CHÁVEZ ABARCA: Sorry, I didn't hear you.

CRUZ LEÓN: I decided not to leave on Saturday because of the surveillance.

CHÁVEZ ABARCA: Why?

CRUZ LEÓN: Looks like the police have a physical description of the suspect. That's why I decided not to leave. I got fixed up with a girlfriend here and been spending these days with her in a private house. She doesn't know anything about me, but she has relatives who work at the airport who told her they're checking all the foreigners leaving Cuba really thoroughly. I moved out of the hotel when the package ran out and came to this house near where Odalys lives: she's the owner of this phone, a friend of my girl's.

One of the officers scribbled a dollar sign on a piece of paper and held it in front of the prisoner's eyes. He resumed the conversation:

CRUZ LEÓN: Another thing, Big Paunch, my money's run out.

CHÁVEZ ABARCA: But how do you expect me to send any money?

CRUZ LEÓN: How do I know? And money is not the only thing I need. For fuck's sake, I want to know how you're going to get me out of here, godammit!

CHÁVEZ ABARCA: Can I ask you a question?

CRUZ LEÓN: Shoot!

CHÁVEZ ABARCA: Does your girlfriend know the suspect's description?

CRUZ LEÓN: Don't think so. All I know is he's a Latino …

CHÁVEZ ABARCA: Don't rely on it, Cubans are big liars …

CRUZ LEÓN: No, I don't think so … I saw myself how the hotels are monitored.

CHÁVEZ ABARCA: You have to find out what their description of the suspect is.

CRUZ LEÓN: Shit, you want me to go to the airport and ask what the guy they're after looks like? Don't fuck with me, man! If I go there, they'll get me!

CHÁVEZ ABARCA: You don't have to go there. Just ask your girlfriend …

At a certain point in the recording, the conversation makes it clear that the Cubans' objective was to lure Chávez Abarca into a trap in Havana:

CRUZ LEÓN: Shit, Big Paunch, why don't you come yourself and get me out of this mess? You know how to do that, for fuck's sake!

CHÁVEZ ABARCA: Don't worry, I won't let you down.

CRUZ LEÓN: Fuck you! You talk like I was safe here! I'm desperate! Your brother told me he sent some money and I should collect it from some woman called Hortensia, works at Joanessa Turismo, in Havana. Hell, you guys think I'd go there to pick up money and get arrested? I don't even know who this Hortensia is. I can't trust someone I don't know.

CHÁVEZ ABARCA: The most important thing now is for you to check the physical description the police have of the suspect.

CRUZ LEÓN: Forget it! I don't give a shit about the suspect's description. The airports are being watched real closely. Even Varadero. The only solution here, Big Paunch, is for you or one of your people to come and get me out of here. Someone who could hide me in some safe place, it could even be under a pile of rocks, and then get me out of here. I talked with your wife on the phone and told her I'd gladly get out of here in disguise or even underwater.

CHÁVEZ ABARCA: My wife? What did you say to my wife, you piece of shit?

CRUZ LEÓN: Fuck, you wouldn't answer my calls, I had to talk to her.

CHÁVEZ ABARCA: For fuck's sake, what did you say to my wife?

Cruz León: Sorry, but I told her everything. She knows everything now.

CHÁVEZ ABARCA: You told her?

CRUZ LEÓN: I had no choice ...

CHÁVEZ ABARCA: OK, OK. Hang in there, and tomorrow I'll call you again.

CRUZ LEÓN: Tomorrow? What do you mean, tomorrow? Sort my problem out now!

CHÁVEZ ABARCA: I need some time to give you a concrete solution.

CRUZ LEÓN: Don't forget, Big Paunch: you're the only one who can help me! You've got to come yourself or send someone to get me out of here. I'm desperate!

CHÁVEZ ABARCA: I'll call you tomorrow between two and six in the afternoon.

CRUZ LEÓN: Don't forget, I'm desperate here, I'm fucked ...

CHÁVEZ ABARCA: We'll talk tomorrow. Good luck.

Big Paunch didn't take the bait or call back, thus evading the ambush. It wasn't yet time for the Cubans to lay their hands on the briber of mercenaries. Published in the September 10 edition of *Granma*, and immediately reproduced by international press agencies and foreign correspondents, the news of Cruz León's capture sent shockwaves through Miami. According to the Cuban authorities, the Salvadoran mercenary was just one end of a tangled ball of twine that took in Francisco Chávez Abarca, in El Salvador, and whose other end was in Miami, where a seventy-year-old, six-foot-tall, blue-eyed and white-haired man was living, known in the underground world of terrorism as Solo: one of Luis Posada Carriles's noms de guerre. The article also affirmed that the funding for the terrorist actions against Cuba—explosives, plane tickets, accommodation and hiring of mercenaries—came from the Cuban American National Foundation vaults. Even after confirming the accusations in an interview to the *New York Times*, Posada Carriles—whose other codenames were Ramón Medina, Ignacio Medina, Bambi, Basilio and Lupo—was still freely walking the streets of Little Havana. A few weeks after the news of Cruz León's imprisonment, Carriles gave an interview to María Elvira Salazar, a journalist from CBS TV, with whom he had this brief and chilling dialogue:

SALAZAR: According to the *New York Times*, the Salvadoran guy arrested in Cuba, Raúl Ernesto Cruz León, was working for you. Is that true?

POSADA: Cruz León was hired by someone who works for me, but I never had any contact with him. He did the job for money.

SALAZAR: Don't you think that this statement of yours may be his death sentence?

POSADA: He signed his own death sentence. Whatever I may say or tell won't change anything.

The imprisonment of Cruz León would be celebrated alone and in silence by the various Wasp Network members in Miami. Not only celebrating a significant victory in the war against terrorism, but also the fact that it had been from them, from the group of agents headed by Gerardo Hernández, that the first reports were sent to Havana raising suspicions of some connection between the bombs and Central American mercenaries hired by Cubans residing in Florida. A month or so after the imprisonment of the Salvadoran, another report issued by the Wasp Network would expose even more clearly the links between the CANF and terrorism. Transmitted through third parties by the Cuban government to the American authorities, information gathered by Gerardo Hernández's team enabled the US Coast Guard to board *La Esperanza*, a cabin cruiser which at dawn on October 27, 1997, was found heading northwest of Puerto Rico, carrying four Cubans based in Florida. When the police asked what they were doing 1,500 kilometers from Miami, where the boat was registered, one of the crew answered:

"We're fishing for lobster."

During the inspection, a policeman went downstairs to the stowage area. He came back holding two Barrett .50 caliber assault rifles, with tripods and telescopic sights, and asked the Cubans:

"You were going to fish for lobster with these?"

Apart from the two rifles, capable of destroying a target at 2,000 meters, the stowage of the twelve-meter cabin cruiser concealed seven boxes of ammunition, six radio communication devices, military fatigues, binoculars, night vision goggles, a satellite-operated cell phone and a huge barrel containing 7,500 liters of fuel. Pressed by the police, the crew finally came clean. Ángel Alfonso Alemán, known in Miami as *Cotorra*—Parrot—confessed what the group's plan was:

"The guns are mine. We were going to kill Fidel Castro in a few days' time on Margarita Island."

The Cuban president would actually be on that Venezuelan islet a week later, for another Ibero-American summit, but the rifles that Alemán claimed were his were in fact registered to Francisco "Pepe" Hernández, interim president of CANF since Jorge Mas Canosa had taken leave of absence for health reasons. Moreover, *La Esperanza*, as verified by the police, was registered in Miami to José Antonio Llama, a member of the executive board of the Cuban American National Foundation. Taken to San Juan in Puerto Rico, the four crewmen were immediately arrested by the FBI whose local director, Héctor Pesquera, mocked the boat owner's flimsy excuse: "It's a little hard to believe that someone goes fishing for lobster with .50 caliber guns." The $50,000 bail per head, set by the Puerto Rican justice department for the prisoners to await the inquiry and the trial in freedom, was paid the next morning "by individuals and groups of exiled Cubans," revealed Alemán as he left prison. Furthermore, *Cotorra* said that the murder of Fidel Castro was a gift the group wanted to give Mas Canosa, to fulfill the last wish of the anti-Castroist movement's patriarch as he lay on his deathbed.

Although Mas Canosa's state of health was a secret restricted to his family and a few CANF leaders, news of his terminal condition had been sent to Cuba by René González eight months before it reached the cafés of Little Havana. Early in 1997, during a routine meeting in a fast-food restaurant, the Cuban agent handed Gerardo Hernández a disk with the information gathered the previous month. In his report to Havana, Giro transcribed an excerpt from René's intelligence concerning the exile community's big boss:

A bit of news was given which Saúl [Rámon Saúl Sánchez, the leader of the Democracy Movement] asked to be kept secret. It is about Mas Canosa, who has terminal cancer, and, according to Saúl, they don't think he will make it to the end of the year. [Another Democracy member, Marcelino García told me that] as a result of the illness, there was conflict among Roberto Martín Pérez and other senior CANF members over who would take charge. I took this news with some reservations, besides the goodness it would do to humanity if a guy like Mas Canosa would disappear. He might be faking the illness as part of a stratagem in which he would undergo a miraculous healing to rally political support. In doing that they could gain sympathy among the people, who would see God's hand and the power of prayer.

Unlike René, Giro believed that Jorge Mas Canosa actually could be ill, and thought René's suggestion slightly unrealistic. Just below the report transcription, he gave his own opinion on the matter with a touch of black humor, referring to René by his usual codename, Castor:

Castor said that maybe this was "pig head's" propagandistic strategy, being tremendously sly. I gave him my opinion that one cannot doubt anything coming from Mas Canosa, but I don't think he's going to get into a story of that kind. And I actually think that if there is smoke, it's because there is fire. [But we were in agreement about one thing:] we united our "faith" in a brief mental "prayer" that the news about the cancer is true, and we hope it cuts him in four pieces as soon as possible. Amen.

Giro was right: it wasn't a performance. The Democracy leader's prognosis on Mas Canosa's life expectancy was accurate. On the gray morning of November 25, 1997, Miami came to a halt to watch what the press called "the funeral of the century." Stores closed their doors and municipal police outriders held up traffic and blocked access to Calle Ocho, in Little Havana, so that the cortege could pass—a cortege worthy of any mafia funeral produced by Hollywood. Black limousines covered in wreaths of flowers followed behind the hearse carrying the remains of Jorge Mas Canosa, who had died two days before. At noon, the coffin was lowered into a grave at Caballero Rivero Woodlawn Park Cemetery. Jorge Mas Canosa was to lie a few meters from the mausoleum housing the ashes of three generations of dictators from Nicaragua—the country where troops had been trained for the invasion of the Bay of Pigs. Next to Canosa lay: Anastasio "Tacho" Somoza (who ruled from 1937–47 and again from 1950–56) and his sons, Luis Somoza (1956–63) and Anastasio "Tachito" Somoza (1967–72 and 1974–79). Another piece of information sent by René to Cuba proved to be true before the corpse was even cold. The hospital had no sooner communicated to the press that Mas Canosa was dead than the war began for control of the CANF, a machine that handled millions of dollars, and had the power to interfere even in American presidential elections.

The succession at the Foundation inspired the Cuban intelligence services to put so-called Operation Deceased into practice, a counter-information campaign aimed at poisoning the selection process and pitting the candidates against each other. Among material related to that subject, the FBI got hold of a leaflet that René was instructed to send anonymously to the CANF's most influential members, disqualifying all the candidates to Mas Canosa's post one by one, starting with his son Jorge:

Who are you voting for as president of the CANF?

For Jorge Mas Santos? He isn't interested in politics. His mother doesn't want him to assume leadership of the CANF. He doesn't have his father's charisma. He's not fluent in Spanish.

For Dr. Alberto Hernández? His extramarital relations don't allow him any time for politics. His most valuable distinction is that he was Jorge Mas's doctor. His health is deteriorating.

For Pepe Hernández? He's a loser. He's under FBI surveillance because he's sloppy. He's not accepted by members of the CANF. He has no leadership charisma. Annexationist. Has prostate cancer.

For Diego Suárez? Conversationalist (even with the enemy). He has little life left.

For Domingo Moreira? Don Domingo Moreira [his father] has prestige but you can't inherit that. He doesn't have the charisma to direct the powerful CANF.

The text ended with macabre irony. The only option was to vote for the leader who had just died:

> Who should you vote for? Vote for Finado.
> [*Finado* is Spanish for "dead person."]

Though depicted as a loser in the pamphlet, as a sick, reckless and uncharismatic man, it was the sixty-year-old Francisco "Pepe" Hernández, owner of the Barrett rifles seized on *La Esperanza*, who ended up taking control of the highly influential political lobby machine. After graduating with an engineering degree in Havana, Pepe had gone into exile in Florida soon after Fidel Castro took over. Arrested in 1961 during the unsuccessful invasion of the Bay of Pigs, he went back to Miami two years later, having been released as part of an agreement between Cuba and the United States. He then enlisted in the US Navy Marine Corps, where he served until 1972, when he was discharged with the rank of captain. The choice of an even tougher hardliner than Jorge Mas Canosa to lead the CANF energized the ultraradical sectors of the exiled Cuban community. In the months to follow, attempts to attack Cuba intensified, but cross-referencing the mountain of information sent to Havana for more than five years by Gerardo Hernández's agents allowed several attacks to be thwarted. In the month of October alone, the Cuban police had disabled two bombs—one of them placed in a tourist minibus and the other under the counter of a duty-free store at the José Martí International Airport. The men behind the frustrated attack, Guatemalan mercenaries Jorge Venancio Ruiz and Marlon González Estrada, had been hired by Ignacio Medina, one of Posada Carriles's codenames.

Before the new year was rung in, the beleaguered Cuban reserves would suffer further bloodletting. The first blow came when a Florida court ordered Cuba to pay an astounding $49 million in indemnity to the families of three of the four Brothers pilots whose planes had been shot down by the Cuban MiGs a year and a half earlier. The money was shared among the families of Armando Alejandre (awarded $17 million), Carlos Alberto Costa ($16 million) and Mario de la Peña ($16 million). Since the fourth pilot, Pablo Morales, had not yet acquired American citizenship, his family was not considered a beneficiary by the judge. The sentence determined that the monies used for the indemnity payments should be taken from frozen Cuban funds—those "blocked assets in the United States" that President Clinton had mentioned after the planes were shot down.

Comments on the unusual amount of the damages were still echoing on the street corners of Little Havana when in 1999 the newspapers announced that Ana Margarita had decided to sue for compensation "for sexual assault"—not by her ex-husband Juan Pablo Roque, but by the Cuban State. That was not the first time the abandoned wife would attend a Florida court. A year before, she had been granted the judicial annulment of her marriage to Roque and the recovery of her maiden name, Martínez, although the only tangible asset she got was the most vivid symbol of his lovelessness, the Cuban pilot's olive-green Jeep Cherokee. Represented by two skillful lawyers, she decided to file a suit not against Juan Pablo Roque, who didn't have a dime and would most likely never set foot again in the United States, but against the Republic of Cuba. Presenting herself as a "fervent anti-communist" and using raw legal terminology, Ana Margarita asserted that "coitus with Juan Pablo had never been consensual," because the man she actually slept with was an agent of Fidel Castro, and not the defector Roque pretended to be and with whom she had fallen in love. "When agreeing to sexual relations with Roque," continued the lawyers, "the plaintiff Miss Martínez had no knowledge that he was a Cuban agent." Since the marriage of the pair had been a sham set up by Cuba, it was the Republic of Cuba that would have to pay damages for the suffering to which she had been subjected.

Her grievances against the Cuban pilot were listed in seventy-three items. Saying that she had been "betrayed and abandoned," Ana Margarita added she had since become shunned by the Cuban community, which did not believe she had genuinely been fooled by Roque. The more radical radio announcers claimed in their programs that as well as knowing everything, she was no doubt helping her husband in his secret activities. During a memorial service for the dead pilots, the father of one of them asked her to leave the church. "You are under suspicion," he said coldly, "and so you're not welcome among us." At the end of the charge sheet, Ana Margarita listed the physical, moral, emotional and material injuries that the Republic of Cuba had inflicted on her: physical harm, pain and suffering from "nonconsensual coitus," mental anguish, medical expenses incurred in the process of emotional recovery, and loss of the capacity to enjoy life. Although her lawyers stated that she would continue to "suffer permanently from many of these ills," they calculated the value of the damages that might mitigate the plaintiff Martínez's trauma at $41 million. Twenty-seven million seemed quite sufficient to Judge Alan Postman, to be paid by Cuba through its frozen assets in the Chase Manhattan Bank.

Ana Margarita would never see Olga Salanueva again. If there was little chemistry between them before, there would be even less after Roque's escape to Cuba. The González couple's life continued comfortably enough, with René dividing his time between his job as a co-pilot at Arrow Air and his activities at the Democracy Movement, Olga selling courses by phone for Inglés Ahora and Irmita happily settled in her school. In late September 1997, amid the excitement caused by Cruz León's imprisonment, the family routine was broken by the news the couple had been awaiting for several months: Olga was pregnant. The joy in the household was not completely unanimous, however, because for the first few weeks Irmita seemed upset by the news. "In the beginning I was a bit sulky, after all, my thirteen-year reign as an only child was coming to an end," she would remember much later on. "But as time went on, I got even more eager than my parents for the baby to come soon." When Gerardo Hernández learned that the González family was going to grow, he became as fatherly as he had been with Tony before he had married Maggie. His first meeting with René after the pregnancy was confirmed, where Olga would also be present, was at the Chinese restaurant Canton, west of Little Havana. After what they called "countersurveillance measures," meaning the usual precautions of checking whether they were being followed, the three of them went in and picked a table. In his report to Havana, Giro said that after they had gone through the usual subjects ("transfer of instructions and receiving information, Castor's general statements and the discussion of political issues") the "spot" turned into a prosaic domestic conversation, "a meeting dominated by the subject of the baby." Nine years younger than René, and with no experience of fatherhood, Giro was holding forth and giving advice like an expert in the subject, as can be seen in his letter to Cuba:

It has been a good pregnancy and she is due towards the end of April or early May. I asked them about their other daughter and they said that she was doing very well in school and she speaks English pretty well. Ida said that the girl is jealous of the baby, but she thinks this will pass. I told her this was normal because up till now she has been the center of attention and now she is going to be "taken off her pedestal," but in my opinion they should handle the situation very tactfully from now on, so she does not become even more jealous.

The report ends by disclosing the baby's gender and making comments on the life of Castor and Ida, Olga's codename in secret communications:

They did an ultrasound and it is a girl, but they have not said anything to the family yet because they want it to be a surprise. Things are going well for Ida at work. She told me that her car was hit while it was parked. It was a company car from her job, but since she had not reported it to the police the moment it happened, that the company probably would not pay because there are no witnesses. As for Castor, they both said that, as a result of the course he is taking [at Arrow Air], he is going through a lot of important and stressful times right now as the exams are very difficult and he has no other choice but to devote himself completely to that. He told us that he did not think that it was going to be this difficult.

The meeting ended at nine o'clock at night with a check of $38 for their chicken with cashew nuts, pork ribs with sweet and sour sauce and fried rice, two beers and a Coke. The standard security procedures were repeated. They left the restaurant one by one; the couple turned to the right and went into the nearest café to ensure that nobody was following them, while Giro walked in the opposite direction and repeated the "countersurveillance procedures," stopping at a drugstore for a last glance around until he was sure that he could depart safely. The permanent fear of being watched would create extremely tense situations, such as on one Saturday morning in January 1998 when Gerardo Hernández was pushing a shopping cart at the Cotsco supermarket, on Biscayne Boulevard, three miles from his home. He was wearing Bermuda shorts, a cap and dark glasses, and was prowling the electronics section looking for a laptop. Although they had been on the market since the beginning of the decade, it was only in late 1997 that Gerardo Hernández, Ramón "Urso" Labañino and Remijio "Marcelino" Luna received permission and money from Havana to buy such equipment.

The agent's heart suddenly started thumping when he saw behind a shelf, less than three feet away, one of the most hated characters of revolutionary Cuba. Wearing a dark-green linen jacket, there was the ex-CIA agent, a Cuban like himself, Félix Ismael Rodríguez Mendigutia: the man who thirty years before had led the hunt for, and authorized the execution of, Ernesto "Che" Guevara in

La Higuera, Bolivia. He'd likely be wearing his prize trophy, the matte steel Rolex watch he stole from the Argentinian guerrilla's dead body. Rodríguez was a veteran of the Bay of Pigs and had shown up again in the news in the late 1970s, involved in the Iran-Contra affair, the covert operation led by Colonel Oliver North, an advisor to President Ronald Reagan, whereby the CIA secretly sold weapons to Iran and passed on the funds obtained to the Contras, the armed movement fighting to overthrow the Nicaraguan Sandinista government.

At the time of the supermarket encounter, Rodríguez was living in Miami where he ran a security consulting firm. "Upon crossing each other's path, we looked at each other, and I knew it was him," wrote Hernández in his report to Cuba. As discreetly as possible, so as not to attract attention, Giro turned around and walked towards the checkout lanes. He paid for his items, crossed the wide, bustling hall, bought an ice cream and chose a small table at the food court from where he could watch Rodríguez when the latter headed to the checkout. A few minutes later, Rodríguez showed up with his cart full of products and picked a line. Hernández stood up, walked toward a phone booth by the exit door, took the pager from his belt and pretended to make a call. From behind his sunglasses Hernández kept his eyes glued on the paunchy sixty-year-old, a far cry from the feared Max Gómez, the alias by which Rodríguez had been known in the 1960s and '70s. From the phone booth Giro saw him pay for his items and move towards the parking lot. Seemingly unaware of being watched, Rodríguez put his purchases in the trunk of a gray Mercedes-Benz with tinted windows. Before getting into the car, he looked round in Hernández's direction. Then he started the car and drove away. Giro's report assured Havana that Rodríguez was alone, but, "because of the characteristics of the jacket he was wearing, it is perfectly possible that he could have been armed." And getting it off his chest, he ended: "You can imagine what it feels like to have a guy so close who is such an SOB and who owes us such a big debt."

Time would show that the constant safety precautions taken by members of the Wasp Network were pointless, since from 1995, or even earlier, the group was being monitored by a squad of FBI agents. Many of their meetings and quick brush passes were photographed from a distance by policemen armed with cameras and telephoto lenses. Incidents like the one inside the Cotsco supermarket might not be mere coincidence, and many of the suspicions that used to haunt them might not be simply paranoid manifestations. In the light of the events that occurred some months later, it is possible that the scare Gerardo Hernández experienced in January 1998 was a sign that the FBI was closing in on the Cuban agents.

12

FIDEL CASTRO SENDS BILL CLINTON A LETTER WITH ACCUSATIONS AGAINST THE EXTREME RIGHT-WING FLORIDA ORGANIZATIONS. THE CARRIER PIGEON IS NOBEL PRIZE WINNER GABRIEL GARCÍA MÁRQUEZ

In the last week of January 1998, Gerardo Hernández wound up one of the trips he made to Cuba every three or four months. For the way back he chose the Havana-Cancún-Memphis-Miami route. When he got to Cancún, on the morning of Thursday, January 22, he found out that problems with later connections would force him to stay in the Mexican seaside resort waiting for a flight that could take him to Memphis—which eventually happened only on Sunday afternoon. In Memphis he was removed from the long line that was forming in front of the immigration windows, along with another half dozen passengers, and led to a separate counter. Everything pointed to his having been chosen in a random selection, but the official who dealt with him seemed particularly grumpy as he asked to see his documents. As on previous trips, Giro was carrying only his driving license and a copy of his birth certificate. In line with an agreement then in force between the United States and its neighbors Mexico and Canada, the two documents were enough for American citizens to travel to these countries without need of a passport—and Manuel Viramóntez (as he was known on his documents) was an American citizen. On all his trips to his own country Hernández repeated the same routine; on arrival in Mexico there was always someone from the Cuban embassy waiting for him with a Cuban passport issued in his real name, with which he continued his journey to Havana. On his return, the passport was taken back on the Mexican stopover, at which point Giro once again assumed the false identity of Manuel Viramóntez and took the plane to the United States. As with the other times, on that Sunday he was clean and had no reason to be alarmed despite the glowering face of the American who approached him at the airport in Memphis. The official asked for his passport, and he explained that he was traveling only with his driving license and birth certificate. The American held the driving license up to the light, confirmed the authenticity of the watermark but, still not satisfied, asked if Hernández had some other document. The birth certificate was also scrutinized by the Cerberus who, while giving no sign that he had found something wrong, put it in his shirt pocket along with the driver's license and ordered curtly:

"Follow me."

Taken to a small closed room, with only the immigration official for company, for the first time in his six years in the United States Giro was challenged to prove that he really was the American Manuel Viramóntez, born in Texas and brought up in Puerto Rico. At the end of two interminable hours of interrogation, full of traps and frustrated attempts to get the passenger to contradict himself, the man did not seem satisfied and continued insisting:

"What did you do in Mexico in the three weeks you stayed there?"

"I was on holiday."

"What hotel did you stay in?"

"I stayed at my girlfriend's house."

"What's her name and telephone number?"

"She's called Agustina and the phone number is 239-5357."

It was a lie, of course, but it had not been made up on the spur of the moment. If the official were to dial the number to check, he would find a woman on the other end of the line who would say her name was Agustina and would confirm the information given. When he received his documents back and was released,

Hernández imagined that the ordeal had come to an end. Going through customs, however, his luggage was meticulously searched by two officers. One of them asked him to switch on the laptop he was carrying and then inspected the programs and files installed in the device. That was illegal in American law, but Hernández knew it would not be wise to enforce his rights, preferring to put up with the arbitrariness in silence. Finally released, he managed to embark for Miami only at nightfall. On Monday morning his first step was to send a brief summary of what had happened to Havana:

> I arrived yesterday, Sunday. It was impossible to fly before then. Please tell David that entry through Memphis is not recommended. They detained me at the Immigration Office for not having a passport. They conducted a thorough interrogation until they confirmed [cover] and I had to show all documents and proof. ... They also detained other people. At the end the guy advised me to get a passport to avoid any problems. Customs was also difficult. They checked all of the baggage completely. ... That was the only place where they made me take out the computer and [they have an] X-ray machine more sensitive than any other airport I went through. ... Will expand in mail. ... Giro, Jan. 26.

When he received an answer from Main Center in the form of a notice reprimanding him for the episode—which would become known between them as "the Memphis incident"—Hernández defended himself in the next message, affirming that he wouldn't be ashamed to admit that everything had happened through his own fault. "If this were the case, I would have told you, honestly, that I gave this or that signal because I got nervous, or because I got tongue-tied, or because I stood in the wrong line," he wrote, "which are things that can happen to me at any time, but not this time." In spite of the formal tone in which the messages were written, he retained his good humor. "Logically, on the side of my analysis, the incident could have been caused by many things, ranging from the official seeing my sweaty bald pate to him being a homosexual and liking me," he finished off, "but unfortunately those and other reasons are just speculation."

Back to his routine, Hernández dedicated his first days at work to reading the reports produced by the Cuban agents during his absence. The eyes of the group remained trained on the recruitment of mercenaries in Central America. Cruz León's imprisonment did not seem to intimidate the Miami organizations of the extreme right, and the information collected from within their circle indicated that the relationship between some of their leaders and Chávez Abarca went on as if nothing had happened. In the middle of February, a report reached Villa Marista that recommended rigorous surveillance at Cuban airports, since there were suspicions that a Guatemalan called Miguel Abraham Herrera Morales, involved with the "friends in Miami," had booked a tourist trip to Cuba. The alert from the Wasp Network coincided with a warning sent secretly by the head of the US Interests Section in Havana, Michael Kozak, to the Cuban foreign ministry. According to Kozak, the American secret services had obtained "sensitive information, supplied by a source whose trustworthiness has not been determined," claiming that a group of Cuban exiles intended to carry out bomb attacks in Havana in the first week of March. It had not been possible to discover where, what time or what the chosen targets were, but, according to the source, the explosives were already on their way to Cuba.

The plot was uncovered on the sultry morning of March 4, when an Aviateca plane landed at José Martí Airport carrying a group of tourists from Guatemala City, via Cancún. Among them was Miguel Herrera, a pale, slim twenty-eight-year-old, with a huge black moustache and prescription glasses. On checking his luggage, customs inspectors found two Casio calculators, nine-volt Kodak batteries, wires and, hidden in two bottles of shampoo, 400 grams of C-4. In police custody, Herrera revealed his real name—Nader Kamal Musalam Barakat, a Guatemalan of Palestinian origin—and said he had not been traveling alone. On the same flight was another Guatemalan, María Elena González Meza de Fernández, who had managed to pass undetected through immigration and by that time was probably at her lodgings in a family home in Havana. Arrested a few hours later, the fifty-four-year-old fortune-teller, a peroxide blonde who owned a tarot stand in the bohemian part of the Guatemalan capital, handed over the hidden material she was carrying in her suitcase to the police—half a kilo of C-4, batteries, wires, four detonators, two calculators, etc. At the end of the interrogation the pair confessed they had been contracted by Chávez Abarca and Ramón Medina—in other words, Posada Carriles—to place four bombs in Havana, in hotel duty-free shops used only by foreign tourists. The pay was the same as that offered to Cruz León: $1,500 per bomb. The operation had been coordinated by María Elena's husband, Jazid Iván Fernández, another Palestinian Guatemalan, who was only twenty-seven years old.

Opting to collaborate with the Cuban intelligence services in exchange for a reduction in his sentence, Miguel Herrera—or Nader Musalam—agreed to repeat the telephonic mise-en-scène used months earlier, in the vain attempt to lure Chávez Abarca into a trap in Cuba. This time the Cubans wanted to catch Jazid Iván, the bridge that would lead to the "friends in Miami." The simulation conceived by the intelligence services claimed that a mugger had stolen María Elena's handbag—her codename was Mary—with her plane tickets and passport, the money reserved for the pair's expenses and the four detonators, which was the reason the bombs had not yet been placed. In the phone calls Musalam had been told to insist that the only solution to the problem was for someone to get on a plane from Guatemala and bring four new detonators and some money to Cuba. The carrier could either be Big Paunch or Jazid. Held in the same room at the Villa Marista where Cruz León had played the role months earlier, the first conversation between Musalam and Abarca was not encouraging. The dialogue began with the Guatemalan passing on the story that had been dreamed up by the Villa Marista agents:

MUSALAM: Something really annoying has happened. They stole Mary's bag in the street. They took the four detonators, the passport and her air tickets and all the money for our expenses.

CHÁVEZ ABARCA: But if they stole her passport, how's she going to get back here?

MUSALAM: She's taking care of that right now, she's at the Guatemalan embassy trying to get temporary travel documents.

CHÁVEZ ABARCA: And the return ticket?

MUSALAM: We already found out that Aviateca will reissue the stolen ticket. The problem is that the money's gone. Can you send us some more?

CHÁVEZ ABARCA: No, I've got nobody available right now.

MUSALAM: Then you come yourself. Come tomorrow, there's a flight that gets here at nine a.m. You could go back on the same plane two hours later.

CHÁVEZ ABARCA: I can't, it's easier if you come here.

MUSALAM: What about Jazid Iván? Tell Jazid to bring the money.

CHÁVEZ ABARCA: No fucking way Jazid is going.

MUSALAM: Fuck, but it's his wife!

CHÁVEZ ABARCA: While Mary's taking care of the passport and the air ticket, why don't you come and pick up everything from me?

MUSALAM: I thought of that, but now Mary's afraid to stay by herself.

CHÁVEZ ABARCA: What do you mean?

MUSALAM: That's right, she's afraid to stay alone here, because the stuff's with her. For safety we thought it better for all that to be with her, and now she's scared to stay alone …

CHÁVEZ ABARCA: I'll call tomorrow with some answers.

He never did. For the second time Big Paunch escaped the risk of ending his days in a Cuban prison—or in front of a firing squad—but for Jazid Iván there was no alternative: he would have to go personally to Cuba to rescue his wife. On the morning of March 20, two weeks after Nader Musalam and María Elena had arrived in Cuba, Jazid was arrested at José Martí Airport. With revelations now made by all three of them, the Cuban authorities put together the pieces that had been stacking up since December 1990, when René had escaped to the United States, and were able to complete the jigsaw puzzle at last. There was no longer any doubt that Chávez Abarca was the link that united on the one hand Central American mercenaries, and on the other Posada Carriles and the big beasts at the Cuban American National Foundation.

The amount and the quality of the information obtained by the

Wasp Network in almost eight years enabled the Cuban government to assert, based on recordings, photos and documents, that a powerful web of terrorist organizations was acting with impunity in American territory with the aim of undermining, through the power of bombs, the tourism industry that had proved so vital for the salvation of the Cuban economy. Fidel Castro continued to believe that if Bill Clinton had access to that information, he would have no alternative but to jail the leaders of what was called in Havana "the Cuban mafia of Miami." The attempt to use the former senator Gary Hart as an intermediary had come to nothing, but Fidel had not lost hope of getting the dossier to the Oval Office somehow. The White House had had at least one demonstration of the efficiency and good faith of the Cuban secret service fourteen years earlier, under the Republican Ronald Reagan, who could top the list of American heads of state most hostile to the Cuban Revolution. In spite of the abyss that separated Cuba from that administration, in mid-1984 Castro personally gave orders to the DSS to deliver into the hands of the ultraconservative William Casey, director of the CIA, a detailed report denouncing the existence of a plot, thwarted in time, to assassinate the president of the United States. Except for a brief public mention of the topic by the Cuban deputy foreign minister, Abelardo Moreno, neither of the two sides ever divulged the slightest detail of the failed operation.

Apparently responding to the threat represented by terrorist groups based in Florida, the White House authorized Michael Kozak, head of the American mission in Havana, to exchange information with the Cuban intelligence services, on the premise that there was a link between the anti-Castroist organizations and the escalation of terror against Cuba. Kozak gave assurances that the US government had already taken "a firm decision to pursue those responsible for these acts and bring them to justice." To that end, the exchange of information with Cuba would be essential since, according to the diplomat, "not all of the suspects lived in Miami and many were operating out of third countries," which cut down on the possibilities of taking action against them. "Any clues or information that might lead us to the people who support or control these activities," affirmed Kozak, "will be of great use to the American government." It seemed a good moment for Fidel Castro to revive his project of getting information on the subject personally to Bill Clinton, but the lack of a reliable channel seemed to delay the plan's fulfillment indefinitely.

A solution appeared at the beginning of April 1998, when the writer Gabriel García Márquez made one of his many trips to Cuba. This time he had come in search of material for an article on Pope John Paul II's visit to the Island that took place in January of that year. Welcomed by President Castro, the Colombian told his old friend that during the last week of April he would be teaching a literary workshop at Princeton University. And he confided that he had asked Bill Richardson, Madeleine Albright's successor as head of the American mission at the UN, to arrange a private meeting for him with Bill Clinton. His intention was to talk with the president about the situation in Colombia, beset at that time by two great problems, the drug trade and the growth of the Revolutionary Armed Forces of Colombia (FARC).

In Havana, a plan was hatched for Gabo to bear a personal message from Fidel Castro which he would deliver directly into Bill Clinton's hands. García Márquez knew it was no simple thing to talk in private with the US president on such a delicate topic. The last time the writer had been in the Oval Office at the White House, seven months before, the encounter had been observed the whole time by Sandy Berger, Clinton's national security advisor. He had a "grim suspicion" that a message like the one he planned to bring would most probably end up with the security services, not the president. Even so, it was decided that the author of *One Hundred Years of Solitude* would be the carrier pigeon for the first missive addressed by the Cuban leader to a president of the United States since that far-off year of 1959.

To spare Clinton the obligation of replying, Fidel decided that it would not be a personal letter, but a concise document written by him, translated into English and typed, but not signed, outlining seven points—some of which were considered by Cuba as essential for the maintenance of a minimally civilized coexistence between the two countries. The first and most important, of course, dealt with the terrorist actions committed against Cuba throughout the previous eight years, planned and financed by organizations legally established in Florida:

> An important subject. The terrorist activities against Cuba continue, paid for by the Cuban American National Foundation, using Central American mercenaries. There were two new attempts to explode bombs in our tourist centers, before and after the pope's visit. In the first case, those responsible were able to escape, going back by air to Central America without achieving their objectives, abandoning equipment and explosives that were seized. In the second attempt, three mercenaries of Guatemalan nationality carrying explosives and equipment were arrested. They were to receive 1,500 dollars for each bomb to explode in Cuba.
>
> Both cases were contracted and sponsored by agents of the network created by the Cuban American National Foundation. Now they plan to explode bombs on planes of Cuban airline companies or any other country's airline that travels to Cuba carrying tourists to and from Latin American countries. The method is similar: place a small device and a powerful explosive charge in some hidden spot on the plane, set the detonator in a digital clock that can be programmed for up to 99 hours later, and leave the plane at its destination. The explosion will take place on the ground or later in mid-flight.
>
> These are truly diabolical procedures: mechanisms easy to set up, minimal training for their use and almost total impunity. The United States police and intelligence agencies have sufficient, reliable information on the leaders responsible. If they really wanted to, they could abort this new form of terrorism on time. But it will be impossible to curb if the United States does not comply with the elementary duty to combat it. The responsibility to do so cannot be left up to Cuba alone. Very soon any country in the world could be the victim of such acts.

The other points in the secret message referred to topics of mutual interest, like the resumption of commercial flights between the US and Cuba, suspended since the downing of the Cessnas two years earlier, and Fidel's thanks for a favorable report from the Pentagon on the military situation of the Island, according to which "Cuba represents no danger to the security of the United States." At the end, Fidel also expressed his thanks "for the comments made by Clinton to Nelson Mandela and Kofi Annan in relation to Cuba." Before the writer left the Palace of the Revolution in Havana, holding the sealed envelope, Fidel suggested that he ask Clinton, "if the circumstances were propitious," two questions that should appear to be García Márquez's own initiative. The marathon of the following weeks would end up yielding a 4,000-word narrative written by the Nobel Prize laureate to Fidel Castro, with details of how he had discharged his mission. Arriving at Princeton on Saturday, April 25, García Márquez telephoned Bill Richardson to inform him that his work at the university would keep him until Thursday, April 30, and that he would remain in Washington, awaiting the audience with the president, from May 1 to 5, when he would return home to Mexico City. At the end of the conversation, he added that he was carrying "an urgent message for President Clinton," without revealing anything about its contents or the identity of the sender.

When the literary workshop at Princeton was over, García Márquez was met in Washington by disheartening news. A Richardson aide called him to say that the president would not be able to receive him: he would be in California until May 6, when Márquez would already have returned to Mexico. As an alternative, the official suggested a meeting with Sandy Berger, the national security advisor at the White House, who had authority to receive the message in Clinton's name. As Fidel had enjoined him to deliver the envelope only to the president in person, the writer proposed another solution: if the cancellation of the audience was just a matter of the incompatbility of dates, he was willing to prolong his stay in Washington until Clinton returned. The official promised to relay the proposal to Richardson and hung up. The phone call left him with a nagging doubt and rekindled the feeling of "grim suspicion." The security services seemed to be maneuvering so that the message would be read first by them and only afterward by the president of the United States.

As he mentioned in his personal report to Fidel Castro weeks later, García Márquez was in no hurry and could wait. Committed to finishing his autobiography, entitled *Living to Tell the Tale*, he made the most of his spare time to work. "I had written more than twenty pages of my memoirs on the idyllic Princeton campus," he wrote to Fidel, "and the pace had not diminished in the impersonal hotel room in Washington where I spent as much as ten hours a day." The real reason for staying days on end in a hotel room, however, was something else. The Colombian got "shivers down my spine" to think that, in his absence, the antiquated safe inside his wardrobe could be secretly opened by someone interested in the contents of the sealed envelope inside. "The safe didn't seem at all reliable," he explained, "because it had no combination lock but a key that looked like it had been bought at a convenience store." The paranoia forced him to stay shut up in his room almost the whole time: "I wrote, had lunch, had dinner and received visitors in the room, always keeping an eye on the safe." He spoke only what was absolutely necessary on the phone, convinced the line was tapped. On the rare occasions he left the room—usually when he'd had enough of the hotel food and made a quick escape to Provence, a French bistro—the writer would carry the key in his pocket and on his return would make sure the envelope was still intact and in the same position. One of the times he went out was for a brief visit to the Cuban Interests Section in Maryland, three kilometers from the White House. With the help of the mission chief there, Fernando Remírez, he sent a coded message to Havana summarizing what had happened. That evening Remírez brought Cuba's reply to the hotel, and from its style García Márquez recognized the author as Fidel Castro. The Cuban president politely requested that he stay in the American capital for as long it took to accomplish the mission, and would appreciate his making sure Sandy Berger did not feel disparaged by being rejected as a go-between. He ended with the kind hope Gabo would use the time to "write a lot" while he waited.

On Monday night the writer left the hotel to have dinner at the home of his countryman and friend César Gaviria, ex-president of Colombia and then secretary general of the OAS. Apparently aware of the existence of the message and the identity of its sender, but not of its contents, Gaviria had also invited Clinton's best friend, Thomas "Mack" McLarty, who had just left the post of presidential advisor for Latin America, but continued to work as a counselor to the president in the West Wing, a few steps from the Oval Office. Before the American arrived at his house, and without disclosing how he had become acquainted with the matter, Gaviria helped García Márquez to "get things straight," as the latter put it. "He explained to me that Clinton's advisors' precautions were normal, because of the political and security risks it would imply for a president of the United States to be handed such delicate information personally, and through unorthodox channels." Although it had been, in his words, "enjoyable and fruitful," the evening brought only the promise that McLarty would intercede with Clinton so that the audience be granted as soon as possible. On Tuesday morning, again via the Interests Section, García Márquez sent another query to Havana: should the president decide not to receive him and delegate the task to McLarty and Berger, to which one should he deliver the envelope? Hours later he found out that Fidel was more inclined toward McLarty, but insisted in taking care "not to offend Berger." The message ended with a phrase that Gabo described as "the most compromising consent" he had ever been given: "We trust your talents." The same day he had a phone call from McLarty's office telling him that he would be received the following morning in the White House, not by the president but by McLarty, to whom he should deliver the message, and by three senior officials of the National Security Council—not including Sandy Berger.

Promptly at a quarter past eleven on the morning of Wednesday, May 6, as scheduled, the presidential advisor greeted the writer with a hug, introduced him to the three officials and ushered them all to the sofas in front of his work desk. He put his hands on his knees and announced with a smile:

"We're at your service."

García Márquez started by stressing that this was not an official visit, to which all four nodded their heads, and went on to describe briefly the meeting with Fidel where the idea had come up to send the missive to Clinton. He took the sealed envelope out of his pocket and handed it to McLarty, asking him to read the typed notes in English and, if possible, to comment on them. As he already knew the text by heart, the Colombian had no written notes with him. However, determined not to rely that much on his memory, he had taken the precaution of noting in an electronic organizer the two questions that Fidel had asked him to put to Clinton "if circumstances were favorable." While McLarty was reading the document, he made two short observations: "That's terrible!" and "We have common enemies …" When the American finished reading and passed on the six typed, double-spaced pages to his colleagues, García Márquez reckoned that now was an opportune moment to ask the first question suggested by Fidel:

"Do you think it's possible for the FBI to make contact with their Cuban counterparts for a joint fight against terrorism?"

Before anyone could answer, the writer added what he called "a line of my own making":

"I'm convinced that this idea would be met with a positive and immediate response by the Cuban authorities."

The first to speak was Richard Clarke, who besides being director of multilateral affairs at the NSC was also Clinton's advisor on terrorism and narcotraffic:

"The idea's very good, but the FBI does not take part in investigations where the results are leaked to the papers. Are the Cubans willing to keep the matter a secret?"

The writer answered with one of his favorite phrases:

"There's nothing a Cuban likes more than keeping secrets."

The impact of the proposal obscured the second question, where Fidel wanted to know if cooperation on security issues could not open the way for the resumption of travel by Americans to Cuba, suspended some decades previously. The indifferent reaction to this of the four men left García Márquez in no doubt that they "didn't have, didn't know of, or didn't want to reveal any immediate plans in that direction." Clarke, who was noting down everything that was said, led the conversation back to the terrorism topic and said that he would instruct the US Interests Section in Havana to prepare a proposal to implement the idea of a joint effort between the two countries' security services to fight terrorism. As had been arranged, fifty minutes into the meeting, McLarty stood up and held out his hand to the visitor. "Your mission was indeed of the utmost importance," he said, "and you carried it out very well." A compliment that, according to the gratified Gabo, he refused to allow to be lost "to the ephemeral glory of the microphones hidden in the flower vases in the room."

In the report that he sent to Fidel Castro, the writer highlighted that at no point during the meeting was there any mention of "democratic reforms, free elections or human rights, nor any of the political sermonizing with which the Americans usually condition any project of cooperation with Cuba." García Márquez left the White House feeling sure that the envelope would be delivered by McLarty to Clinton "in the relaxed atmosphere of the end of some meal." The die had been cast.

13

SIX FBI AGENTS ARRIVE SECRETLY IN HAVANA AND RETURN TO THE UNITED STATES WITH A CRATE FULL OF REPORTS ON THE FLORIDA ORGANIZATIONS PRODUCED BY ORDER OF FIDEL CASTRO

On the eve of Gabriel García Márquez's trip to Princeton, the González family had grown a little more. At the end of the day on April 24, 1998, Olga gave birth to Ivett, a cute, chubby baby with light-colored skin and black hair just like her mother, and greenish eyes like René's. She was born at Jackson Memorial, the same university hospital in Miami where Tony Guerrero—still living with Maggie in Key West, and working at the naval air base in Boca Chica—had been born forty years before. The pregnancy had developed without problems; the only difficulties had been financial. The poor quality of public health services in the United States pushed the couple into exorbitant private medical costs. "At our first appointment in a private hospital, the first thing they asked for was the credit card, even before they asked our names," Olga would remember, shocked to see the receptionist charge them $700, almost half of the monthly family budget. By luck, one of René's student pilots was co-owner of a private clinic where Olga was looked after, free of charge, during her pregnancy. That was not the first nor would it be the last time that the couple resorted to *sociolismo* or "partnerism," a neologism used by Cubans both on the Island and in Miami to refer to informal networks of reciprocal help. It would also be thanks to this practice that, three months after Ivett's birth, they were able to enroll the girl for free in a Kendall day care center. Her status as a foreigner prevented Olga from benefitting from maternity leave, forcing her to return to work when the child was only a few weeks old. Because his schedule was more flexible, René was in charge of taking his daughters to school and the day care center in the mornings and picking them up again at the end of the afternoon. During the week, the mother had a chance to be with the girls only at night when she came home from Inglés Ahora, and most of the time found one, or both of them, sunk in a deep sleep. Besides shuttling back and forth, René shared domestic chores such as washing dishes, bottle-feeding Ivett and changing her diapers.

It was at this time that Cuba's Department of State Security launched the operation that would send in another man to the Wasp Network, short-handed since February 1996, with Juan Pablo Roque's return to Cuba. The role of the new agent would be to replace Ramón "Urso" Labañino, one of Gerardo Hernández's three lieutenants. The big bear had been selected for a "special mission"—apparently to increase surveillance over Orlando Bosch. Since July 1997, Havana had already been preparing his replacement. It was Fernando González—no relation to René, whom he didn't even know—a thirty-five-year-old *habanero*, with a black mustache, light skin and with a resumé very similar to the rest of his colleagues. Joining the Young Communist League aged seventeen, at twenty-three he enlisted as a volunteer to fight in Angola, where he served for two years as a tank driver and from where he returned with a medal, and was admitted to the Cuban Communist Party. From information supplied by his wife—the economist Rosa Aurora, a pleasant, small, blonde woman with blue eyes, three years younger than her husband—we know that like Gerardo Hernández, whom he also didn't know, González had done a course in international relations at the University of Havana, and planned to follow a diplomatic career. Fernando González's official biography, produced by Cuban government bodies, states that between 1989, at the end of his tour of duty in Angola, and 1998, when he moved to Miami, he had worked in economic and diplomatic missions in capitalist countries as part of Cuba's effort to find commercial partners that could fill the hole left by the collapse of the USSR. The correspondence of the Wasp Network agents with Havana affords a glimpse of how his arrival in Miami was anticipated with great excitement by the group already in the United States. In the messages where he was referred to as "the famous Vicky"—one of the aliases he would adopt—nothing suggests, however, that this fame derived from his achievements as a diplomat or as a pioneer in commercial markets. The paperwork amassed by the FBI on the Wasp Network, on the contrary, proves that before moving to Miami, Fernando González lived secretly in Fayetteville, North Carolina, a city where the American police suspected "he very likely had tried to get close to local military facilities." On the eve of traveling to Florida, González sent a message to Key West introducing himself to Tony Guerrero:

> Brother: When you read this, we will have already met in person, which makes me proud because of the political, operational and human quality of the comrades who, like yourself, are carrying out missions in enemy territory so that our families and our people in general can rest easy.

In line with the plan conceived in Villa Marista, González would begin to use the name of Rubén Campa when he moved to Miami. It was not a false name, chosen by chance. As had happened with Gerardo Hernández, whose identity as Manuel Viramóntez had been built on the fake documents of an American who had died in infancy, the real Rubén Campa was born in California in September 1965 and died seven months later. Requested by Cuban agents at the parish records office where the baby had been registered, Campa's birth certificate had made it possible to prepare all the documentation that would be used by Fernando González in the United States. In correspondence with Cuba he would be identified by the code names Vicky, Oscar, Camilo and Hipólito González.

A busy summer was awaiting the new Cuban agent in Florida. At the end of May, information sent by the Wasp Network allowed

Cuba to intercept a speedboat coming from Florida, whose crew had planned to unload their cargo, a shipment of arms and ammunition, on the coast of Minas de Matahambre, in the province of Pinar del Río. On the boat they seized four assault rifles, three American and one Chinese, two 12-gauge shotguns, two Magnum pistols and one Makarov, a high-powered crossbow with twenty steel arrows, 6,000 bullets and cartridges, two bales of camouflage material, ten "ninja" style masks, canteens, canned food, first aid medication, a radio transmitter, a satellite cell phone, three packages containing counterfeit Cuban pesos, inflatable life rafts, packets of leaflets inciting revolt against the Cuban government and a set of nautical charts of the northern Cuban coastline. On being arrested, the crew members Ernesto Abreu Horta and Vicente Marcelino Martínez Rodríguez, both exiled Cubans living in Miami, confessed that they planned to deliver the small arsenal to internal anti-government groups. In the middle of June, also on a tip-off from the Wasp Network, Cuban police arrested another Central American mercenary who had relapsed into crime. Trying to enter the Island among a group of Guatemalan tourists, the Salvadoran Otto Rodríguez Llerena was arrested carrying two detonators, two Casio calculator-alarm clocks and a half a kilo of C-4 plastic explosive—128 grams camouflaged in a tube of shampoo, 112 grams in a stick of deodorant, 67 grams inside a tube of toothpaste and 209 grams concealed in the heels of his shoes. In August of the previous year, Llerena had escaped from Cuba after blowing up the lobby of the Meliá Cohiba hotel in Havana. During the interrogation, the mercenary confessed that he had been recruited and funded by Ignacio Medina, none other than Luis Posada Carriles.

On June 16, one week after Rodríguez Llerena's arrest, an executive jet landed on a noncommercial runway at the José Martí Airport in Havana, out of sight of passersby and passengers. The plane had taken off from Washington carrying on board an FBI chief, the intelligence officers Agustín Rodríguez and Thomas Mohnal, a US Army colonel and two counterterrorist experts. The presence of such an extraordinary delegation on Cuban soil was the first consequence of the operation triggered two months earlier in the White House by Gabriel García Márquez. During the five days they spent in Cuba, under the strictest confidentiality, the group visited only three addresses: the US Interests Section, where they all stayed, the Villa Marista facilities and the seven-story building decorated with a gigantic silhouette of Che Guevara, on Revolution Square, the headquarters of the Ministry of the Interior.

The American agents were able to meet with the jailed mercenaries without any Cuban witnesses, probably for the first time since the triumph of the Revolution in 1959. Apart from that, in the short time they stayed in Havana, the FBI had access to a small crate packed with 175 folders and five audio and eight video tapes with testimony given by the imprisoned terrorists and sixteen hours of telephone conversation transcripts between the Central Americans and their recruiters, in which their relationship to Posada Carriles was laid bare, as was his relationship to the leaders of the CANF. Copies of all the material were already packed and ready for the group to take to the United States. Of the mountain of documents offered by Cuba to the Americans, sixty files contained the detailed personal records of forty exiles—labeled "terrorists of Cuban origin"—directly involved in the planning or execution of the attacks, with names, family affiliations, nicknames, personal and business addresses, biometric data and how to locate each one of them. Another fifty files contained information and copies of documents that tracked the funds supplied by the CANF to various Florida groups to carry out terrorist actions against Cuba. The material also included another bulky portfolio with photographs of the weapons, explosives and equipment seized in each action. A good part of the information from the dossier that Fidel Castro had ordered to be put together was the result, as the Cuban president himself would make public months later, of the eight years of the Wasp Network's activities in the United States. Before they set off home, the FBI directors said they were impressed with the abundance of evidence gathered, and promised to give a reply in a few weeks.

The character most cited in the documentation submitted by the Cubans to the FBI evinced not the least concern to hide his role in the organization and financing of the terrorist campaign against Cuba. Fifteen days after the American agents' secret trip to Havana, Luis Posada Carriles gave a long interview to journalists Larry Rohter and Ann Louise Bardach, published in two editions of the *New York Times*. The reporters' work had been prepared by more than a hundred interviews and by research in CIA and FBI archives. In thirteen hours of recorded deposition from a location "somewhere in the Caribbean," Posada confessed that he had organized the campaign of terrorist attacks against Cuban tourist centers. He also cited CANF as the financial backer of it all and stated that Jorge Mas Canosa, its president, had personally overseen the flow of money and the logistical support for the operations. "Mas Canosa controlled everything," Posada declared to the newspaper. "Whenever I needed money, he said to give me $5,000, give me $10,000, give me $15,000, and they sent it to me." When he admitted to being the financier of Raúl Ernesto Cruz León in the planting of the bombs at the Havana hotels, the journalists asked how he felt about the Italian Fabio di Celmo, killed in the Copacabana Hotel attack. Posada replied that the tourist "was sitting in the wrong place at the wrong time." At his trial years later, the Cuban evaded the issue and alleged that his difficulties with English may have caused the reporters to mistake his meaning.

The American delegation was still in Cuba when Fernando González, duly disguised as Rubén Campa, disembarked in Miami, after a trip that had begun in Havana, had gone through Cancún and then made a stop at Point M-2, as the Mexican capital was known in the agents' jargon. Unknown to him, already waiting at the airport were the FBI agents Joseph Hall, Alex García and Ángel Berlinghieri, entrusted with monitoring him from that moment on. There is nothing to suggest that González was to undertake any fieldwork, like infiltrating organizations or producing reports about anti-Castroist militants. Judging by the information supplied by Cuba and the documentation seized by the FBI, his task was limited to collecting, organizing and passing on the material produced by the group to Gerardo Hernández. During the initial contacts he had with each of the agents who would answer to him, he did not stick to purely professional matters, but also showed some interest in knowing if everything was going well in their personal lives. For the majority of those in exile, in fact, the move from Cuba to Florida had not entailed all-out cultural shock. "The Cubans who escaped the Revolution developed a veritable nostalgia industry in Miami," the writer Noberto Fuentes observed, himself an exile, in his book *An Autobiography of Fidel Castro*. "They sell old postcards of Cuba, they print the Havana phone book of the '50s and reprint old issues of the magazine *Bohemia*," wrote Fuentes. "They make the same brands of beer and soft drinks and give the restaurants the same names they had in the Cuban capital."

The fourteen members of the Wasp Network followed similar routines: participating in anti-Castroist groups and holding a normal job that kept up their disguise. As the organizations' activities were more intense at weekends, there was very little time left for leisure or to spend with their families. Amarilys Silverio, "Julia," for example, braved a ten-hour work day as a receptionist in the Peñalver medical clinic in Little Havana, and still devoted her Saturdays to the meetings of Alpha 66, the organization responsible for various terrorist attacks on Cuba—and whose head, Andrés Nazario Sargén, had given her an autographed copy of his memoirs signed with an affectionate message. In no way did the group's routine have any of the charm and sophistication displayed by secret agents in spy movies. Even the group's leader, Giro, was often obliged to put aside diskettes, pagers and coded radio *pitirres* in order to try and sell his cartoons to the city's newspapers, and more than once complained about the pittance he received for his work. "It's very rare for the *Miami Herald* to buy cartoons from artists who don't work in-house," he wrote in one report sent to Havana, "and if so they pay a hundred dollars at most for each drawing published." Though faced with similar difficulties, René had been able to stabilize his life even on a tight budget and with a growing family. Irmita's memories of those days could not have been better. "René went back to being the same father of my childhood, who used to sit and chat with me and take me and my friends to the movies," she recalled as an adult. "And, since I was so disorganized, he used to clean my bedroom and bathroom and was always helping me to keep my own personal things tidy." When Irma's little sister Ivett was four months old, Olga managed to fix it so she could leave work early on Fridays. This would allow her, at least on this day of the week, to pick up the children from school and the nursery and enjoy their company a little longer. On September 11, 1998, she left the office at the end of the afternoon, collected the children and arrived at their Kendall apartment at nightfall. To the surprise of all three René was waiting for them, unusually for a Friday night, when he normally attended meetings of the Democracy group. When dinner was over, and after helping his older daughter with her homework, the father stretched out on the reclining sofa that became Irmita's bed at night and started playing with the two girls. Sitting nearby, Olga was delighted by the scene and took some photographs of the three of them with the small camera that the couple used to keep a record of their daughters as they were growing up.

At that exact time, the men who would put an end to the González family's peace and quiet and that of the whole Wasp Network were assembled a few kilometers from the Kendall apartment. They consisted of 200 policemen, some in uniforms and heavy black boots, some in suits, massed together in the auditorium of the the spacious FBI headquarters in Florida. Commanded personally by Héctor Pesquera, a sturdy, bearded, white-haired Puerto Rican who, in May of that year, had taken the helm of the state police body, the group consisting of FBI agents and SWAT teams, both men and women, was receiving the final briefing for an operation the likes of which had not been seen in Miami for a long time.

At the stroke of five thirty in the morning, Olga was awakened by the rhythmic sound of helicopter blades beating the air outside her apartment, bathing its interior with the strong bluish beam of a searchlight mounted on the craft. Before the family understood what was going on, the front door was knocked down with a crash. An unknown number of armed officers, between ten and fifteen men and women as far as René, Olga and Irmita could remember, burst into the little apartment. Amid the children's screams, the invaders—some wearing helmets and ninja-type face masks—ran into the couple's bedroom, yanked René out of bed and threw him face down on the floor, cuffing his hands behind his back. In the sights of the others' weapons, agent Mark D'Amico—whom René later referred to as "a courteous and respectful man"—bent down, took a piece of paper from his pocket and, just like in the movies, read the first lines from the Miranda rights, also known as the "Right to remain silent":

"You are under arrest for espionage against the United States. You have the right to remain silent and you have the right to an attorney. Anything you do say from now on can and will be used against you in a court of law."

At the very moment Olga and René's home was invaded, further groups of FBI officers and SWAT police were carrying out identical, equally showy operations at twelve more addresses in Florida. Among the members of the commando that raided Tony and Maggie's little white house in Key West, the American woman was astonished to recognize a man who had been posing as a Cuban exile and who in the last months had become her regular massage client; his real identity was George Quesada, FBI special agent. The raid on the apartment of Gerardo Hernández in Sunny Isles, east of Miami, was directed personally by Héctor Pesquera, coordinator of the entire operation. At three of the addresses the police found no one. By mere chance, that night the Cuban agents Ricardo "Horacio" Villarreal, Remijio "Marcelino" Luna and Alberto Manuel Ruiz, known as Miguel and A-4, were not sleeping at home. By seven o'clock on Saturday morning the Wasp Network no longer existed. The first people to be informed by Pesquera of the operation's success were neither his immediate superior, Louis Joseph Freeh, director of the FBI, nor the attorney general, Janet Reno, who had authorized the invasions, but two Cuban American members of Congress, Lincoln Díaz-Balart and Ileana Ros-Lehtinen.

All those arrested were taken to the Federal Detention Center, a twenty-story prison in bustling Downtown Miami where thousands of foreign tourists daily jostle in search of electronic gadgets. Olga and her daughters remained in their home, without handcuffs but under the close watch of an armed policeman, while his colleagues combed every square inch of the apartment, hunting for evidence that might support the charges. Books, ornaments and even the girls' toys, nothing escaped inspection. Anything that could be regarded as evidence was put into a black canvas bag. When a policewoman approached the shelf where the camera had been left the night before, Olga watched her anxiously and breathed a sigh of relief when the agent took no interest in it, leaving it where it was. The photos of René with her daughters were safe.

It was late afternoon when the group called off the search and withdrew from the apartment, taking the bag of seized material including even kitchen knives. Armed police remained on the premises, one inside the apartment with Olga and the girls, two outside the door, and two more at the building entrance on the first floor. Pretending to be calm, Olga cuddled the girls and comforted them in a low voice, and only spoke to the policeman to ask permission to get them some food from the refrigerator in the kitchen. Going to the toilet or even changing Ivett's diapers in the couple's bedroom was only allowed when accompanied by a policewoman. At one point, the cop who was guarding the three of them asked if he could use the apartment's only bathroom, which opened off the room where they were. Olga nodded and the policeman asked his colleague who was keeping guard in the hall to stay alert while he relieved himself. After a few minutes the mother and the girls heard the toilet flush. The policeman turned the door handle one way and then the other, but the door didn't open. He tried again, at first quietly, and then obviously getting nervous, to no avail: the door remained locked. Irmita said to her mother that she would show the policeman how to turn the door handle correctly, but Olga whispered in her ear: "No, no. Wait a minute, let him get a little scare in there." To see that big man, decked out in black boots and fatigues and holding a threatening rifle, stuck in an ordinary little bathroom, made Olga and Irmita burst into helpless giggles. Hearing the laughter and the desperate rattling of the agent trying to open the door, the man from the hall came into the small living room wanting to know what was going on. Olga finally let her daughter explain to the trapped policeman what the trick was to open the door: just a little push forward on the doorknob, and that was it. Sitting down again by her mother, the girl seemed proud to have helped free her jailer.

It was already night when two men in jackets and ties appeared and identified themselves as FBI agents. With a tape recorder switched on and making notes on paper pads, they announced that her husband was part of a Cuban government spy ring— "something you must know very well"—and that besides him, nine other agents had been arrested. "We came to ask if you're willing to cooperate with the United States government," said one of the policemen. And went on in menacing tones: "One of your daughters is an American citizen, but you and the older one are residents, you can be deported at any time." Olga didn't appear to be frightened by the threat of blackmail and replied she would do nothing before seeing her husband, to be sure he was well. Realizing that they were not going to get any useful information, the agents said that she would not be allowed to talk to him, but she could see him from a distance on Monday at the Miami Federal Courthouse when the prisoners would be presented in court.

Shortly after being taken from their homes, on that day at dawn, the Cubans were put into separate cells at the Detention Center. The same way they had gotten out of bed, without washing their faces, combing their hair or brushing their teeth, the ten detainees spent the Saturday and Sunday undergoing "persuasion interviews": this meant that any who accepted the accusation of spying and agreed to denounce the other members of the Wasp Network would have their sentences substantially reduced, and on release would enter the plea bargain and witness protection programs. All of them were alerted by the FBI interrogators to the fact that, in the United States, the crime of espionage was punishable with life imprisonment. Half of the group capitulated. Before the sun rose on Monday morning, Alejandro "Franklin" Alonso and the couples Linda and Nilo Hernández and Amarilys and Joseph Santos had already betrayed their comrades and made a deal with the prosecutor's office. The remaining five, Gerardo "Viramóntez" Hernández, Ramón "Urso" Labañino, Fernando "Rubén Campa" González,

Tony Guerrero and René González refused the offers of negotiation, denied that they had spied on the United States and declared they were willing to face the risks arising from their actions. Hernández, Labañino and González would keep up their respective covers for many months. In his "persuasion interview," with Pesquera himself in charge, Hernández had the chance, for the first time, to exercise his gifted memory. For hours at a time he recited and repeated the addresses, telephone numbers and names related to the time he had supposedly lived in Puerto Rico. It was no easy task, since Pesquera was a Puerto Rican who had spent most of his life in San Juan, but Hernández didn't leave a single question unanswered. On Sunday night, the director of the FBI gave up, thumping the table:

"So you continue insisting you're a Puerto Rican and not a Cuban? Then get ready to spend the rest of your life inside. You're going to rot in this cell, because the Cuban government isn't going to lift a finger for a Puerto Rican spy."

On Monday morning, the entrance to the United States District Court for the Southern District of Florida was bustling. In the courtroom, separated only by a garden from the Federal Detention Center building where the ten Cubans were being held, anti-Castroist militant organizations fought with journalists for seats in the small auditorium of the room in which the defendants would be presented to Judge Joan Lenard. Olga, who was one of the first to arrive accompanied by her eldest daughter, was approached by an apprehensive leader of an anti-Castroist group:

"Do you know a guy called Manuel Viramóntez?"

She said she didn't, that she had never heard the name before.

"I don't mean to scare you, but a journalist told me that René is involved with a Puerto Rican spy called Manuel Viramóntez."

Under the pretext of securing a good place, Olga excused herself and sat next to Irmita in the front row. As they waited for the judge to arrive, four enormous men in gray trousers, ties and navy-blue blazers showing the "US Marshal" badge roamed around the room, ensuring adherence to the court's strict rules and regulations, such as maintaining low voice levels, and a ban on recording, filming or photographic devices. Newspapers and TV channels that wanted to reproduce court scenes would have to buy the drawings made by Jeanne Boggs, the elderly official court illustrator, who, despite being seated a few steps from the defendants' bench, inexplicably used binoculars to do her work. A journalist was told off for placing his glasses on his head while jotting on a notepad—some nineteenth-century law forbidding the use, within the confines of the courtroom, of "hats, caps, or any other adornments." At nine o'clock in the morning a marshal rang a bell and announced through a microphone that the judge had arrived:

"Her Honor, Judge Joan Lenard."

The public stood up for the entrance of an expressionless young woman with dark hair and eyes. She sat down in her high-backed chair, turned on the microphone and without any initial address, read out in a solemn voice the paper the marshal had placed on the table.

"The United States of America versus Rubén Campa and Associates. The marshals will please bring in the defendants."

Only then did it become clear that among the "Associates" was Juan Pablo Roque, who would be tried *in absentia*. A murmur in the crowd broke the silence when the door to the left of the judge opened to allow the ten prisoners into the room. Accompanied by a group of marshals who also wore gray trousers and blue blazers, the defendants had their hands manacled behind their backs and their feet in chains, which forced them to walk with slow, shuffling steps. With the exception of Gerardo Hernández and his two assistants, none had ever laid eyes on any of their fellow prisoners. They all wore orange uniforms and their physical appearance was terrible, given that brushing their teeth had been the only form of personal hygiene allowed them since the moment of their arrest. They had dark circles under their eyes and their faces were unshaven. "Those sweaty men with the appearance of delinquents," the conservative Puerto Rican newspaper *El Veraz* would publish the next day, "provoked a combination of fear and laughter from the audience." When René entered the room, Irmita broke the solemnity of the court by raising her hand in a thumbs-up and shouting, to the great discomfort of the marshals:

"Daddy! Daddy!"

The guards escorting the defendants unlocked the handcuffs and chains, allowing them to sit down. Apart from René, only Tony had someone in the audience: his girlfriend Maggie Becker, who sat in the front row. This would be the shortest court session of the whole trial and would comprise of the presentation of the defendants, the reading of the felonies imputed to them and the announcement of the names of the prosecutors and of the public defenders selected at random for each defendant. The group stood accused of "conspiracy to commit espionage," "acting as foreign agents not registered with the American government," "falsifying documents," and "perjury in filling Immigration Service forms." The prosecution would fall to the attorneys Caroline Heck Miller, David Buckner, Guy Lewis and John Kastrenakes.

Gerardo Hernández would be defended by Paul McKenna, Ramón Labañino by William Norris, Fernando González by Joaquín Méndez, Tony Guerrero by Jack Blumenfeld and René González by Philip Horowitz. The first three were still being addressed by their respective code names, Manuel Viramóntez, Luis Medina and Rubén Campa. As a mere judicial formality, the judge also announced the names of the lawyers in charge of defending the five remaining prisoners, benefitted by the agreement they had made with the prosecution and the FBI. Considered a fugitive, Juan Pablo Roque did not have the right to a defense lawyer.

The only Cuban American among the group of lawyers named by the judge was Joaquín Méndez. A thin man in his fifties, with a severe face and gray goatee, Méndez had emigrated to Miami with his family shortly after Batista's government was overthrown. The news that he had been selected to defend a secret agent accused of pro-Cuba espionage caused something of a conflict of conscience for him. Méndez feared upsetting his father, an octogenarian who had escaped Cuba and had never stopped being anti-Castroist, despite disagreeing with the violent actions by the Miami groups against the government of his country. Although US legislation allows public defenders to refuse a client, so long as they present plausible reasons to the court, Méndez preferred facing the problem head-on:

by consulting the old man. On the day he received the notification, he went to his father's house and told him what had happened. The elderly man, who had learned of the arrests from the press, took some minutes to think and asked his son if the arrested agents had acted in the United States for money. "No, sir," Méndez replied. "They claim they were here to protect Cuba." The father put an end to the conversation by pronouncing four words: "Then accept the case." Ten years later, while sipping a *mojito* at the Gato Tuerto bar during a trip to Havana, the lawyer would remember this incident with a smile. "On that day I discovered," Méndez would say, "that my father hated Fidel Castro but he abhorred mercenaries."

It was not yet ten in the morning when Judge Lenard closed the hearing. Once again handcuffed and chained, the prisoners were removed from the courthouse and taken back under heavy escort to the Federal Detention Center across the street. The group that had formed at the door of the building, before the session opened, had turned into a small crowd of journalists, curious bystanders and anti-Castroist groups carrying posters and shouting slogans against Fidel Castro, communism and the Cuban Revolution. A paperboy was hawking the extra edition of one of Miami's Spanish-language dailies, with extensive coverage on *los cinco espías* (the five spies). Along with other information, the newspaper published an interview done that morning with Russian immigrant Henry Reizman, manager of the building and owner of the apartment rented by Gerardo Hernández. "Mr. Viramóntez was a very pleasant tenant, a gentleman who was always well dressed, kept the apartment clean and tidy at all times, and I never saw him drunk or anything like that," he declared to the newspaper. "He lived a modest life, always trying to sell his drawings. He used to pay the rent late, up to a week late, but he always paid." Reizman remained convinced that Hernández was from Puerto Rico: "I don't believe this man is a spy, the FBI must be mistaken. The Virámontez I knew can't be a Cuban. I detest Cubans and I know very well how to distinguish a Cuban from a Puerto Rican."

Getting into her car after the hearing, Olga realized that she was being followed and filmed by a news team from Channel 23 that would pursue her up to the door of her building in Kendall, its entrance also crowded by journalists. Not answering any questions she hurriedly climbed the four flights of stairs, hand in hand with Irmita. Arriving home, she saw that someone had spray-painted a hammer and sickle, the symbols of communism, on the door of her apartment. Still shocked by everything that had happened, Olga tried to be calm and organize her thoughts. Without knowing what new surprises destiny had in store for her, she concluded that what was most urgent at that point was to ensure the survival of her daughters and herself—in other words, to keep her job. She knew, though, that the chances of keeping her job in telemarketing were slim. After all, there was no reason to suppose that an exiled Cuban like the owner of Inglés Ahora would continue employing "the wife of a pro-Castro spy." To her surprise, however, the boss reacted with unexpected understanding. "You weren't arrested and you're not even accused of anything, so as far as I'm concerned you're just a mother who needs to provide for two daughters," he said, adding in a confidential tone: "I've had problems with the FBI myself, and I know how disgusting these people are. You can come back to work immediately."

When they were removed from court, the prisoners didn't go back to the normal cells in the Federal Detention Center. They were taken to the twelfth floor, where the Special House Unit is located, known by the prison population as "the hole"—a name that struck dread into the hearts even of hardened criminals. It designated a few dozen solitary confinement cells measuring four meters by two, with a concrete slab covered by a mat for a bed, a small concrete table fixed to the wall, a small metal stool bolted to the floor, a toilet and a basin. The only natural light came from a vertical window fifteen centimeters wide by fifty in length, high up on the wall, sealed by thick armored glass—a needless precaution considering that not even a baby could have wriggled through such a narrow opening. Whenever he had to leave the cubicle, the prisoner was obliged to squat with his back to the door and put his hands through the slot so that the guard on the other side could secure his wrists with the dreaded black box. Unlike conventional handcuffs, attached to each other by a chain with two or three links that allow the hands some mobility, the black box, as the name suggests, is a black metal box the size of a cigarette packet, with two hoops fixed to the sides. Once locked, the black box impedes any kind of movement, inflicting cramps and painful muscular contractions on the prisoner. It was in this hell surrounded by luxury apartment blocks in the heart of Downtown Miami that Gerardo Hernández, Fernando González, René González, Tony Guerrero and Ramón Labañino spent the first seventeen months following their court appearance.

During this period, Olga managed to see her husband only twice. The first time, fifteen days after he went to jail, they didn't allow his daughters to go with her, which forced her to leave Irmita taking care of Ivett inside the car parked in a public lot. Taken by a prison guard to the top floor of the building, Olga was shown into a tiny room divided by a wall in the middle, the lower part made of masonry and the upper part of reinforced glass with a series of small holes that allowed the prisoner to communicate with the visitor. Minutes later, the door in the other half of the cubicle opened up and René walked in. As at the court hearing, he was dressed in an orange uniform, his feet chained together and hands secured behind his back by a black box. Once the iron door was closed, he squatted down and stuck his hands through the small rectangular window behind him, allowing the black box to be removed by the jailer outside the door. Both Olga and René needed to make a big effort to hold back the tears. As the visit was only for fifteen minutes, the time had to be used to deal with small family matters and practical things, like the girls' reactions to everything, and Olga keeping her job at Inglés Ahora. René told her that the police and the prosecution were continuing to insist that he make a deal, like the other five did, in exchange for early release—an offer that was probably being made as well to Hernández, González, Guerrero and Labañino. In his case the FBI had what they believed to be a powerful inducement, which had already been insinuated during several interrogation sessions: Olga and Irmita did not have American citizenship and therefore could be deported at any moment.

In the middle of the conversation, recorded the entire time by a video camera fixed to the ceiling, the guard opened the door and informed them that the visit was over.

Fearful of complicating further the prisoners' already delicate situation, the Cuban press published nothing on the FBI's dismantling of the Wasp Network. However, this discretion turned out to be pointless. Whether through radio or TV Martí, or via the infallible *radio bemba*, the news soon reached all Cubans. A week after the arrests, however, President Fidel Castro had been led for the first time to speak publicly on the subject. The day after his appearance at the 1998 Ibero-American Summit, in Oporto, Portugal, Fidel gave a long declaration to CNN. At the end of the interview, after the Cuban leader had already discussed a variety of topics, the reporter Lucia Newman asked for his opinion on the Cubans arrested in Miami, "accused of spying for your government." He began by saying that he found it "astounding" that the United States, "the country that does the most spying in the world," should accuse Cuba of espionage, "the country most spied on in the world." He continued:

"There's not a telephone call of mine to any political leader abroad that is not picked up and recorded by United States satellites and listening systems."

Fidel recognized that "sometimes" his country had infiltrated "counterrevolutionary organizations" of the United States, with the aim of obtaining information on terrorist activities against Cuba. "I believe that we do have and we will have the right to do this," he underlined, "as long as the United States permits people within its territory to organize armed sabotage, machine-gunning of tourist facilities, the bringing in of arms and explosives, and above all, brutal terrorist attacks." He accused the American authorities of "bad faith" and of setting up "a perfidious trap" by insinuating that the five Cubans were seeking information "on the American Armed Forces and about activities of the United States Army":

"They can say what they like and do what they like, but the only information that interests us relates exclusively to the terrorist acts against Cuba organized on American soil."

The response from Washington to the Cuban president's declarations was silence. In Miami, the solitary confinement of the prisoners whom Fidel had referred to as "men of good faith" had been temporarily lifted so that relatives in the United States could see them. Gerardo Hernández, Fernando González and Ramón Labañino had no family members in the country, and continued keeping up their false identities. Apart from René, the only one of the group to receive a visit was Tony Guerrero. Maggie Becker, who had only become aware of Guerrero's real activity on the day he was arrested, had not severed her relationship with the Cuban. Olga's second meeting with her husband would be permitted almost a year later, in August 1999, but the authorization to take her two daughters only benefitted Ivett, because Irmita was in Cuba on vacation with her paternal grandmother. Recognized in Western popular culture as a sign of bad luck, the date determined by the authorities for the visit—Friday, August 13—had a festive meaning for Cubans on the Island, being the day of Fidel Castro's seventy-second birthday. It also had a special meaning for the González family, because on that day René would turn forty-three. The few minutes that the couple spent together were hardly sufficient for the husband to warn her that the threat of her deportation to Cuba could imminently be carried out. Some days before, René had rejected a new offer by the prosecutor's office, transmitted to him by his attorney, Philip Horowitz, to accept at least to be a witness for the prosecution of the four other comrades in the "hole," without having to admit to spying against the United States. The refusal to accept any bargain would surely be punished with Olga's deportation.

When the visit was over, she went home with one resolution: next day she would leave her youngest daughter with Teté, René's maternal grandmother, an eighty-year-old widow who had lived in the United States since the 1960s. That Saturday morning she drove the 400 kilometers that separate Miami from the city of Sarasota, turned Ivett over to the care of her great-grandmother and returned to Miami. Only forty-eight hours would be needed to confirm she'd made the right decision. Early on Monday morning, as she was preparing to leave for work, Olga was arrested by the FBI and informed that her deportation had been decreed by the American authorities. After spending three months among common criminals in a Fort Lauderdale prison, on November 22 she was put on a US Immigration Services plane to be sent back to Havana, where Irmita was already. On the same flight were ten rafters, who had been posted on the list of "excludable foreigners." Olga would only see Ivett again months later, when Irma, René's mother, received authorization to visit her son in prison and on her return to Cuba took her little granddaughter with her.

Scheduled to begin in September of that year, the trial ended up being delayed for several months due to an appeal lodged by the lawyers of the five. In their petition to Judge Lenard, the defense lawyers applied for the venue to be moved to another city. Their argument was that the climate of hate and intolerance prevailing in Miami against everything that smelt of the Cuban Revolution meant a biased jury, practically guaranteeing a conviction. This was no rhetorical contention or delaying tactic. Among the dozens of public demonstrations of the prejudice that poisoned a good part of the Cuban community in Florida, the incident involving the Brazilian singer Denise de Kalafe was among the most notorious. Acclaimed among the Hispanic public as a performer of romantic ballads since she moved to Mexico in the mid-1980s, de Kalafe had signed a very lucrative contract to participate in the most famous popular festival in Miami, the Calle Ocho Carnaval. A few days before the gig, the artist found out through the papers that her name had been vetoed by the Cuban American businessman Leslie Pantin Jr., the festival organizer, for the simple reason that she had performed in Cuba some months before. Contract in hand, the Brazilian filed a lawsuit against Pantin in the Florida courts, at the end of which she pocketed $3 million in personal damages— money she chose to donate to charities in Miami.

To legitimize their request for a change of venue, the lawyers for the Cuban agents asked Judge Lenard to release funds to pay for a public opinion survey that would evaluate the feelings of the Miami population towards the case of the five. Contradicting the famed agility of American justice, the authorization was granted only a year later, in November 1999, but it was worth the wait. Delivered to the court one month before jury selection, the poll confirmed the misgivings of the defense. Indeed their argument would be endorsed by Robert Pastor, an impartial professor of international relations who had been Carter's national security advisor for Latin America: "Holding a trial for five Cuban intelligence agents in Miami," declared Pastor to the *New York Times*, "is about as fair as the trial of an Israeli intelligence agent in Tehran."

14

A PORTRAIT OF CUBAN MIAMI: THE MILITANT ANTI-CASTROIST RODOLFO FRÓMETA, THE PRO-CUBAN JOURNALIST MAX LESNIK AND THE MARXIST WRITER NORBERTO FUENTES

Sunday mornings in Miami are usually calm and peaceful. In general people like to get up late and go for brunch around midday, not at home, but in restaurants and hotels. In the quietness of dawn, the only noise heard by the few residents jogging in the city's wooded streets and avenues comes from the air conditioners turned on in almost every house. That is, when the long-awaited, well-deserved weekend rest is not interrupted by the loud arrival of *El Jefe*, "The Chief," at the wheel of his big white SUV. The Chief is what the Cuban exile Rodolfo Frómeta calls himself. At five-foot-two, the sixty-year-old Frómeta sports hairy eyebrows, a thick black beard and a flat nose. Confident in the constitutional precept whereby the law of silence is overridden by the freedom of expression, every Sunday at crack of dawn he covers his head with a black beret, takes his Ford Bronco out of the garage, turns on the speakers on the jeep's hood and starts off slowly on his round of anti-Castroist preaching, which always begins with the same battle cry:

"Wake up, fellow countrymen!"

Indifferent to the protests, often couched in bad language, emanating from people's windows, he winds leisurely through the streets that cross the deserted Le Jeune Avenue, one of the city's main thoroughfares.

"Wake up, Cubans! Wake up, for our homeland is in danger!"

Named on one of the index cards in the register of "individuals linked to terrorism" given by Cuba to the FBI, Rodolfo Frómeta is perhaps the character who best represents the stereotype of the exiled Cuban that led the lawyers of the five detained men to request the transfer of the trial from Miami to another city in Florida. The little man dressed in camouflage who introduces himself as "the hero of a thousand battles" is the leader of the F4 Commandos, an anti-Castroist organization installed in a modest room in Little Havana and registered at City Hall under the pompous name of Comandos F4 Partido Uno Inc. In the cafés of Miami's Cuban neighborhood, some people sneer that every battle commanded by *El Jefe* was waged in total safety in the humid swamps of the Everglades. That's where he and his few followers stage combats that almost invariably end with the arrest and summary judgement of "Fidel Castro," impersonated by one of the group members. Over the years, the journalists attending his press conferences have grown ever fewer. In the tiny, stuffy room on West Flagler Street, Frómeta welcomes the press surrounded by a "general staff" made up of his wife, one of her sons, his brother-in-law and a childhood friend, all in camouflage gear. On such occasions he trumpets "the last attack by the organization against the tyrant Castro" or against "the repression services of the dictatorship." If some inexperienced reporter asks to see evidence of the prospective actions, his retort is that "a patriot needs to give explanations to no one."

His comedic features do not mean, however, that the strutting Frómeta is a harmless opponent of the Cuban Revolution. In 1968 he fled the Island by jumping over the wire fence protecting the Guantánamo naval base—the same one José Basulto had bypassed a couple of years previously. He stayed for just one day at the military base before being moved to the United States on a US Air Force plane. He set up residence in New York, where he was recruited by the terrorist group Alpha 66. In October 1981, when he attempted to pull off his first and only clandestine incursion into Cuba, he was arrested and convicted by the local authorities; released nine years later, he went back to the United States, this time to settle in

Miami. In 1994, the Chief was arrested by American police while planning to take a shipment of weapons into Cuba. When he was released that same year, he split from Alpha 66, claiming that its main leader, Andrés Nazario Sargén, was "all talk and no action," and created his own organization, the F4 Commandos. Intending to put his organization on the map with a spectacular operation, he ordered four Stinger 92 portable rocket launchers from a Florida arms dealer, costing $150,000. According to the manufacturer, Raytheon Systems, at least 270 airplanes had been shot down to date, in various parts of the world, through the use of this weapon. On the day set for him to deliver the cash and receive the merchandise, Frómeta was arrested by the seller himself, in reality an FBI agent disguised as a trafficker. Tried and convicted, the Cuban spent three and a half years in prison and was then released on probation, going straight back to his armed activities against Cuba and his Sunday preaching.

Just a few blocks away and a few minutes on foot from the F4 Commandos headquarters, stands living proof that the ludicrous Rodolfo Frómeta does not personify the sentiments of the entire exiled Cuban community. Located on the west side of Little Havana, the Alianza Martiana (named after José Martí, the apostle of Cuban independence) occupies premises as modest as those of the organization run by the Chief. The Alianza Martiana functions as an umbrella organization for four groups in favor of dialogue with the Cuban government—the José Martí Association, the Alliance of Workers in the Cuban Community, the Association of Christian Women in Defense of the Family and the Antonio Maceo Brigade—as well as a group called the Bolivarian Circle of Miami, made up of Venezuelan immigrants favorable to President Hugo Chávez.

The Alianza Martiana owes its public visibility to its chairman, Max Lesnik, a man who is even smaller than Frómeta and yet at over eighty years of age displays all the forcefulness and agility of a young man. The Hispanic community in Florida, especially the Cubans, were used to hearing his strong, hoarse voice on "Radio Miami." Despite the name, always followed by the slogan "An Open Forum at the Service of Truth," this "radio" is, in fact, a one-hour daily slot rented by Lesnik on a local radio station. Between four and five o'clock in the afternoon, from Monday through Friday, he directs and presents what he calls "a radiophonic magazine." Physically this radio program is squeezed into a four-meter-square studio, set up at the back of Alianza's space. Lesnik sits down there every day at the same time, adjusts the earphones on his head where a few scarce auburn-dyed hairs survive, and monopolizes the microphones for the final twenty minutes of the broadcast. The unequivocally pro-Cuban Revolution "Radio Miami" presents itself as an alternative to southern Florida's media "that do not provide truthful, objective information on what is going on in America, in Cuba, and in the world," and usually refers to the anti-Castroist organizations as "the irascible ultrarightists from the ghetto." Three other exiled Cubans assist Lesnik: the sixty-something Lorenzo Gonzalo and Ramón Coll, the latter brought to the United States in the wake of Operation Peter Pan, and the young Sergio Montané, son of Jesús Montané, one of the expeditionary members on the yacht *Granma* along with Fidel and Che Guevara, and also a member of the Cuban Communist Party directorate until his death in 1999. Gonzalo split with the Revolution soon after backing it, was accused of terrorism and sentenced to a thirty-year prison term, at the end of which he moved to Miami.

Four years younger than the Cuban leader, Max Lesnik got to know Fidel Castro in the late 1940s, when they were both studying law at Havana University. Back then, the future president was clean-shaven and always wore a jacket and tie. The fact that they belonged to different wings of the Orthodox Party—Lesnik had never been a communist, and Fidel was already getting close to the Marxists in the student movement—did not stop them from becoming friends. The son of a Polish businessman who had immigrated to Cuba at the beginning of the twentieth century, Lesnik was the only one of their group who had a car, a navy blue Pontiac, a fact that made him the driver of his friend, who had not yet become a communist. And it was in the Lesnik family's apartment, in front of the old presidential palace in the center of Old Havana, that Fidel hid for two weeks from the dictator Fulgencio Batista's police when they were first on his tail.

When the two men finished university, they each went their own way. In 1953, while Fidel was leading the frustrated attempt to take the Moncada Barracks, a show of daring that would cost him two years in prison, Lesnik was taking his first steps in journalism, which would come to be his lifelong occupation. They would not meet again until December 1955, when Lesnik, just married to Miriam, took advantage of his honeymoon in Mexico to visit his friend. Fidel, his brother Raúl, Che Guevara, Jesús Montané and some others were learning the rudiments of guerrilla warfare on the outskirts of Mexico City with the retired Cuban general Alberto Bayo, a veteran of the International Brigades who fought in the Spanish Civil War between 1936 and 1939. Excited by the group's determination to overthrow Batista's dictatorship by force, Lesnik returned to his country and joined the urban cells of the 26th of July Movement that brought together different guerrilla factions.

With the triumph of the Revolution on January 1, 1959, Lesnik fully endorsed the new regime, but turned down invitations to participate in government, preferring to remain "safely in journalism." The political and personal bonds between the two old friends would be tested for the first time a few months after the bearded men took office. The creation of revolutionary courts and the execution by firing squad of allies of the old regime, accused of murder and torture, shocked the young journalist. "The shootings left a bitter taste," he would remember half a century later, in his comfortable house in Coral Gables. "It was not just a matter of humanity; I thought the *paredón* [the execution wall] would tarnish the Revolution's image, which in fact it did." The last straw, causing a definitive break with Fidel, was Cuba's increasing closeness to the Soviet Union. Lesnik knew, of course, that the increasingly radical Revolution did not tolerate dissent, not even from someone like himself, a friend of almost all the top members of the government and an active militant in the fight against Batista. In December 1960 he decided to leave the country. He sent Miriam and their two daughters to Miriam's parents' house, and in January 1961 took refuge in the residence of the Brazilian ambassador, Vasco Leitão da Cunha. Shortly after, he secretly boarded a small motorboat and made the dangerous nineteen-hour trip to the United States. His fellow escapees were Eloy Gutiérrez Menoyo and Andrés Nazario Sargén, who two years later would become the main leaders of the Alpha 66 group. After two months, Miriam and the two girls landed safely in Miami.

Even far away from his homeland and from the friends he had helped to power, Lesnik still felt himself to be one of them. "I never ceased being a revolutionary," he would repeat to whoever was listening, "but as I'm a revolutionary who worships intelligence, I can't be a communist." Despite its declared anti-communism, that statement was enough for him to be branded a "traitor to the homeland" and "a spy at Fidel Castro's service" by some sectors in the already numerous Cuban community in Florida. Indifferent to what they thought of him, he plunged headlong into journalism where he felt like a fish in water. His new start in the United States was low-key. As he would do again some years later with "Radio Miami," he rented space at a local station where he broadcast a daily program in Spanish. In the mid-1960s, Lesnik decided to launch the tabloid *Réplica*, intended to rival the weekly newspaper *Patria*, a clearly anti-Castroist newspaper funded by the overthrown Fulgencio Batista, who was enjoying a sweet exile on the island of Madeira under the protection of the Portuguese dictator Antonio de Oliveira Salazar. Unlike the dogmatic *Patria*, whose texts read like anticommunist rants, *Réplica* championed pluralism, publishing opinions from both sides of the Florida Straits. Compared with its slick rival, Lesnik's *Réplica* had a poor graphic appearance, but it was handed out for free, often by Lesnik himself, in the cafés and Cuban meeting places of Little Havana.

The formula worked. Launched with only eight pages, a few months later *Réplica* was circulating with two forty-page sections, half of which were taken up with advertising. A year after the launch, the success inspired Lesnik to issue a second publication with the same name but in magazine format, and with a color cover. The tabloid continued to circulate on Tuesdays, while the magazine arrived at the kiosks on Thursdays. The magazine proved even more popular than the original newspaper. By the time *Réplica* was two years old, in the middle of 1968, Max Lesnik had four publications on his hands: besides the tabloid and the magazine, he had launched a tourist guide, distributed free of charge in hotels and airports. However, the greatest success, both with the public and financially, would come from a little magazine called *Guía de TV*; it was a Spanish copy of the ubiquitous American *TV Guide*, the weekly listings magazine which also gave the inside gossip on the stars.

When Lesnik was owner of just the *Réplica* newspaper, he didn't seem to bother the more radical sectors of the exiled Cuban community. But the rapid evolution from an almost handmade publication to a small media empire turned on a red warning light for the *verticales*, the "upright" anti-Castroists. In response to the first death threats, made in anonymous phone calls, Lesnik discreetly began carrying a Colt .38 revolver on his belt. A few weeks later, a bomb destroyed the front of the building where his publishing company operated. When he went to the police to file a complaint, he heard a chilling warning from the chief officer on duty:

"We will investigate the attack, Mr. Lesnik, but if you intend to keep up your present editorial line, then you're a dead man."

Over the following months, eleven bombs exploded at his publishing house, Réplica Editorial, but since the headstrong Cuban would not give in, the extreme right-wing groups then began attacking his supporters. They targeted the newspaper stands and kiosks that sold or distributed Lesnik's publications, then the advertisers. One of these was the cigar manufacturer Padrón Cigars, owned by the exiled Cuban millionaire José Orlando Padrón, an advocate of maintaining a dialogue with Havana's communist government. As well as advertising regularly in all of Lesnik's publications, Padrón offered the two versions of *Réplica*, the tourist guide and the TV magazine for sale in his tobacco stores—a degree of solidarity punished by four bomb attacks. The terrorist campaign would eventually yield results. Max Lesnik ran out of advertisers and distributors, and eighteen months after the first threatening phone call, he closed the doors of his publishing house. Consistently committed to détente between Cuba and the US, Lesnik went back to Cuba for the first time in the mid-1970s. When he was received for an audience at the Palace of the Revolution, Lesnik joked with the friend he had hidden in his house twenty years before:

"How should I address you: as Commander, President or Prime Minister?"

The Cuban leader answered with a smile:

"For you, I will always be Fidel."

From then on Lesnik started to pay regular visits to Cuba, where he was invariably received by Castro. Through another exiled believer in renewing the dialogue between Cuba and the US, the Cuban multimillionaire Charles Dascal, owner of the Continental Bank of Miami, Lesnik got close to the former American president, Jimmy Carter. For a long time the journalist acted as a go-between between the Cuban leader and Carter, who would become an active advocate of the normalization of relations between the two countries. This process culminated in a visit to Cuba by Carter in May 2002, the first by a former president of the United States since 1959; it required special authorization from President George W. Bush. The visit would end with a scene that would have been unthinkable at the height of the Cold War: before a crowd of 50,000 people in Havana's Latin American Stadium, Carter threw the first pitch with Fidel Castro as batter in an unprecedented baseball game between a Cuban and an American team.

However, the diametrically opposed profiles of Lesnik and Rodolfo Frómeta are insufficient to convey an even slightly reliable picture of Cuban Miami. A third point is needed to complete the triangle with "Radio Miami" and the F4 Commandos, and this can be found in the sixty-eight-year-old writer Norberto Fuentes, who lives in a penthouse apartment on Boulevard Ponce de León. The grandfather of five children and the father of four daughters from four different marriages, Fuentes didn't hide his irritation upon discovering that he would be sharing this chapter with Lesnik and Frómeta. "Please, put me in some other company," he protested. "Frómeta's a ridiculous character and Lesnik's an opportunist." His opinions about the Cuban exiled community as a whole are equally caustic. "Cuban immigration turned Miami into an independent republic, a typical banana republic," he scoffs, with a laugh that dispels any suspicions of resentment. "This place is shit." Asked why he elected to live among compatriots whom he seems to despise so much, he answers that he doesn't live in Miami, "but in the United States." As a matter of fact, no one has ever seen the writer at any functions organized by the Alianza Martiana and much less in the company of anti-Castroist *verticales*, whom he doesn't even want to hear about:

"I was, and still am, a revolutionary. I'm a Marxist, I didn't come to the States to take part in a counterrevolution. I came here in search of the rebelliousness and iconoclastic spirit of William Faulkner, Ernest Hemingway and John Wayne in *Rio Bravo*."

Considered even by his enemies on the Island as one of the greatest Cuban writers alive, Fuentes was only fifteen when Fidel Castro came to power. If fate walked in a straight line, the natural thing would have been for him to leave the country in the first migration waves to the United States. His father, the advertising executive and lawyer Norberto Fuentes, represented the interests of none other than Santo Trafficante in Cuba, one of the most famous American gangsters of the 1950s. According to documents disclosed by the CIA in 2007, Trafficante, who owned two casinos, one nightclub and four hotels in Havana, among them the Capri, delivered 10 percent of his establishments' takings every night to one of Fulgencio Batista's messengers. Once the dictator was overthrown, Trafficante was arrested and deported to the United States as an "undesirable alien." Fuentes Sr. chose to stay on in Cuba, "doing the business he could and the business he couldn't," according to his son, until his death in 1978.

Educated at Candler College, a traditional American Methodist school established in Cuba, the writer-to-be grew up listening to Elvis Presley and Cole Porter. Joining the Revolution at the precocious age of seventeen, he started to work for a magazine published by the Communist Youth, a job that allowed him to travel all over the country writing articles on the radical changes implemented by the new regime. Fuentes made his debut as an author in 1968, at the age of twenty-three, with *Condenados de Condado* (The Condemned of Condado), a collection of short stories inspired by his coverage of the repression of a hotspot of armed resistance to the Revolution in the Escambray Mountains. Although the book had been awarded a prize by the Casa de las Américas, the most traditional cultural institution in post-Batista Cuba, and had become a national bestseller, *Condenados* was considered a "dissident work" by the government and as such caused what the writer called "my first collision with the Revolution." Leaders of the Revolutionary Armed Forces had been stung by what the author called "my irrepressible, unalterable lack of respect." According to Fuentes, when Fidel Castro finished the book he threw it so hard against the wall that "its puny one hundred and fifty pages" were scattered all over the floor.

In 1971, well after the unruly Fuentes and the Revolution had "forgiven each other" for the incident, they clashed again, more noisily. The writer Heberto Padilla had been arrested on vague charges of subversion following the publication of his prize-winning book of poems *Fuera del Juego* (Out of the Game). There was an international outcry and a strongly worded petition from sixty-two intellectuals including Jean-Paul Sartre, Simone de Beauvoir, Mario Vargas Llosa, Susan Sontag and Carlos Fuentes, after Padilla was forced to perform a humiliating act of public self-criticism before the Writers' Union. He included in his mea culpa his wife and other colleagues who were present. When Norberto Fuentes heard his name, he jumped up and protested:

"Just a moment, Heberto! Take my name off that list! Besides repudiating self-criticism, I can't regret any counterrevolutionary activities which I never engaged in!"

Such insolence proved costly. Although no explicit punishment was meted out, Fuentes endured some years of ostracism, during which he devoted himself to his next book, *Hemingway in Cuba*. With a foreword by Gabriel García Márquez, the work was published simultaneously in Cuba and the United States in 1984, and its success was instrumental in reconciling the author with the Cuban Revolution and its leadership, whose favorite writer he became. Fuentes experienced the Angolan Civil War as both journalist and combatant, and was part of the Cuban delegation to Cairo that negotiated the peace treaties in 1988 with representatives of Angola, South Africa, the United States and the Soviet Union. As well as being awarded the Internationalist Combatant Medal, First Class, Norberto Fuentes had built a solid friendship in Angola with Antonio "Tony" de la Guardia, a colonel in the Ministry of the Interior with a long record of services rendered to the Revolution, not only in Africa, but also in the war that brought the Sandinista National Liberation Front to power in Nicaragua.

On the morning of June 14, 1989, the people of Cuba awakened to an unbelievable piece of news on the front page of *Granma*: the day before, General Arnaldo Ochoa, who had led the hundreds of thousands of Cubans in the Angolan and the Ethiopian campaigns, Colonel Tony de la Guardia, his twin brother of the same rank, Patricio de la Guardia, and another dozen officials had been arrested. The accusation against them could not be more serious: between 1987 and 1989 the group had supposedly used Cuban airplanes, boats and military facilities to smuggle six tons of cocaine, in an operation that had brought in over $3 million in commission. The drug was acquired from the Colombian drug trafficker Pablo Escobar, carried to Varadero beach in Cuban airplanes and loaded onto speedboats heading towards the islets at the extreme southern tip of Florida. When he read of the arrests, Norberto called one of his powerful friends, Carlos Aldana of the Ideology Secretariat, with a staggering revelation: three months before, Tony de la Guardia had asked him to stash some bags full of dollars, and the money was still hidden in his house. At dawn on June 16, a group of officers of the Ministry of the Interior showed up at Fuentes's apartment, in the Vedado district of Havana, and seized half a million dollars hidden under his bed. According to the police report drafted on the spot and signed by the writer, there were "564,000 dollars, separated into wads of different denominations, stored in black nylon Samsonite bags."

When de la Guardia asked him to conceal such a sum in his

house, Fuentes suspected that it might be *"plata mal habida"* (ill-gotten gains), but he never dreamed that his friend could be involved in corruption, let alone drug trafficking. After all, this was a respected war veteran who since 1982 had been occupying a post of vital importance at the Ministry of the Interior—the department in charge of all the dollar transactions for setting up joint ventures with foreign companies and circumventing the US economic embargo. Although the authorities accepted the writer's innocence when he insisted that he was unaware of the provenance of the money, his honeymoon with the top echelons of the Cuban political hierarchy was over. Tried by a military court including forty-five generals, brigadier generals and admirals, the fourteen defendants were stripped of their ranks, medals and decorations, among them that of "Hero of the Republic of Cuba" bestowed on General Arnaldo Ochoa. Fuentes's name did not arise during the trial. According to the verdict, published on July 10, ten of the defendants were sentenced to prison terms ranging from ten to thirty years. Ochoa, Tony de la Guardia, Major Amado Padrón and Captain Jorge Martínez were sentenced to death and executed at dawn on July 13, 1989.

Interrogated several times at Villa Marista over the weeks following the "Ochoa case," Norberto Fuentes would spend four years in political and professional limbo. He remained free but would never again be "the columnist of the Revolution," as he was called by the Cuban press. He spent his time working on a new version of his bestseller *Hemingway in Cuba*, wrote a book on the Angolan war and compiled a selection of his best articles—but no Cuban publisher was interested. He received invitations to give speeches and seminars abroad but couldn't get the necessary exit visas. In the second half of 1993 Fuentes decided to escape from Cuba via the only means available to someone in his circumstances: by sea.

Perhaps because it had been conceived by a writer, the escape plan seemed like the screenplay for a Hollywood thriller. With the help of some friends in the United States, Fuentes pitched a story to the conservative daily the *Washington Times* that so far only had a title—"The Rafter"—and which would describe the getaway to Miami that he intended to carry out. In order to complete the project, however, he would need $10,000 in advance to cover travel expenses. The newspaper, owned by the South Korean religious leader Sun Myung Moon, jumped on the offer, and days later the requested amount reached him in Havana. Fuentes next hired the services of Boomerang, the nickname of a sailor who had ferried many exiles across the Florida Straits and done several stints in prison for it. Via the *bolsa negra*, as the black market is known in Cuba, the writer used Reverend Moon's money to buy an old Soviet inflatable launch, big enough for twelve people, with a 135 hp Yamaha engine. To document the adventure he invited the Italian photographer Luca Marinelli, a frequent visitor to the Island. Young, bohemian and adventurous, Marinelli had become a celebrity photojournalist the year before, when he captured the dramatic execution of an Italian soldier by a rebel in Somalia.

The first setback was when Boomerang decreed the inclusion of six more passengers on the crossing, making it even more lucrative for the sailor. Although Fuentes disliked the idea of being part of a group escape, with people he'd never seen before, he had no alternative. Before departure, however, he spent a few weeks recording memories and information onto diskettes that would be invaluable if he decided to write about his troubled story one day. By the end there were fourteen megabytes of notes on ten disks, the equivalent of 2,000 pages of a book. He stored the disks in a plastic bag weighted down with a little lead bar he used as a paperweight. If the worst came to the worst and they were caught by the police, the first thing he would do would be to throw the bag with his precious memories into the sea.

On the evening of Sunday, October 10, 1993, Fuentes and his wife Niurka de la Torre, a doctor three decades younger to whom he had been married for some years, met up with Marinelli and together they walked for an hour until they reached the small, stony Jaimanitas beach, located a few blocks beyond the twin hotels Tritón and Neptuno, in Miramar. Around ten, Boomerang showed up in the dark, steering the boat that already had his quota of six passengers on board. Although the dangerous trip in such a rickety vessel could take well over twenty-four hours, the trio's only supplies were a few packs of cookies kept in a backpack along with the disks. Marinelli, who seemed to have drunk too much rum, was carrying nothing but two Nikon cameras around his neck plus his Italian passport and an air ticket for Miami-Cancún-Havana in the back pocket of his jeans. When the adventure was over, he intended to resume his vacation in Cuba.

Everything went wrong. At one o'clock in the morning, when the lights of Havana were still visible from out at sea, the boat slowed down and began to go round in circles. The vibration had caused a piece of wood from the stern to come loose, making the engine sag down into the water and minutes later stop working. The skipper and his passengers remained adrift for forty long, hushed minutes, until the boat was swept by a beam of light coming from an approaching vessel. When Boomerang saw it was the Cuban Coast Guard patrol, he put his hands on his head. "Assholes!" he muttered. "Another New Year's Eve in the cooler!" Fuentes reached surreptitiously into his backpack, grabbed the bag with the disks and threw it into the sea, blithely copied by the photographer who didn't hesitate to throw overboard two cameras that were certainly worth as much as the writer had paid for the boat and the engine that had left them in the lurch. Dawn had not even broken yet when they found themselves locked away inside the cells at Villa Marista.

In less than a week, Boomerang's six customers were freed and the photographer had been packed back to Italy on the first available flight. One month later, Fuentes and Niurka were released and the seaman, just as he had foreseen, started off 1994 in jail. In the writer's opinion, his release was due to the Cuban government's fear they might be "creating a new Solzhenitsyn in the Caribbean"—a reference to the Russian writer Alexander Solzhenitsyn, a sworn enemy of the Soviet Union (in 1970, after spending years in Soviet prisons, the author of *The Gulag Archipelago* was awarded the Nobel Prize for Literature). Fuentes spent the following ten months at large. He didn't know, however, that an operation was underway in the United States to get him out of the country.

After some informal discussions, though it is not certain on whose initiative, the Colombian Nobel Prize winner Gabriel García Márquez and presidents Clinton and Salinas de Gortari of Mexico decided to act to get Fuentes out of Cuba as soon as possible. Besides the three of them and the writer Carlos Fuentes, only two others were aware of the plan: Felipe González, the president of Spain, and the American writer William Kennedy, who was then on the board of trustees of PEN International. Under absolute secrecy, over the following weeks Gabo traveled three times to Cuba and Fidel got at least four phone calls from Salinas de Gortari, who always stressed that he was talking entirely for himself, not on behalf of Bill Clinton. With such powerful sponsors, results were not long in coming. On the morning of August 24, 1994, a jet with the Mexican president's insignia painted on its fuselage landed at Havana Airport carrying only two passengers: García Márquez and an official from President Salinas de Gortari's Cabinet. A passport was hurriedly issued to Norberto Fuentes and on August 25 he boarded the plane to Mexico, where he stayed for ten days and then left for Miami, where he would settle.

And it was as a lonely, silent observer that Fuentes read the news of the Cuban intelligence agents' arrest in Miami—unlike Max Lesnik and Rodolfo Frómeta, who led noisy pressure groups lobbying at the courthouse door, respectively in favor of the Cuban prisoners and against them. The thirty years of his tumultuous relationship with Castroism had left deep wounds—"the Cuban Revolution was very, I mean very ungrateful to me," Fuentes never tired of repeating—but these wounds had not turned him into a typical *miami cubano*. On the contrary, as became apparent a few days after he arrived in Florida. Invited to speak before the Cuban Committee for Human Rights, he disappointed the audience, who expected to hear him vituperate against Fidel Castro. "Those people were hoping that I would do there what I had refused to do in the Padilla case: self-criticism," remembers Fuentes, with roars of laughter. "They wanted me to write an exile version of *Condenados de Condado*." The Cuban agents' trial would again pit him against the mainstream of the Cuban community in Florida. "For the first time, this society poisoned by defeat had the chance to strike a blow against the Cuban Revolution and against Fidel," maintained the writer. "From the first day, the trial was pressurized by public opinion and by the media toward a single result: conviction." Nor does Fuentes believe this was an isolated opinion:

"It was clear that if the trial were held in Miami they would be convicted. I knew that, the five prisoners knew that, and Fidel knew it too."

15

LEONARD WEINGLASS, ATTORNEY TO JANE FONDA, ANGELA DAVIS AND THE BLACK PANTHERS, JOINS THE DEFENSE OF THE CUBAN FIVE, BUT FOR THEM THE DIE HAD ALREADY BEEN CAST

The poll results would confirm Norberto Fuentes's opinions about the prevailing atmosphere in Miami. It was only in March 2000—one and a half years after the five Cubans were imprisoned—that the results of the survey measuring the degree of animosity in the city's population towards the Cuban Revolution and the five prisoners arrived on Judge Lenard's desk. Coordinated by the American demographer Gary Moran, professor at Florida International University, the poll showed that half of Miami's Cuban population was in favor of a military attack by the United States to bring down the Cuban government, while 74 percent supported the armed actions waged against Cuba by Florida's anti-Castroist organizations. Repeated among the Cuban Americans of Broward County, forty kilometers from Miami, the survey came up with some very different responses. In this part of Florida, two-thirds of the interviewees replied they were against any violent action against Cuba, either by the American government or by the exiles in Florida. Fort Lauderdale, the county seat for Broward County, was precisely where the defense lawyers had moved to transfer the trial. The statistics were delivered to the court accompanied by an opinion issued by the Cuban-American anthroplogist Lisandro Pérez, a professor at Florida International University, exiled in Florida since 1970. "Even if the jury were composed entirely of non-Cubans," the academic stated, "the possibility of selecting twelve citizens of Miami-Dade County who can be impartial in a case involving acknowledged agents of the Cuban government is virtually zero."

The study was promptly rejected by the prosecution. Disregarding both the research and expert opinions, the government prosecutors asked the court to reject the motion for a change of venue. Miami "is an extremely heterogeneous, diverse and politically non-monolithic metropolitan area," argued the counterplea. "This is not a backwater, but a city immune from the influences that could preclude a fair trial." These arguments seem to have been sufficient for the judge, who on July 27 dismissed the motion for the change of venue. It was the second defeat for the defense before the trial had even begun. Months earlier Lenard had denied a petition by the lawyers requesting bail arbitration so that the accused could remain at liberty during the judicial process. New petitions and objections on both sides delayed the start of the proceedings, which finally got under way during the second week of November, more than two years after the arrests.

The first five days of the court's work were taken up with the monotonous selection of the twelve members of the jury who would decide the fate of the Cuban agents. Of the list of seventy-two names put forward by the District Court, thirty asked to be excused on grounds of health, for family or professional reasons, or for being less than impartial. Of these last, two had done business with José Basulto, leader of the Brothers to the Rescue, one was acquainted with the family of the pilot Mario de la Peña, killed in the attack by Cuban MiGs, and two were friends of Silvia Iriondo, the anti-Castroist militant who was on the plane with Basulto when the Cessnas were shot down. Another two were excused because they knew the journalist Hank Tester, from the NBC television network, summoned as a witness for the prosecution. Tester had taken part in countless flights carried out by the Democracy Movement, some of which were piloted by the now accused René González. Of the forty-two remaining candidates, seventeen were vetoed by the defense and thirteen by the prosecution, leaving at last the twelve jurors—six men and six women, seven of whom were caucasian and five of Hispanic origin. Once the selection process was complete, Lenard decreed a two-week recess, after which the trial would commence.

The thermometer marked 64°F, a glacial temperature by Miami standards, when the doors to the court were opened on the morning of November 27, 2000. In spite of the cold, groups of demonstrators had been gathering in front of the building since early morning, carrying banners and posters with slogans for and against the accused. Separated from each other by uniformed marshals were the two opposing groups: on one side the anti-Castroist militants and the families of the four pilots killed in 1996, who wore mourning attire; on the other, in smaller numbers but equally vociferous, the activists of the Alianza Martiana led by the excited Max Lesnik. Prohibited from taking pictures inside the courtroom, photographers and cameramen were interviewing demonstrators and any high-profile personalities.

At nine o'clock sharp, the occupants of the packed courtroom on the twelfth floor of the district court stood up for Judge Joan Lenard. All seventy seats in the public area were taken, twenty of them by journalists. Dressed in a black robe, the judge spent the first forty minutes explaining what the trial calendar would be. Court sessions would be daily, from Monday to Friday, beginning at nine in the morning, with a fifteen-minute coffee break, and at one o'clock they would adjourn for lunch. Sessions would begin again at three in the afternoon and finish at six. It was just before ten o'clock when Lenard declared open the first session of the judicial proceedings known as "The United States of America versus Rubén Campa and others," or Criminal Case 98-CR-721-Lenard. The twelve jurors were called in and sat down in the two rows of seats perpendicular to the judge's desk and to the auditorium. Next came the ten prisoners. The presence of the five Cubans who had made a plea bargain fulfilled a mere legal formality. Transformed from defendants into "witness collaborators," they had already been given minimum sentences, with no need for the jury's opinion.

With the time spent in prison deducted, months later they would be pardoned and released, entering the American Justice Department's witness protection program.

As in their first appearance two years and two months earlier, the accused were wearing orange denim clothes and cotton sneakers. On the judge's order the marshals removed the handcuffs and chains that bound their hands and feet. And also as in 1998, only two of the accused saw family members among the public: Maggie Becker, Tony Guerrero's partner, and Roberto González, René's younger brother, were there. Thanks to his American citizenship and status as a lawyer, Roberto had moved from his home in Havana to Miami, and managed to register himself as an assistant not only to Phil Horowitz, René's defense counsel, but to all the other attorneys as well. Ten years later, in the Cuban capital, Roberto would remember the tight spots he'd been in when he started work in the United States. "Apart from encountering a legal system with which I was completely unfamiliar, I could hardly speak English," the lawyer would recall, puffing on a strong *Popular* cigarette. "As time went by, however, it became just as easy to read legal texts as a menu in a restaurant." Even so, the first task he and his American colleagues faced was to peruse the almost 10,000 pages of the indictment. The confidential nature of most of these papers led Lenard to prohibit any prosecution document being taken out of the court, which obliged the defense attorneys to work in a small room in the basement of the building—a "lugubrious" place according to Paul McKenna, Gerardo Hernández's lawyer—and always under the watchful eye of the marshals.

Soon after proceedings got under way, and even before the indictment was presented, the audience witnessed a demonstration of the climate of intolerance revealed in Gary Moran's research. With the consent of the judge, Paul McKenna, an American who had never been to Cuba, was forced by one of the prosecutors to declare formally that he was not a communist nor did he work secretly for Fidel Castro's government. With that cleared up, the floor was taken by the prosecutor David Buckner to present the charges against the five Cubans who had refused the offer of a plea bargain. Buckner's intervention took up all the remaining time of the morning session, was resumed after the lunch recess and finished only at the end of the day. Still referring to Gerardo Hernández, Ramón Labañino and Fernando González by their code names, the prosecutor held forth on the activities of each one of the accused, highlighting that the work of the FBI had "prevented the accused just in time from obtaining secret information." In the daily letter he would write and send to Olga by post—duly censored by the prison authorities—René recognized that Buckner had not done "a bad job," but criticized the fact that the indictment "overstated the activities of the five and glorified the work of the FBI"; he accused the prosecution of referring to the Brothers and to the Democracy Movement as if they were "Mother Teresa of Calcutta charities." Buckner saved the most serious novelty for the end of his exposition, when he added a fresh indictment to those that had been announced by the judge three days after the arrests. Gerardo Hernández was now formally accused of "conspiracy to commit murder" in connection with the four downed pilots. According to Buckner, papers seized by the FBI in the Cubans' houses proved that it was Hernández who had transmitted the information to Cuba about the Brothers' flights that made the shooting down of the Cessnas possible.

Except for a brief recess for the end-of-year vacation, the trial went on without interruption for seven months. Throughout this time the prosecution's strategy focused on three objectives: to demonstrate that the anti-Castroist groups infiltrated by the Wasp Network were organizations of a pacifist and humanitarian nature; to prove that the Cuban agents had tried to obtain classified information by penetrating American military installations, like the naval base at Boca Chica, where Tony Guerrero was employed; and to incriminate Gerardo Hernández for the death of the four pilots. In response the defense argued that many of the exile organizations were fronts for terrorist activities against Cuba, and that the Cuban agents had never laid hands or eyes on any paper considered confidential, restricted or secret. As for the accusation against Gerardo Hernández, Paul McKenna exhibited documents captured by the FBI to prove that on February 24, 1996, when the attacks took place, the head of the Wasp Network was not even in Miami. On that day Giro was personally finalizing Operation Starlet, accompanying Juan Pablo Roque to Fort Lauderdale and Tampa so that the pilot could fly to Cancún and on to Cuba. The lawyer also pointed out that Hernández could hardly be accused of secretly sending information to Havana that was known the day before to journalists and to at least two top officials of the American government—the director of the FAA, Cecilia Capestany, and the special advisor for Cuba, Richard Nuccio. Furthermore, McKenna went on, it had been the FBI agent Oscar Montoto himself who had advised René not to fly on February 24, "because Cuba was determined to shoot down any plane that invaded its airspace."

Half of the quota of twenty-one witnesses to which the defense had a right was taken up with American government officials, in a list that went all the way from big shots like Nuccio down to Timothy Keric, Tony Guerrero's workmate at the Boca Chica base. The list also included Cecilia Capestany, agents from the FBI's anti-terror squad who for years had monitored the radical Alpha 66 and Omega-7 groups, and Dalila Borrego, the employee who had suggested that Guerrero apply for a job at Boca Chica. Also called as witnesses for the defense were two generals, an admiral and a colonel from the US Armed Forces. Rodolfo Frómeta and José Basulto were also on the list. The Brothers to the Rescue leader had been called as a "hostile witness"—a term in American law for a person who is obliged to testify while being opposed to whoever proposed his name. Summoned as a witness and cited by the defense as "a member of the CANF's clandestine military apparatus," the notorious Ángel Alemán, the lobster fisherman, refused to appear in court, invoking the Fifth Amendment of the American Constitution, which states that "no person can be legally compelled to answer any question in any governmental proceeding if that answer could lead to that person's prosecution." The last three witnesses lined up by the defense were Cuban government employees: Fidel Arza, from the Institute of Civil Aeronautics, Percy Alvarado, a retired intelligence officer who in the 1980s had infiltrated the Cuban American National Foundation, and Colonel Roberto Caballero from the Ministry of the Interior, who had overseen the mercenary Raúl Ernesto Cruz León's interrogations in prison. So that they could be heard, Judge Lenard had to authorize the journey to Havana of nine members of the defense and prosecution, accompanied by interpreters and sound technicians to record the testimonies in situ.

On the list of prosecution witnesses presented by attorneys Caroline Heck Miller, David Buckner, Guy Lewis and John Kastrenakes were nine FBI agents who had taken part in the operation to dismantle the Wasp Network, three leaders of anti-Castroist organizations, the Cuban intelligence agent Joseph Santos, who had made a deal with the prosecution, the naval officer Bjorn Johansen and Captain Linda Hutton of the American Navy, who commanded the naval station at Boca Chica during the period that Tony Guerrero worked there. The testimony of at least two of these witnesses resulted in a setback for the prosecution. The repentant Joseph Santos, extremely nervous, became so confused answering the defense's questions that the prosecution chose to excuse him for a few minutes after the start of questioning. And then Linda Hutton threw a wet blanket over the spying accusations against Tony Guerrero. After saying that throughout her administration the installations at the base remained open for public visits, the captain affirmed that Guerrero had never had access to information that might compromise "the defense, national security and the interests of the United States."

Johansen's testimony raised a subject that would provoke heated debates in court: the difference of opinion between the governments of the United States and Cuba, and by extension, between the prosecution and the defense, about the exact location of where the two Brothers planes had been shot down. As far as the Americans were concerned, the Cessnas were over international waters; the Cubans insisted that the two planes were within the twelve-mile limit of Cuban territorial waters and airspace, and had thus committed an intrusion. Although the difference between one claim and the other was a matter of meters, the argument went on for weeks. One of the prosecution's strong cards in support of the downing in international waters thesis was the September 1999 report by the Inter-American Commission on Human Rights of the OAS. Signed by the body's chairman, Robert Goldman, and by its vice-chairman the Brazilian Hélio Bicudo, the document found that the aircraft had been shot down in international airspace and therefore held Cuba responsible for the death of the pilots Carlos Costa, Pablo Morales, Mario de la Peña and Armando Alejandre. The basis of the OAS's argument was a report by the ICAO, the United Nations agency that regulates air traffic standards, according to which the shooting down had happened outside Cuban air space. And the ICAO, in turn, had reached this conclusion based on the logbook of the young Bjorn Johansen, a deck officer on the liner *Majesty of the Seas*, the one the MiG pilots themselves had noticed below them in the Straits of Florida on the afternoon of February 24, 1996.

Testifying for the prosecution, Johansen recognized that his certainty regarding the location of the incident, which according to him took place in international waters, originated from visual observation and not from the electronic registration of the exact position of the *Majesty of the Seas*. Cornered by McKenna, he revealed that only on the following day had he transferred the details to the logbook from a piece of paper where he'd noted them down. He also said that between the shooting down of the Cessnas and his registering of the event in the logbook, he had been interrogated by FBI agents. Protected by objections from the prosecution which the judge accepted, the sailor and the ship's owners refused to present to the jury either the logbook or the piece of paper he had scribbled on when the planes were shot down.

In a moment of apparent carelessness by the defense, one question was not asked: who owned the ship? A superficial check in newspaper archives and in CANF's files would have provided the lawyers—especially McKenna, Gerardo's defender—with a crucial piece of information. Of Norwegian origin and resident in Miami, Bjorn Johansen was an employee of Royal Caribbean Cruises, the group that owned *Majesty of the Seas*. And in February 1996 the number two in the company hierarchy was the American Peter G. Whelpton, an enemy of the Cuban Revolution who had never made a secret of his views. Far from it. In his official resumé, the executive vice president of Royal Caribbean (until 1999) presented himself as "an advisor to the Cuban American National Foundation's Board of Governors" and "a Member of the Foundation's Blue Ribbon Committee for the Reconstruction of Cuba." In a series of articles published by the *New York Times* in 1995, the president of the CANF, Francisco "Pepe" Hernández, had revealed to journalist Larry Rohter that Royal Caribbean was one of forty companies that had helped finance the creation of the CANF—each company had contributed $25,000. Bjorn Johansen's boss went further. "We want to help the Cuban community in their efforts to overthrow Castro," affirmed the entrepreneur to Rohter, making clear his preference for CANF as the strongest group, "with whom we will be able to move forward when the time comes." Whelpton's implication with anti-Castroism, however, was inexplicably never investigated or brought up by the defense lawyers of the Five.

What lay behind the mobilization of the Cuban community and the pressures exerted on the court, with ample support from the local press, was an undisguised hunger for revenge, due to a family drama that had climaxed months earlier. On the morning of November 25, 1999, two fishermen had rescued a five-year-old boy clinging to an inner tube in the waters off Fort Lauderdale's Pompano Beach. The boy, whose name was Elián González, had left Cuba three days earlier in a dinghy accompanied by his mother, Elisabeth, and twelve others. Halfway across, the fragile vessel sank, leaving three survivors hanging onto the only two inflatables brought by the group. A young couple was on one of the buoys, and on the other was Elián, whose mother had drowned along with the remaining fugitives. Elián was handed over by the American authorities to a paternal great-uncle, Lázaro González, who had gone into exile years earlier and lived in Little Havana.

The case would have been just another statistic in the long history of Cuban migration—were it not for the fact that Juan Miguel, Elián's father back in Havana, at once asked the Cuban government to request the United States for his son's return. On January 5, 2000, the attorney general, Janet Reno, ordered the boy's repatriation.

In defiance of the federal order, and incited by Miami's anti-Castroist organizations, Lázaro González decided that "he would not return Elián to the tyrant Fidel Castro." As of that moment the small wooden house where he had taken in his grand-nephew was guarded day and night by militant pickets and barricades, fearful that the government would remove the boy by force, which is what ultimately happened. On April 22, by order of Attorney General Reno, SWAT policemen armed with rifles took Elián into custody under the lights of flashbulbs and TV cameras. Juan Miguel had already arrived in Miami to reclaim his son, but Lázaro González, supported by lawyers hired by exile organizations, had succeeded in getting the 11th Circuit Court of Appeals in Atlanta to revoke the repatriation order. Pitched battles were fought in the streets of Little Havana between anti-Castroist groups opposed to the removal and groups linked to Max Lesnik's Alianza Martiana, in favor of the boy's return to Cuba. With widespread international media coverage, the tension provoked by the case led the Justice Department to place father and son under the protection of the armed forces, installing them in a house inside Andrews Air Force Base, in Maryland, while the wrangling continued in the courts. On June 28 the Supreme Court upheld the government's decision and later that same day Elián and his father were greeted at Havana Airport by the Cuban president in person. The general feeling in Miami was that the exiles' battle had been lost due to an uncommon alliance between Fidel Castro and Bill Clinton.

When the trial of the Wasp Network men began, the Elián case still rankled for the radical groups of the Cuban diaspora. This time, however, the attorney general was on their side. Janet Reno, in charge of the FBI and the Immigration Service—the two main bodies involved in the boy's repatriation and in the imprisonment and indictment of the five Cubans—had an interest in the Cuban agents' conviction that went beyond the call of official duty. Born in Miami, she was planning to run as the Democratic Party candidate for governor of Florida in 2002. To be blamed twice for thwarting the will of the Cuban community was certainly not the best way to win an election in that state. These factors were noted with apprehension across the Straits. Dismayed at the course the trial seemed to be taking, and faced with the prospect of Gerardo Hernández's conviction for murder, the Cuban government decided in 2001 to reinforce the defense of the Five. So that Havana could be party to the case, however, it was necessary for Giro, Ramón and Fernando to reveal to the court their real identities, a secret that in any case was no longer justified.

A heavyweight celebrity attorney, Leonard Weinglass, was chosen for this task. The owner of an expensive and renowned New York law firm, the sixty-seven-year-old "Lenny" Weinglass had become famous as a defense attorney in some of the most controversial cases in the United States. Among his clients were the actress Jane Fonda, prosecuted by the Nixon government for making a solidarity trip to North Vietnam; the military analyst Daniel Ellsberg, who released the top-secret Pentagon Papers; the activist Angela Davis; the leaders of the Symbionese Liberation Army, responsible for the kidnapping of the millionairess Patricia Hearst; and the Black Panthers, the revolutionary party founded by Huey Newton and Bobby Seale. The youngest of all his clients had been nineteen-year-old Amy Carter, daughter of the former president, prosecuted in 1987 for denouncing CIA recruitment of students at the University of Massachusetts Amherst. Before replying to Cuba's invitation, Weinglass went to Miami to read through the entire proceedings, and decided that he would participate in defending the Five. He informed Havana that he would work pro bono, as indeed he had done in the majority of the cases cited.

The trial carried on over the following months, alternating periods of tedious stagnation, when even the defendants would doze off, with fierce verbal jousting between the prosecution and the defense, forcing Judge Lenard on repeated occasions to order short adjournments while she summoned the attorneys to the bench for consultation out of earshot of the jury and the public. When the defense described the simplicity in which the Wasp Network agents lived, even the anti-Castroist newspapers were surprised. "The life of Fidel Castro's agents in Miami had definitely nothing to do with the glamorous world of James Bond," wrote a reporter in the *Sun-Sentinel*. "None of them was like those superspies we see in the movies. Far from cocktail parties and luxury cars, they led very simple lives, on tight budgets."

The two tensest moments of the trial, around the shooting down of the Brothers planes, were not provoked by witness testimony but by two cockpit recordings. The first was presented by the federal prosecutor, Caroline Heck Miller, and reproduced the dialogue between the control tower in Cuba and the jet fighters. Transmitted over loudspeakers, the voices of the pilots rejoicing over the destruction of the two planes in foul language echoed round the courtroom. The public and the jury's horrified expressions were the most visible signs that the prosecution had scored a major point. The riposte would be delivered days later by Paul McKenna, Hernández's lawyer, when he played a recording of only a few seconds but that also caused a major stir in court. It was José Basulto's voice, letting out a resounding burst of laughter the moment he saw the plane manned by Armando Alejandre Jr. and Mario de la Peña being pulverized by the MiG's missiles. The laughter was followed by a shout. "Fuck, let's get out of here!" exclaimed Basulto to his three companions, as he swung the plane around towards Florida. The recording was one more piece of evidence with which McKenna aimed to show the leader of the Brothers as the true culprit for the death of the four pilots. The lawyer alleged that, intent on provoking a military incident between Cuba and the United States, Basulto had not hesitated to entice four young men on a suicide flight, saving his own skin the minute the Cuban MiGs attacked the Cessnas.

At the end of May 2001, when the trial was close to its hundredth session, all the witnesses had been heard and tense expectation surrounded the impending decision of the jury. Media with no links to the Cuban community reflected the anxiety with which the public awaited the verdict. "Months of testimony, recesses and verbal confrontations tiresomely prolonged the trial without throwing any light on the central issue," said a dispatch from Agence France-Presse, which ended with the question: "Finally, are these people dangerous spies who tried to penetrate American military installations, or merely infiltrators of Florida's anti-Castroist organizations?" The defense still hoped that the jurors would go for the second alternative. "The prosecution failed to prove that the accused had even tried to gain access to United States secret documents," Fernando González's lawyer, Joaquín Méndez, would say years later. "And came up with no evidence of any involvement of Gerardo Hernández in the downing of the Brothers to the Rescue planes."

After a week of closing statements by lawyers and prosecutors, on Friday, June 8, 2001, Judge Joan Lenard summoned the foreman of the jury to pronounce their verdict. A middle-aged biologist in a suit and tie approached the microphone, took from his pants pocket a piece of paper, and read out the words that would seal the fate of the Cuban agents:

"We, the jury, unanimously find the defendants guilty as charged on all counts."

Lenard had to press the bell and strike the table several times with her gavel to demand silence from the relatives of the dead pilots and the militant anti-Castroists who were whooping and cheering the jury's verdict. It would now be the judge's task to determine the sentences that would be handed down, but the commotion the case aroused in Miami would resonate for some time yet. Before closing the session, Lenard decreed a recess of six months, at the end of which she would announce her decision.

Once back in the Federal Detention Center, across the sidewalk from the court, the five Cubans decided to appeal to American public opinion. In a three-page document made public by their lawyers and entitled "Message to the People of the United States," the agents explained the reasons why they had infiltrated the anti-Castroist organizations in Florida, and rejected the accusations of espionage and murder. "We do not regret what we did to defend our country," they concluded, "and we declare ourselves totally innocent." Considered a disciplinary infraction, the proclamation would be severely punished. On June 26 the Five were taken back to "the hole," which they would leave only in December when Lenard reconvened the court to deliver her sentence.

At nine o'clock on the morning of December 11, the judge declared the sentencing hearing open. The defense team clung to a slender hope of leniency. Three months earlier to the day, the United States had been the victim of Al-Qaeda suicide attacks on the Twin Towers in New York City. Despite Judge Lenard's severity, the lawyers recognized that she had acted with dignity throughout the proceedings. They thought it possible that she might have come around to their view, that the work undertaken in Miami by the Wasp Network was exactly the same as that being done by American agents since October 7 in the mountains of Afghanistan: identifying terrorists and preventing further attacks.

Discussions between the prosecution and defense on legal formalities took up the entire morning, affording no opportunity for Lenard to announce her decision. Among the Cubans present who had managed to get US entry visas was Irmita, as well as the mothers of Gerardo Hernández, René González, Tony Guerrero and Fernando González. When the proceedings were reopened after lunch, the judge ordered Hernández, the first defendant, to stand up, and went on to read the sheet of paper that a bailiff had put before her eyes:

"The defendant Gerardo Hernández Nordelo, also known by the alias of Manuel Viramóntez, was found guilty by the members of the jury of the United States District Court for the Southern District of Florida of the crimes of conspiracy to commit murder, conspiracy to deceive the United States, the collection and transmission of defense data, the falsification and use of identity documents, fraud and improper use of visas and entry permits to the United States and conspiracy to act as a non-registered foreign agent. For all these offenses, this court sentences him to two life terms plus fifteen years in prison."

At that, the elderly Carmen Nordelo, Giro's mother, who had been standing to hear the sentence, had to be propped up so as not to collapse. Meanwhile the judge rang her bell to silence the groups on the other side of the auditorium, who were celebrating the conviction with shouts of "Long live free Cuba!" Closed for a few minutes, the proceedings were reopened for the announcement of Ramón Labañino's sentence of life imprisonment plus eighteen years. The liturgy was repeated in the following weeks for the declaration of the penalties handed down to René González, condemned to fifteen years, to Fernando González, nineteen years, and to Tony Guerrero, condemned to life. The longest and one of the most controversial trials ever to take place in Miami came to an end. After four decades of a bloody war, the Cuban community exiled in Florida had succeeded in inflicting its first defeat on Fidel Castro.

AFTERWORD BY RENÉ GONZÁLEZ

On October 7, 2011, René González was released from the Jackson County jail in Marianna, Florida, on condition of remaining in the United States on probation for three years. In 2012 he was granted permission to travel to Cuba for two weeks to see his brother Roberto, who had been one of his defense attorneys and was terminally ill with cancer. René then returned to the United States to continue his probation. In April 2013, after the death of his father, he again obtained permission to visit his family on the Island. On May 11 of the same year René González abdicated American citizenship before the US Interests Section in Havana, remaining in Cuba thereafter.In an exclusive interview with Fernando Morais for the purposes of this book, René González describes his nineteen months on probation, living in semi-hiding in Palm Beach until at last he was able to return home.

The story of my return to Cuba begins exactly one year before I got out of jail. One year before I got out, my attorney, Philip Horowitz, filed a motion before the federal judge for me to serve out my probation in Cuba. Before filing a motion, the standard procedure is for the attorneys to check with the prosecutors to find out where they stand on the matter. Because if the prosecution doesn't object, there's no problem. So my attorney wrote to the prosecutors to see what they thought of the motion. At first they said they'd consider agreeing to it so long as I gave up my American citizenship. Meaning that the idea of giving up my citizenship actually came from the prosecution. In fact I didn't accept, initially, because it seemed to me it was a birthright, and I couldn't see that I should renounce it just because the prosecution wanted me to. Later, though, weighing up the pros and cons, I said to my attorney: Let's accept. I don't want to fight with those guys over the citizenship question because what's on the line, what's at stake, is my personal safety and on the other hand my family. I wanted to be with my family. Well, if it was a choice between American citizenship and three years living with my family in Cuba … So that's what we did. My attorney told the prosecution I was willing. I was still in jail. The idea was, by the time I came out the decision would be taken already and I could go to Cuba to serve my probation. So in the end I told my attorney to concede, and he submitted the motion to the judge in writing, about eight months before I was due for release, I don't remember exactly, requesting permission to serve my probation in Cuba. The government, in other words the prosecution, wrote back opposing the motion. That document doesn't mention anything about citizenship yet. The prosecution opposed us …

Their argument at that stage was, first, the technical one that the sentence couldn't be changed once it had been pronounced, etc., etc. And another point, the one eventually adopted by the judge, was that it was a little premature for me to be asking for that. Because the judge needed time to see if my conduct outside was satisfactory, all that. But right when those motions were before the court, the prosecutors were negotiating under the table—I'm not saying they shouldn't, it's no problem—with my attorney over the conditions of my giving up US citizenship in exchange for changing my probation. To be clear: the motions have been filed, the judge has got them in front of her, and behind the scenes the prosecutors are still negotiating with my attorney over the logistics of renouncing my citizenship so that I can serve probation over here. Because when it comes to renouncing citizenship there's this small legal hitch, which is that you can't do it on United States territory.

You have to be outside the country. If a US national wants to renounce his nationality he has to leave the country and apply in a US consulate. Those negotiations dragged on for months. Two options were proposed at the outset: one was for us to go to the US embassy in the Bahamas, and give up my citizenship there. The other was to come to Havana and do it here, in the US Interests Section. But the prosecution appealed against that; they said, "If he goes off to Havana, how can we be sure he'll really do it?" I also think the prosecution was trying to link my case to that of Alan Gross.* Trying to establish a parallel in order to exchange me for Gross—a suggestion I was indirectly made aware of, and which I rejected, of course. So the months went by, until, around two weeks before I was due for release, the prosecution suddenly said to my lawyers, just like that, out of the blue: no, we're not interested. And simultaneously, equally out of the blue, the judge backed the prosecution's position and said that indeed the motion was well premature and it was necessary to watch me on probation for a while and assess my conduct and all that. She approved the prosecution's motion and rejected mine.

That's why when I came out I had to start probation in the United States. My experience of supervised release involved a pretty atypical, unusual supervision. I'd say that in some respects it was even worse than prison. Because I was in southern Florida and had to make sure the Miami terrorists didn't track me down. I mean, well, the terrorists were protected from me; the judge protected them by forbidding me to approach them, but they were free to approach me. As a result I had to lead a virtually clandestine life indoors, thanks to a Cuban friend, in a fairly exclusive neighborhood. I

---

* The American Alan Gross, a subcontractor with the US Agency for International Development (USAID), was arrested in 2009 after entering Cuba with a range of satellite phones and computer equipment. Accused of spying for the US intelligence services, he was sentenced in January 2010 to fifteen years in prison for "acts against the independence or the territorial integrity of the state."

couldn't introduce myself, I couldn't meet the neighbors. I couldn't take a steady job, or own a driving license, because that would reveal my address. I couldn't have a bank account or a credit card. In effect it was like living underground, shut away inside that house.

The system normally requires a probation officer to interview you at fairly frequent intervals. They made an exception for me. The probation service behaved as well as it could in my case, and I can't say a word against the officers, especially the first one, who passed away while I was here visiting my brother … That first guy was very professional, he did his best to protect me and make my life easier every way he could. He knew about the case and respected me and I respected him back, I can't say I didn't. The officer was an Italian American named Antonio Gagliardi. He'd been in Miami and he'd known those terrorists, he told me so. We developed a good, working, cooperative relationship. He cooperated with me and I with him. But, let's face it, his capacity to protect me was pretty limited. He couldn't provide bodyguards. All he could do was collect information, and, well, see whether … So we carried on in those conditions. My lawyer and I decided we'd file the motion again at the end of four months, because I had to demonstrate my good behavior.

In February 2012, as the four months drew to an end and my attorney and I were preparing to meet to draft our motion, that's when my brother Roberto's health took a turn for the worse, here in Havana. On the same day I told my attorney: "Look, forget about that motion, let's file another one applying to visit my brother for two weeks." This is standard procedure, meaning, you're not asking a special favor from the judge. If you're on probation and a family problem arises, it's normal to apply for permission to visit and they have to grant it if you've been on good behavior. So in February we filed a motion to go see Roberto. The prosecution rejected it, formally opposing the motion. I recall their reasons very well. Like how I might abscond in Cuba, stupid stuff like that. But this time, fortunately, the judge did the right thing and approved my request. The prosecution put in various demands. One of their arguments, I remember now, trite as can be and very stupid as well, was that I might meet up for instruction with the Cuban intelligence service and then begin spying in the United States. Total garbage! They're shameless, those guys, they'll use any excuse, regardless of logic or whatever. That's the way they are. And seeing as the judges follow suit, and are pretty lacking in shame as well, they all understand each other perfectly. That was their main objection. So they asked the judge to impose a number of restrictions to keep me from hooking up with intelligence people here. She imposed a few, but not many and not too harsh. I'd have to tell my probation officer and give him a copy of my itinerary, a contact number in Cuba, an address, all that. That's how cooperative Gagliardi and I were, we worked together. He went out of his way to be helpful, he said to me, "Listen, you just call me every other day." And when I was over here sometimes I didn't call for days, and afterward he'd say, "It doesn't matter, don't worry." The two of us really had a great working relationship.

Well then, I came over here, and stuck faithfully to all the restrictions the judge had imposed. For two weeks. I'd come to see Roberto, I saw him and I went back. And on the way back an interesting and amusing thing happened, which I'll tell you, for the first time I believe. It seems there were a lot of people over there who wanted me to break my word and not go back to the United States. They have no morals, they never did. That's why they're always hunting for ways to take a swipe at our morals. Apparently it occurred to some such people over there—because vile as they are, they're constantly projecting themselves—that I was going to do the same as they would, stay here and betray my word. When what mattered was respecting the judge and so forth. As well as the prosecution. So of course, when I came over here I complied with everything I'd promised. Because with us, morality grows even stronger in such cases.

Now then, when it came time to leave I obviously had to come back via the Bahamas. Luckily it had occurred to me to ask my lawyer to come meet me there, just in case. I arrived in Nassau and there he was, with the Cuban ambassador. They'd already spoken to the customs men to make sure I got through, the procedure, you know. I went to Customs, and was led to an office they have in the airport. And while I was in there a Bahamian immigration officer turned up looking for me. I stepped forward and he said, "No, you can't come through the Bahamas, you'll have to return to Cuba on the plane that brought you."

And I said, "No, I can't do that."

"You show up on my computer as a person who is banned from entering this country."

Off we went to the immigration office to talk to his boss. This gentleman, the supervisor, was pretty rude: "Nope, you've got to go back to Cuba."

"Hold on a second. What do you mean? Look, here's my US passport, I came through here in transit fifteen days ago, and nobody told me then that I had any problem in the Bahamas. How come all of a sudden I've got a problem in the Bahamas?"

"Well, that's what shows up on the computer."

The Cuban ambassador began calling the Bahamian government. My American attorney came in and said, "Look here, I'm his lawyer, I'm from the United States and he is obligated to go back there by judicial order." At that they moved in between my lawyer and me, and we began feeling corralled.

And I said, "I was just here fifteen days ago, and you're going to send me back to Cuba? Because I have to go to the States. You should let me go to the States, because no way am I going back to Cuba."

I told my attorney that if they forced me back to Cuba I'd grab a boat and paddle to Miami. I wasn't going to let them throw a big party in Miami because I'd violated my probation. I'd be imprisoned again in front of the whole world. Anyhow we managed to work it out in the end, the guy allowed us to stay in the Bahamas under the supervision of that other officer who'd come to find us. Eventually we reached the American part of the airport, where you can board a US flight. What I mean is that somehow, in some way, someone was trying to fix it so I'd be sent back to Cuba. Obviously someone from the United States, not a Bahamian.

So, I returned to the US and started to work with my attorney on renewing the motion to change my supervision rules and be allowed to go back to Cuba. We submitted our motion to the judge and we said to her, "Listen, Your Honor, this man"—well, by then I'd been back eight months, this was in June—"has displayed an exemplary conduct, there hasn't been one single complaint about him, he's done everything you told him and now we're filing the motion again." And that's when for the first time we put it to the judge that I'd hand back my citizenship, in exchange for … I mean, that was the first official document from us that featured the offer of my citizenship in exchange for the judge's permission to go to Cuba. We submitted the motion and the government rejected it again. Their excuse this time came down to: "This guy is a spy and a nasty piece of work. There's no guarantee that when he gets to Cuba he will be true to his word and offer his citizenship to the American embassy."

After a few months the judge asked to examine some memos and regulations relating to the process for giving up citizenship, to see what could be done. In my view, she did so to delay the process. What's more, in the middle of all this paperwork my father fell ill. He grew sick in December and died in April, of a stroke, while the case dragged on. My father died on April 1. We were still working on changing my probation conditions, and I said to my lawyer, "Look, we have to request another compassionate visit to Cuba, because he has passed away." My attorney filed a new motion modeled on the previous year's, requesting leave to attend the old man's funeral. This time the prosecution didn't object. They just asked the judge to impose the same conditions as last time. Before leaving the US I said to my attorney, "Here's what I suggest. Since the prosecution opposed my motion to hand back my citizenship on grounds that once I was back in Cuba I would not go to the embassy, here's what we do. Soon as I'm in Cuba, right away you file a motion telling the judge that I'm well and truly going to the embassy." That's how we dealt with the judge. I came to Cuba for my dad's funeral and that's when my attorney went to the court and said, "Your Honor, my client is in Havana. And from Havana he wants you to know that he is going to the American embassy to hand back his citizenship." So the government had no choice but to say, well, what can we do? They appointed another prosecutor to handle the matter with my attorney. My attorney got in touch, our communications went very smoothly, we made all the arrangements and he came over. He came over from the US and the two of us went to the Interests Section, and there, well: that all came out on TV. I went through the process of renouncing citizenship, and once they gave me the certificate saying I wasn't an American anymore, then the judge went ahead and modified my probation. So that's basically how it happened.

I was living, like I said, in a house in Palm Beach. I'd go out in the morning running or cycling. I lived alone in the house. My security was to be anonymous. Nobody knowing I was there; nobody suspecting that the person who lived there was René González. I grew a beard, which disguised my face a little, but the important thing was not to show myself around too much. I didn't go to bars or hire any home help, and because I was a bad cook I had to learn how to grill all kinds of things and to heat up food in the microwave. I learned how to prepare hash browns, rice, beans, and I was real good at soups … Apart from me and the owner of the house, the only people who knew I was there were three friends of his, Americans, who used to take me out sometimes. We'd go out in disguise, sometimes they'd take me to the theater or to some other place where they were going. What I mostly did was read and study, on the computer, doing Internet searches, connecting to the blogosphere in Cuba.

I can't figure how the Miami terrorists didn't know where I was. Especially seeing the complicity there's always been between them and the FBI. My biggest fear in terms of safety was that they were waiting for me to be nearly free before moving in on me. They would've felt so satisfied to make me go through three years' probation and then, when I had a month or two to go, to do something to me. Me, of course, I couldn't appear in public, couldn't give interviews, couldn't do anything of what I wanted. I'd have wanted to start fighting for my brothers as soon as I got out of jail. That was one of the toughest parts, not to hardly show my face or go on TV; it upset me a lot.

This story will only be finished when all five of us are free. There are two legal paths toward that. The first is habeas corpus, which was applied for more than two years ago now. The other is for the president to sign a pardon. The trouble is that the case has been politically manipulated from day one. And every decision that was ever taken in the case has been political. Not one decision has been juridical. My opinion is that it's going to continue the same way. And if the judge finally gets around to deciding the matter this way or that, it'll be because a political decision was taken to resolve the case. But in the last instance, it'll always be a political decision. A decision they'll take in the White House, the way they always do. To date, all the judges have acted in line with the wishes of the White House.

I don't know how they communicate, with smoke signals or by telephone. That's their business. But what I'm hearing is that it's a White House decision. We know it, the prosecutors know it, everybody knows it. Anybody who cares to know, knows. The people in Miami know, Ileana Ros knows, the Díaz-Balart brothers know. That's why I think it's important to keep putting pressure on the American government to take the right decision. After all, the only thing we've ever asked the judges to do, from the start, is to apply the law. We don't expect favors or anything like that. No. Just for them to apply the law. The five of us met when the trial began, and agreed that our rule of conduct here would be respect for the law. We know very well we're here as unregistered foreign agents. There's a body of statutes that constitutes the law of the land, and we will respect it. We will respect the judges, we will respect the attorneys, and we will respect the law. We maintained this conduct from the outset. That's why I went along with what the judge asked of me; I could have stayed in Cuba, but we'd vowed to respect the law. What we want the White House to do is to proceed along legal channels, to call the judges and tell them, go ahead, apply the law, examine the evidence and rule accordingly. That's where we're at now. I've said it before and I say it again: This story will only be finished when all five of us are free.

René González

EPILOGUE

In 2008, the attorney Leonard Weinglass appealed to the US Court of Appeals for the 11th Circuit in Atlanta, based on material and procedural flaws he had found in the trial. The court complied with some of the defense arguments and ordered Tony Guerrero's, Fernando González's and Ramón Labañino's penalties be reviewed. In late 2009, Judge Joan Lenard revoked the three defendants' life sentences, reducing Labañino's sentence to thirty years, Guerrero's to twenty-one years and ten months and González's to seventeen years and nine months. After serving his entire sentence, Fernando González was released from Safford Federal Prison in Arizona on February 27, 2014. Gerardo Hernández's and René's penalties were not reviewed.

Despite continued protests against the miscarriage of justice and the vindictive restrictions on visits by relatives—sent to the White House by the World Council of Churches, Amnesty International, the European Parliament, the UK House of Commons, thirteen American city mayors and the trade unions of nine countries—the remaining prisoners continued serving their sentences: Gerardo Hernández in California, Tony Guerrero in Colorado and Ramón Labañino in Georgia.

On December 17, 2014, months of secret diplomacy mediated by Canada and the Vatican culminated in unexpected simultaneous televised announcements from President Barack Obama and President Raúl Castro. Acknowledging the failure of decades of confrontation, they vowed to work towards the normalization of diplomatic relations and expanded communications and cooperation through a more constructive engagement on both sides. This thaw would provisionally operate within the limits of the economic, commercial and financial embargo, whose suspension would require congressional approval.

That same day, as a powerfully symbolic token of the new goodwill, a prisoner swap had taken place: the American subcontractor Alan Gross was released from Cuba, along with the US spy Rolando Sarraff Trujillo. The last three incarcerated Cubans made the opposite journey. Raúl Castro told the nation: "Gerardo, Ramón and Antonio have arrived today in our homeland." The story was finished: all five of them were free.

In 2002, the former attorney general, Janet Reno, campaigned for nomination for the Florida gubernatorial race, but was defeated by Bill McBride in the Democratic primary. The elected governor would be the Republican Jeb Bush, brother of the then President George W. Bush.

Sentenced to death by Cuban courts, the Salvadoran mercenaries Raúl Ernesto Cruz León and Otto René Rodríguez Llerena had their sentence commuted to thirty years in 2010.

A court in Havana tried and sentenced the Guatemalans Nader Kamal Musalam Barakat (twenty years), Jazid Iván Fernández Mendoza (fifteen years) and María Elena González Meza de Fernández (thirty years).

Weighing twenty kilos less, on July 1, 2010, the Salvadoran Francisco "Big Paunch" Chávez Abarca was arrested attempting to enter Venezuela using a false name and passport. He confessed that he intended to plant bombs in the offices of oppositional political parties and organizations, so that the attacks would be attributed to followers of President Hugo Chávez. Extradited to Cuba, which had already requested Interpol to capture him, Chávez Abarca was tried and sentenced to thirty years in prison.

The lawyer Leonard Weinglass died on March 23, 2011, at the age of seventy-eight, as he was petitioning for a writ of habeas corpus for Gerardo Hernández. His last client was the Australian Julian Assange, creator of the WikiLeaks website.

In March 2011, a federal court in El Paso, Texas, unanimously acquitted Luis Posada Carriles of immigration fraud and perjury. Posada lives unmolested in Miami.

There has not been any further news of Alejandro *Franklin* Alonso or of the couples Linda and Nilo Hernández and Amarilys and Joseph Santos, the five agents who signed a plea bargain agreement with the FBI and entered the United States federal witness protection program, after serving sentences of between three and seven years.

Orlando Bosch died of natural causes in Miami, on April 27, 2011, at the age of eighty-four.

ACKNOWLEDGMENTS

The idea of telling the story of the Cuban intelligence agents who infiltrated anti-Castroist organizations in Florida was born in September 1998, when I was listening to the car radio and heard they had been arrested by the FBI. In the following years, I tried in vain to break through the wall of silence that surrounded the matter in Cuba; the secrecy surrounding everything related to the Wasp Network was such that the Cuban press mentioned the case for the first time in June 2001, when the agents were convicted in the United States. Even after that, the affair remained a state secret for years.

This book would only take its first steps one February evening in 2005, when I traveled to Cuba to take part in the Havana Book Fair. The night before my return to Brazil, during dinner at the historic restaurant La Floridita, the president of the National Assembly, Ricardo Alarcón, told me that the intelligence services' documents on the network of secret agents whom Cuba had infiltrated into the heart of Florida's extreme right-wing organizations would finally be released to me. As I was involved in another work project, three years passed before I could at last begin the fieldwork that resulted in this book.

Although everything in here is, of course, my entire responsibility, I must acknowledge my true gratitude to so many people who helped me in Cuba, in the United States and in Brazil. In the person of Alarcón, I would like to thank all the Cuban authorities and officials, both civilian and military, without whose patience and goodwill this book would not exist.

I thank Marina, my wife, for the affection with which she put up with me in these three years of work and for her implacable reading of every chapter I wrote.

I also thank the talented young journalists Leslie Salgado in Cuba, Alejandra Chaparro in Miami and Daniella Cambaúva in Brazil, for their professional assistance in the work of research, organization of files, and transcription of the dozens of interviews I did in the three countries.

Although some names will inevitably be missing, I would like to express my gratitude to all my interviewees and furthermore to: Abel Prieto, Abelardo Blanco, Alquimia Peña, Ana Mayra Rodriguez Falera, Breno Altman, Camila Morais Cajaiba Garcez Marins, Carlinhos Cecconi, Carlos Parra, Claudio Kahns, Eduardo dos Santos, Emir Sader, Eric Nepomuceno, Fabián Escalante, Firmeza Ribeiro dos Santos, Frei Betto, Juliana Horta, Kirk Nielsen, Lucas Figueiredo, Lucia Haddad, Luciana Bueno Netto, Lira Neto, Mac Margolies, Marcello Veríssimo, Marcio Valente, Mariana Chirino, Marilia Morais Cajaíba, Max Altman, Maximilien Arvelaiz, Mônica Kalil, Reinaldo Morais, Ricardo Schwab, Ricardo Setti, Roberto Koltun, Rogério Teixeira, Rui Ferreira and Wilson Moherdaui.

Fernando Morais
Ilhabela, Brazil, March 2011

LIST OF INTERVIEWEES

Cuba

Adriana Pérez O'Connor
Elisabeth Palmeiro Casado
Irma González Salanueva
Irma Teodora Sehwerert
Jesús Arboleya
Juan Pablo Roque
Magali Llort Ruiz
María Eugenia Guerrero
Michel Marín
Mirta Rodríguez Pérez
Nuris Pinero Sierra
Olga González Salanueva
Raúl Ernesto Cruz León
Ricardo Alarcón
Roberto González Sehwerert
Roberto Hernández Caballero
Rosa Aurora Freijanes Coca

United States

Ana Margarita Martínez
Charles Dascal
Edmundo García
Francisco Aruca
Joaquín Méndez
Joe García
John H. Cabanas
José Basulto
Juan Manuel Salvat
Larry Rohter
Leonard Weinglass
Lorenzo Gonzalo
Margareth Becker
Max Lesnik
Norberto Fuentes
Rafael Anglada
Ramón Coll
René González Sehwerert
Tony Yansó
William Schuss

Mexico

Denise de Kalafe

BIBLIOGRAPHY

Books, theses and documents

Aguirrechu, Iraida. *Atlanta y el caso de los cinco: La larga marcha hacia la justicia*. Havana: Editora Política, 2005.
———. ed. *La tormenta perfecta*. Havana: Editora Política, 2005.
Alfredo, Zhores; Máiread Corrigan Maguire; Dario Fo; Nadine Gordimer; Günther Grass; Rigoberta Menchú; Adolfo Pérez Esquivel; José Ramos-Horta; José Saramago and Wole Soyinka. *Petición de revisión al Tribunal de Apelaciones del onceno circuito de los Estados Unidos, Tribunal Supremo de los Estados Unidos*. Havana, 2009.
Arboleya, Jesús. *La revolución del otro mundo: Cuba y Estados Unidos en el horizonte del siglo XXI*. Bogotá: Quebecor World S. A, 2007.
———. *La ultraderecha cubano-americana de Miami*. Havana: Editorial de Ciencias Sociales, 2000.
Causa 1/89—Fin de la conexión cubana. Havana: Editorial José Martí, 1989.
Clinton, Bill. *My Life*. New York: Alfred A. Knopf, 2004.
Dávalos Fernández, Rodolfo. *Estados Unidos vs Cinco Héroes: Un*

juicio silenciado. Havana: Editorial Capitán San Luís, 2005.

Escalante Font, Fabián. *Nicaragua sandinista: Un conflicto de baja intensidad*. Havana: Editorial de Ciencias Sociales, 2009.

————. *Operación Exterminio: 50 años de agresiones contra Cuba*. Havana: Editorial de Ciencias Sociales, 2008.

Fuentes, Norberto. *The Autobiography of Fidel Castro*. New York: W. W. Norton, 2010.

González, Ana Margarita and Rafael Hojas. *La historia que me ha tocado vivir*. Havana: Editora Política, 2011.

Guerrero, Antonio. *Desde mi altura / From My Altitude*. Havana: Editorial José Martí, 2001.

————. *Firme y romántico*. Havana: Ediciones Logos, 2007.

————. *Inseparables*. Havana: Editorial Letras Cubanas, 2005.

González, Fernando; Gerardo Hernández; Ramón Labañino and René González. *Desde la soledad y la esperanza*. Havana: Editorial Capitán San Luis, 2007.

Hart Santamaría, Celia. *Les debo verlos libres*. Havana: Ediciones Especiales, 2009.

Lamrani, Salim. *Fidel Castro, Cuba y los Estados Unidos: Conversaciones con Ricardo Alarcón, presidente de la Asamblea Nacional del Poder Popular*. Havana: Editorial José Martí, 2007.

Lawrence, Matt and Thomas Van Hare. *Betrayal: Clinton, Castro & the Cuban Five*. New York: iUniverse, 2009.

Lemoine, Maurice. *Cinq cubains à Miami: Le roman de la guerre secrète entre Cuba et les États-Unis*. Paris: Don Quichotte Éditions, 2010.

Martínez, Ana Margarita and Diana Montané. *Estrecho de traición: La historia de la fatídica unión entre Ana Margarita Martínez y Juan Pablo Roque*. Miami: Ediciones Universal, 1999.

Roque, Juan Pablo. *Desertor*. Washington: Cuban American National Foundation, 1995.

Ros, Enrique. *La fuerza política del exilio cubano*, vols. 1 & 2. Miami: Ediciones Universal, 2007 and 2008.

Santos Ferreira, Marcos Alan Fagner dos. "O impacto da política externa dos EUA nas relações entre Brasil e Cuba (1996–2004)." A master's dissertation in the "San Tiago Dantas" International

Relations Program, a partnership among Unesp (Universidade Estadual Paulista Júlio de Mesquita Filho), Unicamp (Universidade de Campinas) and PUC-SP (Pontifícia Universidade Católica de São Paulo). São Paulo, 2006.

Schuss, William. *Día tras día con los Hermanos al Rescate*. Miami: D'Fana Editions, 2007.

Torres, Sonia. *Nosotros in USA: Literatura, etnografia e geografias de resistência*. Rio de Janeiro: Jorge Zahar, 2001.

Ubieta Gómez, Enrique. *Por la izquierda: Veintidós testimonios a contracorriente*. Havana: Editorial José Martí, 2007.

Vargas Llosa, Álvaro. *El exilio indomable: Historia de la disidencia cubana en el destierro*. Madrid: Editorial Espasa Calpe, 1998.

Vázquez Montalbán, Manuel. *Y Dios entró en La Habana*. Madrid: Ediciones El País, 1998.

Wyden, Peter. *Bay of Pigs: The Untold Story*. New York: Simon and Schuster, 1979.

Newspapers, magazines and periodicals

ABC, Spain
Diário Las Américas, United States
El Mundo, Spain
El Nuevo Herald, United States
El País, Spain
Escambray, Cuba
Granma, Cuba
Juventud Rebelde, Cuba
La Jornada, Mexico
Miami Herald, United States
Miami New Times, United States
Newsweek, United States
New York Times, United States
Southernmost Flyer, United States
Sun-Sentinel, United States
Trabajadores, Cuba

Veja, Brasil
Washington Times, United States

Films and Documentaries

Del otro lado del cristal, Guillermo Centeno, Manuel Pérez, Marina
    Ochoa and Mercedes Arce, ICAIC, Cuba.
El proceso: La historia no contada, Rolando Almirante, Cuba.
Rompiendo el silencio, Carlos Alberto García, Cuba.
Man of Two Havanas, Vivien Lesnik Weisman, United States.
Fidel! Saul Landau, United States.
Will the Real Terrorist Please Stand Up? Saul Landau, United States.
Shoot Down, Cristina Khuly, United States.
The Flight of Pedro Pan, Joe Cardona, United States.
The Specialist, Luis Llosa, United States.
They Killed Sister Dorothy, Daniel Junge, United States.

Internet

Cuba
antiterroristas.cu
cubadebate.cu
granma.cu

Spain
elmundo.es/america
elpais.es

United States
cnic.navy.mil/regions/cnrse
elnuevoherald.com
foia.ucia.gov
freethefive.org
gwu.edu/~nsarchiv

huffingtonpost.com
miamiherald.com
nsarchive.chadwyck.com
pedropan.org
thecuban5.org